Michel Schooyans

The Gospel Confronting World Disorder

Preface by
Joseph Cardinal Ratzinger

Translated by Rev. John H. Miller, C.S.C., S.T.D.

Copyright 1999
Central Bureau, CCVA
All rights to the original French,
L'Évangile face au désordre mondial,
reserved to Arthème Fayard, Paris, 1997

ISBN 1-887567-09-7
$17.50

Cover design by Chris Pelicano

Published by
Central Bureau,
Catholic Central Verein of America

Printed by
St. Martin de Porres Lay Dominican Community

ABBREVIATIONS

BPCL   *Bioethics and Population: The Choice of Life*
CA   *Centesimus Annus*
CNE: Center for New Europe
DC   *Documentation catholique*
DLC   *Démocratie et libération chrétienne*
TTL   *The Totalitarian Trend of Liberalism*
EPA   *L'Enjeu politique de l'avortement*
EV   *Evangelium Vitae*
UNFPA: United Nations Fund for Population Activities
GS   *Gaudium et Spes*
IIS: Interactive Information Service
IPPF: International Planned Parenthood Federation
WHO: World Health Organization
RN: *Rerum Novarum*
SC   *On Social Concerns*

TABLE OF CONTENTS

PREFACE i
INTRODUCTION: TIDINGS OF GREAT JOY v
CHAPTER I: HUMAN LIFE THREATENED 1
   A DISTRESSING TABLEAU 1
      Abortion 1
      Abusive Medical Practices 2
      Euthanasia 3
      Life Dried Up at its Sources 3
      Practices having Harmful Repercussions 4
      AIDS and Suicide 4
   DO NOT FORGET THE PAST 6
      History 6
      The Recent Past 7
      In the Name of "Higher Interest" 8
   POWERFUL AGENTS OF DISSEMINATION 9
      Public International Institutions 11
      National Governments 11
      Private Organizations 12
      The Media 13

CHAPTER II: THE IDEOLOGICAL COALITION OF GENDER . 17
   SOCIALISM AND LIBERALISM REVISITED 17
      Socialist Ideology 17
      Malthus and Liberal Ideology 18
      Eugenics and Neo-Malthusianism 19
      Joining Socialism and Liberalism 20
   THE IDEOLOGY OF GENDER 21
      Class Struggle Reactivated 21
      The Influence of Structuralism 22
      Deconstruct and Reconstruct Society 23
      Gender at the UN 24

CHAPTER III: THE NEW PARADIGM OF WHO 29
  WHO AND THE WORLD BANK 29
    Political and Economic Dimensions of Health 29
    The Thrust of the Cairo Conference 31
    Toward a Reform of the UN? 32
    The World Bank and the Burden of Global Morbidity 33
    "Public" Health? Health "for All"? 34
    A Deceitful Indicator 35
  THE AXES OF A NEW ETHIC 37
    Hippocrates Surpassed? 37
    Ethics and Fairness 39
    The "Special Event" in 1998. 40
  AUTHORIZED CONFIRMATIONS 41
    Health: A Product Subordinated to the Economy 41
    Criteria of Priority 42
  THE "NEW PARADIGM" AND THE LOGIC OF EVIL 43
    Sources or Analogies? 44
    Ethics and Responsibility 45
    Procedural Justice 45

CHAPTER IV: THE NEW AGE:
ITS PARADIGM AND NETWORKS 49
  THE NEW AGE IN ITSELF 49
    The "Gentle Conspiracy" and Its Network 52
    Toward a World Directorate 54
  THE GREATEST MENACE SINCE ARIANISM 55
    The Return of Gnosticism. 56
    Disparate Components 56
    A Millenarian Pantheism 58
    Networks and Hermetic Freemasonry 58

CHAPTER V: DANGERS TO MAN'S RIGHTS 63
  THE UNIVERSAL DECLARATION OF 1948 63
    Originality 63
    Fruitfulness 64
  THREATS TO THE DECLARATION 64
    The Half-Open Door 64
    The Inclusion of "New Rights" 65
    The Tactic of Derogation. 66
    From Consensus to Law 66
  DISTORTIONS OF MEANING 67
    From Equality to Fairness 67

  The "Polymorphous" Family.............................. 68
THE RELATIVIZATION OF RIGHTS..................... 68
  Relativization According to Women's Status 69
  Relativization According to the "Quality of Life" 71
  Relativization According to Cultures 72
  Relativization of Time 72
WHAT KIND OF SOVEREIGNTY?
WHAT KIND OF DEVELOPMENT?...................... 73
  Flexible Sovereignty. 73
  The Excessive Role of Some Nongovernmental Organizations.... 73
  What Kind of "Right to Development"? 74
  An Audit of the UN. 76
  Europe in the Globalist Nebula 76
PERVERSION OF HUMAN ACTIVITY 78

CHAPTER VI: TO LOVE IS HAPPINESS................... 83
SOME REASSURING FACTS............................ 83
HEART OF GOD, HEART OF MAN 88
THE BODY, PLACE OF LIBERTY........................ 89
A NEW ANTHROPOLOGICAL ERROR 91
DEATH AS HORIZON 92
  From the Love of Death to the Death of Love 92
  Warlike Order 94
"THE STING OF DEATH IS SIN" 94
  The Era of Sin 95
  The Deification of Violence 96
AT THE SERVICE OF MAN'S HAPPINESS 96
  Pluralism and Agnosticism............................. 97
  Love, the Future of Man 97
LIBERTY THROUGH DEATH? 98
  The Disintegration of the Person......................... 98
  Compromised: Fidelity and Fecundity..................... 99
  Machismo and Feminism............................... 100
  Obligation of Purpose 100
  Abortion: Prototype of Gratuitous Violence 101
  The Unfaithful Steward................................ 103

CHAPTER VII: WE WERE ALL ONCE A BABY IN THE WOMB .. 105
A DEEPLY MOVING DISCOVERY 105
  The Joy of Expecting 105
  Common Ground..................................... 106

    Defending the Man in the Unborn Baby 107
LOVE DISARMED 108
    In the Image of God 108
    The Good Samaritan 109
    Rejection of the Two Commandments 111
A PERSON? 112
SOME CONVERGING TRADITIONS 113
COMMUNION IMPOSSIBLE 114
    Salvation in Peril 115
    Structures of Sin Approved by Law 116
SOME "INDICATIONS" THAT CARRY NO WEIGHT 116
CHAPTER VIII: WE WILL ALL PASS THAT WAY, OR DEATH TODAY 121
EUTHANASIA IN PRACTICE 122
    Studying the Arguments 122
    Foreseeable Consequences of the Practice of Euthanasia 123
    Alternate Proposal: Palliative Care 125
    Euthanasia: "Active" or "Passive"? 126
REFLECTION ON THESE PRACTICES 127
    Clarifying the Debate in the Light of Contemporary Experience . 127
    Put in Philosophical Perspective 128
    Philosophers and the Dignity of Man 129
    Contribution of Christians 130
CHAPTER IX: TAKING THE FIRST STEP 133
HAPPINESS AND SOLIDARITY 133
    An "Intermediate" Relationship 133
    The Blinding Sign of the Times 134
TOWARD A POLITICS FOR LIVING TOGETHER 135
    The Slippery Slope of Totalitarianism 136
    Controlling the Fertility of Couples? 137
    Moral Degradation 138
LAW, PROTECTOR OF THE WEAK 139
    The Need for Values 139
    Resistance to Unjust Law 140
    Nondisposability of the Body 140
MEDICINE IN THE SERVICE OF LIFE 141
ADJUSTING THE AGRO-ALIMENTARY SECTOR 143
    Sensational Progress 143

 Patents and the Rights of Farmers 144
 An Agriculture Against the Farmer 145
A MARKET ACCESSIBLE TO ALL 145
 Toward a Global Economy? 145
 Indebtedness 147
A HUMAN ECOLOGY 148
SHARING KNOWLEDGE 149
 The Advantage of Knowledge 149
 The Faces of Poverty 149
THE RISK OF LOVING 151

CHAPTER X: THE NEW DEMOGRAPHIC ORDER 153
CONTRASTED SITUATIONS 153
THE INHUMAN COST OF DEVELOPMENT 158
 Two Trends: Malthusian and Hedonist 158
 The Example of Mexico 159
 Curb the "New Enemy" 160
 By What Right? 161
FOR AN "ELITISM" OF SERVICE 163
 Interdependence: An Opportunity and a Risk 163
 The Cost of a Child 164
 Development and Demographic Density 165
 Supporting Capacity: Relative 167
 From Privileges to Service 167
BACKWARD FLOW AND EXCLUSION 169
 Demographic Winter 170
IMPOSSIBILITY OF SILENCE ON
THE PART OF THE CHURCH 172
 Superfluity and Necessity 172
 Demographic Police 173

CHAPTER XI: FOYER OF LOVE: THE FAMILY 177
WHEN LOVE SPEAKS TO US OF GOD 177
 Man and Woman 177
 The Twofold Fruitfulness of Love 178
 To Love Unconditionally 180
INVINCIBLE BASTION AGAINST TOTALITARIANISM . 181
 The Family: Seat of Resistance 181
 The Role of the Media 182
GUIDELINES FOR A FAMILY POLICY 184

CHAPTER XII : PROCREATION AND DELEGATED WORLD POWER 187
IMAGE OF THE CREATOR 187
HUMAN PARENTHOOD, RESPONSIBLE PARENTHOOD . 188
EXPANDING MAN'S HEART 192

CHAPTER XIII: WHAT IS TO BE DONE 195
HOPE IN THE HEART OF THE POOR 195
"NO DISPARATE COUPLINGS!" 195
Liberty in the Face of Idols 195
Refusing Conformity 197
LIFE, LIKE DEATH, NEEDS INSTITUTIONS 198
Public and Private Institutions 198
Doctors 199
Lawyers 200
Farmers 200
Economists 201
Demystifying Malthus 202
Workers 202

CHAPTER XIV: FAITH AND WORKS 205
UNITY OF FAITH, UNIVERSALITY OF LOVE 205
Signs of the Times 205
Education for Life 207
Option for the Poor 208
FOYER OF HAPPINESS: THE FAMILY 210
FOR AN AUTHENTIC FEMINISM 211
What Kind of Liberation for Women? 211
From Power to Love 213
THE CHURCH, SIGN OF HOPE 214

ACKNOWLEDGEMENTS 217
BIBLIOGRAPHY 219
INDEX OF NAMES 229
INDEX OF SUBJECTS 233

PREFACE

From the very beginning of the Enlightenment, belief in progress has always set Christian eschatology aside and eventually replaced it entirely. Happiness is no longer anticipated in the afterlife but rather in this world. The attitude of Albert Camus, who resolutely opposes to Christ's words "my kingdom is not of this world, his affirmation that "my kingdom is of this world," is emblematic of modern man's disposition. If in the last century belief in progress was still a generic optimism that anticipated progressive betterment of the world's condition and an ever closer approach of a kind of paradise from the triumphant march of the sciences, such faith in our century has taken on a political turn.

On the one hand, there have been systems of Marxist orientation that promised the attainment of the desired reign of man by way of their ideologically-driven politics; an attempt that obviously failed. On the other hand, efforts to build the future have been made by attempts that draw more or less profoundly from the sources of liberal traditions. Under the title New World Order, these efforts take on a configuration; they increasing and characteristically relate to the UN and its international conferences, especially those of Cairo and Beijing that transparently reveal a philosophy of the new man and of the new world, as they endeavor to map out the ways of reaching them.

Such a philosophy is no longer utopian, in the sense of the Marxist dream. On the contrary, it is very realistic: it determines the limits of the well-being sought from the limited means for attaining it. This philosophy recommends, for example, without seeking to justify itself, not worrying about taking care of those who are no longer productive nor have any hope of a quality life. Furthermore, it no longer expects that people, used to riches and well-being, be ready to make the requisite sacrifices, on the contrary, it recommends ways of reducing the number of participants at humanity's table, so that at least the so-called happiness, already acquired by some, will not be touched. The typical character of this new anthropology, which is at the basis of the New World Order, is revealed above all in the image of woman, in the ideology of "Women's empowerment," proposed at Beijing. The goal is the self-realization of women for whom the principal obstacles are the family and maternity. Thus woman must be liberated above all from what characterizes her and very simply makes for her specificity: this must disappear before "Gender, fairness and equality," before an indistinct and uniform human being, in whose life sexuality had no other meaning than as a voluptuous drug that can be used in any manner conceivable.

In the fear of maternity that gripped a great number of our contemporaries, there is something more profound at play. The other person is always, in the end, a competitor who takes away a part of my life, a menace to my Ego and my free development. Today we no longer have a "philosophy of love," but only a "philosophy of egotism." The notion that I can enrich myself simply in the gift that I can find beginning with the other and through my being-for-another — all that is rejected as an idealistic illusion. But it is precisely there that man is deceived. In effect, when he is advised against loving, he is actually counseled not to be man.

And so, at the stage of the present development of a new image of a new world, we reach the point where the Christian — not only him but especially him — is obliged to protest. We must thank Michel Schooyans for having, in this book, given energetic voice to the protest needed. He shows us how the idea of man's rights that characterize the modern epoch, which is so important and positive in many ways, suffers right at the very beginning from the fact that it is founded on man alone and therefore on his ability and his will to carry out the general recognition of these rights. If, from the start, the reflection of the luminous Christian image of man protected the universality of rights, new questions arise to the degree that this image becomes blurred. How will the rights of the humblest be respected and promoted when our conception of man so often is based, as our author says, "on jealousy, anxiety, fear and even hate? How can such a dismal ideology, that recommends sterilization, abortion, systematic contraception and even euthanasia as the price of an unbridled pansexualism, bring men to the joy of living and loving?" (Ch. 6)

It is here that we clearly find that the Christian has something positive to offer in the struggle for future history. In effect, it is not sufficient that he opposes eschatology to the ideology of "postmodern" constructions of the future, Certainly he must do this and do so resolutely. But our voice has become all too feeble and timid in this regard over the last decades. In fact, in his earthly life man is but a straw without meaning if our gaze is turned away from eternal life. The same thing holds true for history as a whole. In this sense, reference to eternal life, if it's made correctly, never has the character of a flight. It simply gives to earthly existence its responsibility, its grandeur, its dignity. But precisely these repercussions on the "intramundane" must be articulated. It is certain that history must never be simply reduced to silence: one cannot, it is not allowed, reduce liberty to silence. That is the illusion of the utopians.

We cannot impose on tomorrow today's models, which will then be yesterday's models. Nevertheless, we must plan the proposals for a path to the future, proposals for generally overcoming the new historical challenges. That is what Michel Schooyans does in the second and third parts of his book. Above all, he proposes, in contrast to the new anthropology, the essential traits of the Christian image of man and then applies them in a concrete way to the big problems of the future world order (especially in Chapters 10-12). He thus gives a concrete and politically realistic and realizable content to the idea of a "civilization of love," so often expressed by John Paul II.

Michael Schooyans' book thus goes to the heart of the great challenges of our historic moment with vivacity and great competence. We hope that it will be read by people with varying orientations, that it will stir up lively discussion and thus contribute to prepare the future with models worthy of the greatness of man, as well as insure the dignity of those who are unable to defend themselves.

Joseph Cardinal Ratzinger
Rome, April 25, 1997

INTRODUCTION
TIDINGS OF GREAT JOY

"Behold, I bring you tidings of great joy that shall be to all the people" (Lk 2:10). These words addressed to the shepherds by the angels remain forever engraved on our hearts since the Son of God chose to be born of Mary in order to come closer to men and dwell among us. At the dawn of salvation, the message proclaimed is the good news of a birth, that of the Savior of the world. By associating man with His work of giving life, by delegating to him the responsibility of transmitting to other men the gift of human life, God invites man to make a celebration of every birth, a celebration which among all generations, would mark the history of humanity.

The shepherds were hardly let down: they went in haste, full of joy, to see the newborn. And St. Luke tells us how their eagerness was rewarded. In effect, these poor shepherds were the first, after Mary and Joseph, to perceive that the newborn, naked and powerless, came to fulfill God's promises.

By making His entrance into the world in this way, Jesus therefore anchored salvation in the joyous newness inherent in every human birth. But He also revealed that every human birth was the bearer of new meaning. From the moment the Child is seen, He is offered for the "shepherds'" appreciation; they approach to look upon Him and marvel. But the Child is also the *sign* through which the witnesses are led to acknowledge the image of God. Path of God to men, the Child is also path of men to God.

Ever since Bethlehem, a solidarity between the children of men and the Son of God is affirmed, for better or worse. For the better, because all the children of men are called to become children of God and brothers and sisters of Jesus. For the worse, because all the children of men are exposed, as Jesus was, to being rejected and being put to death.

In this regard, contrasted with that of the shepherds, Herod's reaction, reported by St. Matthew, is revealing (Mt 2). Unlike the shepherds, Herod doesn't let himself be called by the Child. He thinks that the Infant Jesus has come to rob him of his power; he believes his security is threatened. Thus if the Child makes Herod tremble, it is simply because, by His fragile presence, the unjust character of the tyrant's power is unmasked: Herod rules only for himself. And desiring to get at Jesus, he exterminates all the infants who reflect His image. By attacking the innocent infants, Herod himself demonstrates the wickedness of the power he exercises.

Thus, in His infancy the Son of God shows that between the smallest and Himself a solidarity is sealed which nothing through the centuries will contradict. Henceforth, the quality of power will be evaluated on the basis of the quality of attention given to the weakest in human society.

In the 19th century, Leo XIII revitalized this quality of attention on behalf of the most underprivileged. The Church celebrated in 1991 the centenary of his encyclical *Rerum Novarum*, in which, we know, he denounced with such prophetic accents, the "undeserved misery of the working class" (RN 2). If the prophetic words of Leo XIII had been better heeded and put into practice, humanity would be spared many of the evils that have punctuated this century which is coming to a close.

It is important that the intention of this great encyclical be reactivated today. The challenge which was advanced over a hundred years ago was the relief of workers' oppression and exploitation. By way of fidelity to this heritage, it is urgent for Christians and all men of good will, presently to take up the major challenge of our time, namely releasing from oppression those in our society who are the weakest and most vulnerable: first of all unborn babies (those given the beautiful name *nascituri*, those about to be born); then the incurably sick, the handicapped, elderly persons; finally, the innumerable hordes of poor and oppressed who are abused in so many ways as their ignorance is taken advantage of.

In fact, for many years now we observe, an accelerated lessening of respect owed to human life. This development alone justifies a priority commitment on the part of all men of good will. What makes this commitment not only justified but urgent are the campaigns to gain total control over human life. These campaigns are led, on the national and international level, by public as well as private organizations. We are struck, in particular, by the number of international conferences aimed at the realization of this goal.

Just as the Church could not remain silent in the 19th century, so the Christian community cannot remain silent at the present moment when some are attempting to organize the "New World Order" and when the profile of the 21st century is being defined.

These actions against human life have assumed such a magnitude that numerous people, coming from a variety of spiritual, religious and philosophical backgrounds, have begun to become aware of them, to become anxious about them and even to react against them. They know that the respect owed to human life is rapidly deteriorating, openly and in diverse ways. These people and all other men of good will long to be enlightened and directed.

We see the evil in whose name some would refuse the Church the freedom to speak out in a domain so decisive for the future of humanity. To make use of this right is even an imperative duty.[1] This duty is pressing due to the fact that respect for human life is first of all a problem of natural morality; still more, obviously, Christian theology also has a specific contribution to make to this subject. But when, even among Christians, moral conscience is darkened to the point of no longer perceiving the most elementary demands of justice, it becomes an integral part of the service which the church owes the human community to revivify in it the sensitivity of this moral conscience. The Church, which loves all men, could not resign herself to the idea of the mutilation or elimination of even one innocent human being.

The actual situation facing this notion is particularly serious in that, often without thinking, men of today, Christians included, flirt with ideologies of death. Before this hopeless perspective the Church must deflate all the myths which are the source of it. More than ever the world needs to hear a word of hope. To ward off this obsession with death, to return to men the joy of living and loving, the Church must help men rediscover the fact that their life has meaning, that it is beautiful, since God loves us and calls us to love.

---

[1] See Paul VI, "Discourse to the American Bishops," May 16, 1978, in *DC* n. 1744 (June 18, 1978) 553 f; John Paul II, "Discourse to the Congress of Catholic Doctors," October 3, 1982, in *DC* n. 1840 (November 21, 1982) 1029-1032; *On Social Concerns*, 41; *Veritatis Splendor*, 27029; *Evangelium Vitae*, 19, 40,61, 65, 101.

CHAPTER I

HUMAN LIFE THREATENED

In our first chapter we are going to pinpoint and analyze the principal threats presently menacing human life. This chapter will comprise several points. We will first of all indicate the threats; then we shall examine their origins and propagators. We will then be able to uncover the "justifications" habitually invoked in favor of controlling life, and these "justifications" in turn, will have to be carefully analyzed. To end this chapter, we will highlight the perverse consequences of these practices and their "justifications."

A DISTRESSING TABLEAU

Abortion

Procured abortion occupies the first place among these menacing practices. Abortion is the major attack on human life, essentially because the victim is totally innocent and totally without defense. Now three aggravating circumstances have recently appeared and have transformed what was the act of one or two people into a "fact of society." Although the facts pertaining to this subject must be accepted with caution, one can first of all recall that, according to the U.N., there are between 40 and 60 million abortions performed each year in the world.[1] For metropolitan France alone, according to the French Ministry of Social Affairs, there were 183,551 abortions in 1993.[2] Then, in a certain number of countries, abortion is authorized by law and even presented as a "new right." Finally, costly research is financed and programed, aimed at spreading this practice and making it commonplace. After surgical abortion, mechanical abortive techniques were developed. In this regard, we must point out the dissemination on a wide scale of the intra-uterine device that notably acts by impeding nesting, thereby dooming the infant to death by expulsion from the natural milieu on which its development depends.

More recently, chemical techniques have been developed. First among these figures the abortive pill RU 486, produced by the multinational pharmaceutical firm of Hoechst-Roussel-Uclaf with the help of the World Health Organization (WHO). This preparation has already spread throughout Europe and has been authorized in the United States. In the latter country, its exploitation is assured by the Population Council, which entrusted its commercialization to the firm Advances in Health Technology. This product would be called upon — according to Dr. Etienne Baulieu, who presents himself as its inventor — to "help" the poor countries, like China, to "control" the growth of their population, the preliminary condition, we are assured, to any development. Other multinational pharmaceutical firms are in the process of producing similar preparations, e.g. the Schering Company.

Alongside the abortive pill, research has been in progress for many years to produce anticonception vaccines.[3] This research also benefits from substantial support coming notably from the World Health Organization and from the United States. Diverse and convergent indications permit us to state that this research has now entered an experimental phase on a large scale. Among the victim countries of these experimental campaigns are the Philippines, Nicaragua, Brazil and Mexico.

Abusive Medical Practices

Human life is equally threatened by *In Vitro* fertilization, which was the subject of the instruction *Donum Vitae* published in 1987 by the Congregation for the Doctrine of the Faith.[4] Beyond the moral qualification that applies to *In Vitro* fertilization properly so-called, we should realize that this practice unjustly runs the risk of causing death to some embryos. In the case of a multiple pregnancy one doesn't hesitate to have recourse to selective abortion, and surplus embryos are used for experimental or commercial purposes.

Experience also shows that prenatal examinations can lead to abortive conduct. We are not calling into question the lawfulness of these examinations if they are used to detect and cure a disease. Actually we should rejoice in the remarkable progress of prenatal surgery. But when prenatal examinations detect an anomaly in the infant, all too often they result in a decision to abort the child. The very existence of the infant is then subject to the realization of a dependent condition: it is permitted to live on condition that it is not afflicted with malformation.

Human life is still threatened by abusive medical experiments, performed at all ages, and which are not excused by either scientific research or even the intention of seeking a remedy for a disease.

Recourse to grafts, their excision and their transplanting must be done with the enlightened consent of the donor, and the chances of proportional success must be explained to him or her. Experience, however, shows that abuses are not rare in this area. Haste in excising organs for grafting from "warm cadavers" often calls for great moral reservations. An international market for fresh organs already exists whose victims are the poor or those without defense.[5]

Euthanasia

Already practiced openly or discreetly in many countries, euthanasia tends to spread. In Holland, according to the report of the general prosecutor Remmlinck, 15% of deaths are brought about by euthanasia.[6] As recently in the case of abortion, the practice of "fait accompli" is used — according to the desire of some — to anticipate "legalization." To facilitate things, they erase the difference between licit palliative care and euthanasia properly so-called, and they endeavor morally to excuse this practice by confusing the latter with the former.

Euthanasia consists, for the one who procures it, in deliberately putting an end to the life of someone, whether at the request of the person concerned, his entourage, or at the decision of the one who does it. The causes for "excusing" this are well known: an incurable disease, compassion, the suffering of those near, uselessness, for the sake of society, to avoid great expense for the sick in a terminal stage, etc.[7]

Life Dried Up At Its Sources

Before conception, life is threatened at its living source by *sterilization*, the practice of which also tends to become commonplace.[8] Men and women have recourse to it in order to enjoy sexual pleasure without the risk of procreation. We observe, nevertheless, the appearance of a new motivation. In the Third-World and, more recently, in developed countries, some enterprises demand that women produce a certificate that they have been sterilized when they are hired (see Illustration 1).[9] This practice is observed even in some countries in which the replenishment of the population is no longer assured. One can point to it in Germany, which would appear victim to the condemnation of its own memory (*damnatio memoriae*).[10]

Contraception must also be mentioned here, for even if it only procures reversible sterilization in principle, it also reveals an attitude of being closed to life. It detaches the unitive end from the procreative end of conjugal union, somewhat like the decadent Romans who had recourse to *vomitorium* in order to immerse themselves in the "big meal" and thus disconnect the tasting end from the nourishing end of eating.

Presently, some international organizations pride themselves on the increasing extension of the number of those who use contraception.[11] Now, even in the opinion of abortion activists, the contraceptive mentality opens the way to the abortion mentality:[12] In case of failure of contraception, one must have recourse to remedial abortion.

Practices having Harmful Repercussions

To this lamentable enumeration we must, alas, add other practices that have harmful repercussions on human life and the respect owed to it.

Homosexuality, with the moral specification it implies, involves actions and life-style behavior that reject life.[13] Furthermore, groups of homosexual persons frequently effect an alliance with movements favorable to abortion.

Drug addiction, unfortunately very widespread, entails personality problems among its users, creating anti-social behavior hostile to life, and eventually may lead even to self-destruction.

AIDS and Suicide

AIDS has had an alarming spread.[14] According to the data released on November 17, 1995, by the World Health Organization, 10 million people have been infected, and this number could reach 40 million by the end of the century. Since 1970 the number of deaths due to this disease would be in the order of 4 million.

Now AIDS evidently plays a restraining role in demographic growth. It happens that we are in the presence of what is sometimes called "deferred suicide" through a frantic plunge into pleasure and/or despair.

The *suicide of young people*, pitiful indicator of society's malaise,

Illustration 1

Percentage of Couples Who Presently Use Contraceptive Methods

World Region	Sterilization		Pill	Injections	IUD
	Women	Men			
Percentage of couples where the woman is of procreating age					
World	17	5	8	1	12
Developing Countries	20	5	6	1	14
Africa	1	0.1	6	2	4
Asia & Oceania	23	6	4	1	16
Latin America & Caribbean	21	1	16	1	7
Developed Regions	8	4	16	0.1	6
Percentage of users of contraception					
World	30	8	14	2	21
Developing Countries	37	9	11	3	26
Africa	8	0.4	36	10	20
Asia & Oceania	39	11	7	2	28
Latin America & Caribbean	36	1	28	2	11
Developed Regions	11	6	22	0.2	8

Source: *Informe conciso sobre la situación demográfica en el mundo en 1995* (New York: U.N., 1995) 21.

sometimes reaches a very high index that attests to the failure of the search for happiness among a great number of youth. The most recent data indicates 10,000 suicides a year in France, principally among the young.[15]

Recourse to *psychiatry* and to other medical disciplines for policing, coercive or repressive purposes, so frequent among contemporary totalitarian regimes, has also contributed to the creation of a civilization of death.[16] A perverse use of psychiatry, for example, can lead victims to such self-disdain that they come to commit suicide.

And so it appears that these different threats are consistent with a general context of declared hostility to life. How could our society have reached the point of succumbing to this fatal tendency?

DO NOT FORGET THE PAST

Unfortunately, we must assert that contempt for human life is constantly attested to in humanity's history and even in its recent past.

History

History teaches us that cases of extermination, genocide, infanticide, exposure of infants, etc., are, so to speak, recurrent throughout the centuries. The Old Testament itself contains reports of massacres that surprise us.

Without doubt, we have to seek the origin of this behavior in the aggressiveness that smolders in the heart of man. But we must also seek it in the tendency to find a "scapegoat," that is, to make someone else bear the responsibility for our own misfortunes.[17]

Ever since the advent of industry, new forms of disdain for human life have seen the light of day. Leo XIII denounced the lack of respect on the part of employers for the life of their workers: He denounced job insecurity, unhealthy working and living conditions and, above all, the violence of the structures in industrial society. This violence, he reminded us, is explained by the lure for gain that leads to the maximum exploitation of workers. Echoing the tone of *Rerum Novarum*, numerous later pontifical texts, especially *On Social Concern* and *Centesimus Annus*, have shown that these criticisms were always topical.

During the 20th century, contempt for human life was also expressed by particularly monstrous political regimes. Just think of Soviet Communism! How can it be forgotten that this political system, first in the USSR and then in China, legalized abortion for population control, and presented it as a requirement of the imperative planning of production? How can it be forgotten that in the name of the same ideology entire populations, especially the peasants, have been massacred? And what shall we say about fascism which reduced man to being a simple impersonal "member" in the body of the State? How can we let the memory be erased of a Naziism that, not content with having made sterilization and euthanasia commonplace, and after having encouraged cruel medical experiments, exterminated millions of innocent people for racial, philosophical or religious reasons?[18] The nearly total *black-out* that surrounded the fiftieth anniversary of the Nuremberg trial (1946) fully reveals the embarrassment into which this commemoration would plunge the anti-life circles.

The Recent Past

The atomic bombing of Hiroshima and Nagasaki in 1945 and the "justifications" afterwards invoked in an attempt to excuse them, have contributed toward acclimatizing the public and some leaders to the idea that in modern warfare the massive destruction of innocent populations poses no special moral problems.[19] Solely because they possess the means of incomparably greater destruction, the strongest think they are justified in using these means with abandon and impudence.

The Gulf War (1991) confirmed this callousness. Some found it "normal," on the one hand, that the victors had suffered relatively low human losses and, on the other, that in the camp of the vanquished the human losses, both military and civil, were relatively high. They even prided themselves on this situation.

The death industry has never been so prosperous. Men compete in ingenuity when it comes to preparing for the mass elimination or even extermination of the human race. This funereal ingenuity, however, has some surprises in store: The cost of removing anti-personnel mines is ten times higher than planting them. We think that we've settled accounts with Communism, Fascism and Naziism, but we have not removed from our mentality the worst aspect of these ideologies, namely, the obsession with death.

In fact, the ideologies of death are experiencing a present revival and even have the tendency of becoming refined. After the rout of Fascism and Naziism in 1945 and despite the implosion of Soviet Communism, the spectre of total war still hovers over the world. International relations are always profoundly impregnated with the idea that war is not only the affair of the military; it is being waged everywhere, by every means and in all domains.

Thus, while continuing the production of classical armaments, contemporary society has witnessed the birth of new ideological "indications" that "legitimize" attacks on life. One sees the means for suppressing life or drying up its sources multiplying. The new methods are produced in laboratories and are used in dispensaries, clinics and hospitals.

Contemporary totalitarian regimes have had recourse to effective methods of individual and group *mental conditioning*. They have frequently used lies to maximize the effects of violence. These techniques for deprograming-reprograming have become more and more effective thanks especially to the complicity of some psychiatrists. This results often in the weakening or inhibiting of the ability to make personal judgments and free decisions among individuals as well as society.[20]

The effectiveness of these methods is even perceptible in the role the media has assigned to itself. It not only has the ability to select or distort information; it also possesses the means to condition public opinion by inculcating lies that are absorbed without discernment. It is recognized that the media has thus contributed to making practices disdaining life acceptable to a public opinion too easily manipulated. In the mass media, and even in scientific publications, every procedure is followed in order to abuse public opinion, condition government officials, and manipulate minds. Henceforth the lie becomes an "aid for decision making."[21]

Finally, alas, we find at the source of this disdain for life factors such as silence, abdication of responsibility, and even the connivance of some theologians and pastors. With regard to the campaigns hostile to life some are so fearful that they hardly feel concerned over what is at stake. Others take refuge in casuistic or semantic acrobatics, and their subtle ambiguities, besides supporting immoral practices, have the effect of creating confusion and error. It even happens that some confessional groups refuse to teach entire parts of morality.[22]

Thus in the contempt of which life is presently the object, the responsibility of spiritual leaders is seriously indicated, as much by reason of omission as by their complicity.

In the Name of "Higher Interest"

Etienne De Greef (1989-1961), who was professor of psychiatry at the University of Louvain, wrote:

Higher interest suffices to dry out at its source all sympathetic reaction toward the most innocent and pitiable victims.... The notion of higher interest instantly desensitizes our consciences, which offer only minimal resistance to this anesthetic.

It is in the name of freedom, of justice and morality, and even for love of one's neighbor, that people commit the worst crimes on earth.

Today we know that civilized people can, without fearing the least serious condemnation on the part of another civilized nation, terrorize, steal from and destroy an ethnic minority, provided they succeed, not by hiding the fact, but by preventing the victims' cries from being heard and their despair from being perceived.

The same author adds:

Hitler did but push to their ultimate limits the battle against life, the negation of the concept of good and evil, and the repudiation of all moral law. Why and with what right are people scandalized by these ideas which are taught in the greatest number of Western Universities?[23]

POWERFUL AGENTS OF DISSEMINATION

The attacks on human life at its source as well as in its development unfortunately are led or supported by entities in possession of powerful means.[24] These means are shown in illustration 2.

Public International Institutions

Certain public international institutions — which otherwise render appreciable services to the human community — encourage and program, as they themselves proclaim, practices opposed to human life. The United Nations Fund for Population (UNFPA), for example, doesn't hide its support either for hormonal contraception or for sterilization. If it is discreet about abortion, it doesn't hesitate, however, to recommend the IUD as well as the more recent drugs whose effect is either contraceptive, obstructive and even antinidatory.[25] UNFPA also contributes its copatronage to several anti-life programs at other international organizations, such as WHO or IPPF.

A specialized agency of the U.N., WHO had for years sponsored research programs concerning human reproduction. These programs are concerned, among other things, with new methods of contraception and sterilization.[26]

Illustration 2

Expenses for Population Programs 1982-1991

Channel of Distribution	1982	1983	1984	1985	1986	1987	1988	1989	1990	1991
Bilateral					Thousands of US $					
	101,587	98,565	134,383	161,046	129,336	145,297	163,330	208,437	231,325	286,487
					Percentage of the total					
	28	28	32	34	36	36	29	40	38	39
Multilateral					Thousands of US $					
	153,897	153,267	171,878	182,641	105,070	112,129	161,755	142,822	169,646	249,376
					Percentage of the total					
	42	43	40	39	30	28	29	28	28	34
Nongovernmental Organizations					Thousands of US $					
	111,761	100,933	118,936	125,170	121,022	149,813	242,029	165,813	200,822	196,022
					Percentage of the total					
	30	29	28	27	34	37	43	32	33	27
Total					Thousands of US $					
	367,246	352,766	425,198	469,216	355,427	407,241	567,113	517,072	601,794	731,885

Source: *Review and Appraisal of the World Population Plan of Action. 1994 Report.* (New York: U.N., 1995) 131. The multilateral channel does not include the World Bank because the disbursements of the Bank for population activities was not available at the time of the inquiry.

Many of these institutions try to obtain U.N. support for the policies they put into effect.

It happens also that some international officials, paid by educational, scientific or other agencies, are little by little being diverted from their proper tasks to programs for controlling life. Furthermore, some institutions like UNICEF do not hesitate to go beyond their mandate in order to give their endorsement to programs hostile to life.[27]

Other diverse international organizations attribute economic "justifications" for these practices. The dissemination of contraception, and limiting the birth rate using the most effective means are, for poor countries, an indispensable prerequisite for their development. This theme appeared especially in the discourse of Robert McNamara to the U.N. in 1991,[28] as well as in various reports of the World Bank and the International Monetary Fund. We see them also in the reports of specialized agencies of the U.N., such as the Program for Development and in the publications of UNICEF.

We must again point out that some initiatives are undertaken to sensitize the heads of State and members of parliaments and rally their support for activist programs determined by public and/or private international organizations.[29]

National Governments

Now it happens that national governments actually provide documents that reveal their intentions about controlling life. Particularly noteworthy among those issued in the United States, is the dossier entitled NSSM 200 produced in 1974 at the request of Henry Kissinger, then Secretary of State.[30] A document of major importance, it analyzes the implications of world demographic growth for the security of the United States and its interests abroad. On the governmental level, the chief architect of North American demographic policy is the United States Agency for International Development (USAID).[31]

National governments' interest in programs that control life is also shown by the financial contributions they pour into organizations which specialize in the field.[32]

Moreover, the example for controlling human life domestically given by the wealthy countries has often been presented as a necessary prerequisite for controlling life in poorer countries. According to some, it was necessary to make abortion commonplace in wealthy countries in order that, by way of imitation, it would be accepted by the poor countries.[33] To crown it all, it unfortunately very frequently happens that officials in poor countries themselves organize campaigns to control the procreative activity of their citizens.[34]

Finally, poor countries are called upon in a more and more insistent manner to finance themselves the campaigns to control life which have been undertaken among them![35]

Private Organizations

With ramifications that almost always spread to international society, some private groups also act with determination. They often have recourse to the practice of lobbying. This consists in acting informally on the margin of official meetings in view of influencing the participating members.

One of the principal groups is the International Planned Parenthood Federation (IPPF), whose members are active in very many countries.[36] The organization prides itself on working with the grassroots, but it also intervenes with those who make the decisions. It disseminates all the available methods for preventing the transmission of human life. The sources for funding the IPPF and its affiliates leave no doubt about the fact that this "private" organization is widely used by wealthy nations. Various elements in the USA, in particular, use it to carry out policies on demographic control. The NSSM 200 dossier, already cited, explicitly confirms this connivance.

Many other organizations act in the same way. In the United States examples are: the Population Council, the Rockefeller Foundation, the Ford Foundation, the National Organization for Women, Catholic Pro-Choice, the National Abortion Rights League and many others. Mention should also be made of what many universities do, among them John Hopkins University and Columbia University. These universities receive governmental funding to conduct research on controlling life.[37]

Many of these organizations have begun to spread all over the world. They habitually present themselves as beneficent associations for aiding women, the family and their rights, aid for development, etc.

To these organizations aiming at controlling the transmission of life must be added those that fight for sterilization or euthanasia. Among the first figures is the Association for Voluntary Surgical Contraception; among the second we should mention the Euthanasia Society of America.

Special attention should be focused on the informal clubs whose influence is sometimes noted among political and economic decision-makers and which receive a considerable hearing before public opinion. In some famous reports, the Club of Rome, for example contributed toward sensitizing minds to the "problems" of poverty and population.

According to certain of its most qualified members, Freemasonry has played a prime role in the international promotion of contraception and abortion.[38] We see this, for example, in the book, *De la vie avant toute chose*, by Dr. Pierre Simon, obstetrician-gynecologist and former Grand Master of the Grand Lodge of France.[39]

Some doctors are also wondering what role they could or should play when faced with abortion. Especially significant in this regard is the action of the Association for the Study of Abortion. The acts of the congress organized in 1968 by this organization are the expression of a real change of attitude in some medical circles regarding abortion, and, consequently, human life.[40]

We should also mention the role of pharmaceutical firms. The Hoechst-Roussel-Uclaf and Schering laboratories are involved in preparing abortifacient drugs.[41] Some of the most important firms of the world fight over the contraceptive market. Such is the case of Parke-Davis and Johnson & Johnson, American Home Products, Akzo Pharma, Syntex, Upjohn, etc.

Curiously, these firms are developing projects which, in the end, are going to limit their own expansion. In effect, every infant born is one of the potential sick people on whom the expansion of the pharmaceutical market depends.

The Media

The responsibility of the media is greatly apparent in the dissemination of methods aimed at controlling human life and their justification.[42] Frequently the media presents contraception, sterilization and abortion with an insistent sympathy, and it encourages international projects of demographic control in the poor world.

At the same time, the media easily passes over in silence the work which discloses the multiple risks of contraception, sterilization, abortion, etc. In the same way, the demographic studies that refuse to go along with the anti-life alarmism of the international establishment are hidden.

[1] See the three volumes prepared by the Department of Economic and Social Development of the U.N., *Abortion Policies: A Global Review* (New York: U.N., (1992, 1993,1995). This publication can be completed by reference to *Abortion, A Tabulation of Available Data on the Frequency and Mortality of Unsafe Abortion*, 2nd edit., document WHO/FHE/MSM/93.13 (Geneva: WHO, 1994). One can wonder about the origin and reliability of the data put forward in these two publication.

[2] According to the demographer Chantal Blayo, of the National Institute for Demographic Studies (INED), this number is underestimated and should be rectified by adding 16% which brings the total to 218,514. See the INED's review, *Population*, May-June 1995.

[3] On vaccines see the report of WHO, *Challenges in Reproductive Health Research. Biennial Report 1992-1993* (Geneva: WHO, 1994) esp. 43, 67, 71 f., 124-128, etc.; David Griffin et al., "Anti-Fertility Vaccines: Current Status and Implications for Family Planning Programmes," in *Reproductive Health Matters*, (Geneva: WHO) n.3 (May 1994) 108-114. David Griffin applied himself to showing the link between the "anti-fertility" vaccine and the "burgeoning population" in "The Immunoregulation of fertility — Changes in Perspectives," the *American Journal of Reproductive Immunology*, n.35 (1996) 140-147. Together with Julie Milstien and J. W. Lee, he published "Damage to Immunization Programmes from Misinformation on Contraceptive Vaccines, "*Reproductive Health Matters* (Geneva) n.6 (November 1995) 24-28. The authors protest the denunciations made by pro-life movements against the vaccine. Their protest would be more convincing if they explained why the vaccination campaigns are above all directed at the female population of reproductive age. This program is criticized by Judith Richter in *Vaccination against Pregnancy. Miracle or Menace*? (Amsterdam: Health Action International (Jacob van Lennepkade 334 T, 1993); the video of U. Schaz and I. Schneider, *Antibodies against Pregnancy* (Hamburg, Bleicherstrasse 2, 1991). The controversy over the vaccine has developed above all in Mexico: see, among others, Rodrigo Vera, "Controversia en torno de la vacuna antitetánica," *Proceso* (Mexico D.F.) n.971 (June 1995) 32-35; James A. Miller, "Baby-Killing Vaccine: Is It Being Stealth Tested?" *HLI Reports* (Gaithersburg, MD) 1, 2, 8.

[4] Text in *DC*, n.1937 (April 1987) 349-361.

[5] See *DTL*, 124-126.

[6] See Philippe Schepens, *L'Euthanasie. Pourquoi en Hollande*? (Ostende: World Federation of Doctors Who Defend Human Life: 1995); on the Remmlinck report see pp.29 f and 42. One of the reference works on euthanasia is due to Karl Binding and Alfred Hoche, *Permitting the Destruction of Unworthy Life*, a rare work whose translation was published in *Issues in Law and Medicine*, vol.2 n.2 1992, reprint series, P.O. Box 1586, Terre Haute, IN, pp.231-165.

[7] We will return in detail to this question in Chapter III.

[8] The reference work on this subject is that of Stephen Trombley, *The Right to Reproduce. A History of Coercive Sterilization* (London: Weidenfeld and Nicolson, 1988). See the monograph of Fenneke Rysoo and al., *The Incentive Trap. A Study in Coercion, Reproductive Rights and Women's Autonomy in Bangladesh* (Leiden: ed. Rijks Universiteit, 1995).

[9] A film made for North American television by Ed. Kaplan, *For Their Own Good*, takes up this problem.

[10] Karl Jaspers devoted a famous work to *La Culpabilité allemande* (Paris: Minuit, 1948). The scope of this reflection is such that it goes beyond the case of Nazi Germany and is of great interest for the present situation.

[11] Of many other examples, see *The State of World Population 1995* (New York: UNFPA); See also the tableau entitled *World Contraceptive Use 1994* (New York: U.N.). the *Plano estratégico. Visión año 2000* (London: IPPF, 1993), etc.

[12] See *EPA*, 81; *BPCV*, qu.122.

[13] Magaly Llaguno in 1994 joined two collections of documents devoted to *Homosexualismo y Sida*. These collections are available from Vida Humana Internacional, 4345 S.W. 72nd Ave. Suite E, Miami, FL. 33155.

[14] Of the abundant literature on AIDS one should take note of *Exposé fait à l'Académie des sciences de Paris*, Nov. 16, 1992, by William A. Haseltine. The text of the Harvard professor's address was translated into French by René Bel and is available in manuscript form from the translator, Via Aurelia 218, I-00165 Rome. René Bel himself has prepared several substantial dossiers on this pandemic, especially as it developed in Africa. These dossiers, compiled with exemplary rigor, are available from the author and deserve widespread distribution.

[15] See the despairing "testament" of someone who committed suicide in Stig Dagerman, *Notre besoin de consolation est impossible à rassasier* (Actes Sud, Hubert Nyssen, 1981). According to WHO, it is estimated that 779,000 people committed suicide in 1993. See the *Rapport du la santé 1995. Réduire les écarts* (Geneva: WHO, 1995), esp. pp. 19 and 35.

[16] See *DTL*, 213 f.; *BPCV*, qu.142.

[17] The word of René Girard can cast a bright light on the "culture of death." Let researchers who lack a topic for a thesis take note! See specially *Le Bouc émissaire* (Paris; Grasset, 1982) and *Quand ces choses commenceront...* (Paris: Arléa, 1994).

[18] A catalogue — always yet to be completed — of genocides of the 20th century was compiled by Yves Ternon, *L'État criminel. Les génocides au Xxe siècle* (Paris: Le Seuil, 1995).

[19] See Karl Jaspers, *La Bombe atomique et l'avenir de l'humanité* (Paris: Buchet-Chastel, 1963).

[20] Totalitarianism's objective is to destroy the "Ego." This is explained by Jean-Jacques Walter, *Les machines totalitaires*(Paris: Denoël, 1982).

[21] One can find an illustration of the danger represented by ensnaring language in the astonishing repertoire of Janice Miller and Claire Bahamon, *Family Planning Management Terms. A Pocket Glossary in Three Languages* (Newton, MA: Management Sciences for Health, 1996). This work curiously omits a few "sensitive" words like abortion, race, holism, paradigm, etc.

[22] Cardinal Ratzinger points out in this regard that "relativism is today the central problem of faith and theology;" see the text of a conference bearing that title in *DC* n.2151 (January 5, 1997) 29-37.

[23] Cited in Jacques Verhagen (ed.) *Licéité en Droit positif et Références légales aux valeurs* (Brussels: Bruylant, 1982) 165 f.; other quotations on pp. 159-167.

[24] We analyze these problems in a more detailed way in *DTL*, 59-90 and *passim*.

[25] UNFPA publishes about every two years an *Inventory of Population Projects in Developing Countries Around the World*; see, for example, the 1995 edition, New York: United Nations Population Fund. This publication is of capital importance as a source of information on birth control projects. See also Gaston Legrain and Pierre Delvoye, *La Planification familiale pratique et opérationnelle* (Paris: Hatier, 1994); Elizabeth Wollast and Marcel Vekemans, *Pratique et gestion de la planification familiale dans les pays en voie de développement* (Brussels: De Boeck, 1995). These two books were supported by UNFPA and explain its goals and practices. See also *The State of World Population 1995* (New York, U.N.).

[26] See the *Rapport sur la santé dans le monde 1995. Réduire les écarts* (Geneva: WHO, 1995) 33-45. More revealing still is the report entitled *Reproductive Health: A Key to a Brighter Future* (Geneva: WHO, 1992). The same WHO explains "what health workers need to know" concerning vasectomy and female sterilization in two brochures published in Geneva in 1994. WHO doesn't stop there: it is preparing a new ethic which we will examine later in Chapter III.

[27] The report of UNICEF on *La situation des enfants dans le monde 1996*, published in New York, intermittently touches on these questions, especially on pp. 55, 64-66. UNICEF takes responsibility for dissemination, through educational channels, of the "justifying" reasons for controlling the transmission of life.

[28] This address of Robert McNamara is entitled *A World Demographic Policy to Promote Human Development in the 20th Century*; it was given on December 10, 1991 and published by the U.N. in New York in same year.

[29] There exists a Global Committee of Parliamentarians on Population and Development; its address is 304 E. 45th St., New York, NY 10017. This committee disseminated in 1985 a *Statement on Population Stabilization by World Leaders*, signed by forty heads of state from the Third-World. It organizes congresses to sensitize members of parliaments to the necessity of controlling the population.

[30] This document, codified as NSSM-200/1974, has the title *Implications of Worldwide Population Growth for U.S. Security and Overseas Interests*. Circulating in diverse forms, the text can be found in the violently anti-Christian work of Stephen D. Mumford, *The Life and Death of NSSM 200* (Center for Research on Population and Security P.O. Box 13067, Research Triangle, NC 27709, 1994) 45-186.

[31] The publications coming out of this agency are completely clear as to its objectives and means. See, for example, Elizabeth S. Maguire, director of the Office of Population of USAID, *Evaluating Reproductive Health Programs: Perspective for the U.S. Agency for International Development*, a manuscript of 11 pages, prepared for the Annual Meeting of the Population Association of America, San Francisco, CA, April 1995. On the resources allocated see *Overview of USAID Population Assistance* 1993 (Washington, D.C.: Office of Population of USAID, April 1994).

[32] Some of these financial contributions appear in the annual reports of the U.N. and its agencies as well as the reports of non-governmental organizations.

[33] This thesis is explicitly defended by René Dumont in *L'Utopie ou la mort* (Paris: Le Seuil, 1973) 47-51.

[34] The example of China is far from being unique. See the *Programa Nacional de Población 1995-2000* fixed by the *Poder Ejecutivo Federal*, (Mexico City: 1995).

[35] See *DTL*, 72-73.

[36] See, for example, the *Informe Annual 1994-1995* published by IPPF in London. See also *Plano estratégico. Vision año 2000* (London, 1993 f.).

[37] See, for example, Stephen Isaacs (ed.), *Politique de population. Un manuel pour les planificateurs et les responsables politiques*, 2nd ed. (New York: Columbia University Press, 1991). Published in many languages, this booklet was subsidized by USAID, the North American agency for international development. For further related reading, see *EPA* 137-141.

[38] See *DTL*, 218. See also "Les secrets des francs-macons," in *Le Vif-L'Express* of Brussels, n.2081 (May 24-30, 1991) 37.

[39] Pierre Simon, *De la vie avant toute chose* (Paris: Mazarine, 1979).

[40] The acts of this congress were edited in two volumes by Robert E. Hall under the title *Abortion in a Changing World* (New York: Columbia University Press, 1970).

[41] See above under **A Distressing Tableau**, *Abortion*.

[42] The role that the media plays and can play with a view to controlling the transmission of life is shown in the work of Sandra Colvier, *The Right to Know, Human Rights and Access to Reproductive Health* (University of Pennsylvania Press, 1995).

CHAPTER II
THE IDEOLOGICAL COALITION OF GENDER

The reasons habitually given to "justify" practices aimed at controlling human life are derived from two ideologies, socialist and liberal, which have affected the contemporary world the most. But these two ideologies are presently given a double interpretation. It revolves around two themes: "gender" and the "new paradigm." Because of its importance, the latter will be treated in Chapter III.

SOCIALISM AND LIBERALISM REVISITED

Socialist Ideology

Currents hostile to life borrow many fundamental themes from the socialist ideology.

Among them, we find the idea of generic humanity coming from Feuerbach (1804-1872). The only thing that really counts is the "human race"; the individual human is but a momentary manifestation and doomed to death. The life of humans, including their corporeal and physical aspect, will have to be useful for generic humanity and organized according to the needs of collective humanity, and it is only as such that the human "survives" after death. The glorious society will be achieved via planning based on the scientific knowledge of the principals that govern matter. Individuals will be cogs, sometimes useful, sometimes harmful, in the social machine; and they should be treated accordingly.

This ideology also comprises a sensualism which is moderated only by the requirements flowing from the transcendence of generic humanity. Humans will have the right to the most total individual pleasure, provided that this pleasure is compatible with the species's accepted standards.

We also find the influence of Marx (1818-1883) with his theory of class struggle. Between the proletariat and the capitalists, the weak and the strong, the poor and the rich, struggle, even violent, is inevitable.

The reinterpretation of internationalism is also derived from the Marxist tradition. National identities and regional peculiarities must dissolve so that the New World Order can blossom.[1]

It is also from Marx that the reinterpretation of messianism is derived. In virtue of this, it is entrusted to the so-called enlightened minority to explain to ordinary mortals what they must think, will and do. This minority is the heir to the enlightened despotism of the 18th century, and one finds it henceforth in the international technocrats who determine the programs with which we are familiar.

Finally, it is mostly from Lenin (1870-1924) that the idea of a bureaucracy is derived which, duly organized by the enlightened technocrats, is going to establish a network of international organizations at the service of the planning of human life.

Malthus and Liberal Ideology

Currents advocating control of human life owe their utilitarian conception of man also to liberal ideology. However, despite a fundamental relationship, this conception of man is presented differently than in the socialist ideology; it nevertheless leads to conclusions similar to those of the socialist ideology. In the "justifications" invoked for controlling human life we find a permanent influence of a few classical themes of liberal ideology.

In the reformation which is presently given to it, liberal ideology is firstly dependent on a heritage that, at least in some aspects, goes back to Plato. In fact, we know that the great philosopher recommended a strict quantitative and qualitative control of the population. The city must limit its inhabitants and conduct a eugenic policy.[2]

Malthus (1766-1834) is the heir to this ancient tradition: he appears as the major theoretician of security in food resources. According to him, the gap deepens fatally between the arithmetical increase of food resources and the geometrical growth of the population. Penury emerges and, with it the spectre of famine. One must not, therefore, interfere with Nature's mechanisms that bring about a wise "natural" selection. One must allow the brakes to operate, thanks to which the less endowed and poor are eliminated. In their interest and in that of everybody else, it will also be necessary to counsel late marriage and continence.

Malthus, then, contributes toward consolidating the essentially utilitarian vision of man developed by Bentham (1748-1832). The poor person is vanquished by free competition; he is simply surplus because he does not produce anything, or if he does, not enough, and yet still needs to eat.

Malthusianism is going to spread, but the contemporary currents that attack human life will always make its hard essence a principal reference point. From this Malthusian heritage is also retained the idea that poverty as well as riches are a "natural" phenomenon which should not give anyone a complex or cause a feeling of guilt; this phenomenon is determined by the unequal aptitudes of individuals.

Eugenics and Neo-Malthusianism

On the heels of Malthus, others will take an important step: selection — they will recommend — will have to be artificial and doctors will be in charge of it. *Galton* (1822-1911) will be one of the most influential theoreticians of this eugenics. For him, there are considerable inborn differences among individuals, and these differences are determined by the genetic capital of each person. It is, therefore, vain to hope that the environment, especially education, will ameliorate the less apt performances. And so it is necessary to favor transmission of life between more talented partners and to curb it among the less endowed.

Eugenics programs of Galton's inspiration are actually practiced in diverse countries. While they are discreet in Singapore, they are made official in China, where couples may procreate following the quotas that are variable according to the "quality" of the parents determined by the biocratic bureaucracy.[3]

Furthermore, present liberal ideology also owes much to the neo-Malthusian tradition. Man has the right and even the duty to exercise control over the transmission of life, but to this Malthusian thesis, neo-Malthusianism adds the thesis of the right of the individual to pleasure. This thesis finds its origin in *hedonist* morality, that is to say, that which gives pleasure — in this case, sexual — an object of man's good par excellence.

In their most radical expressions, feminist currents will apply to women the neo-Malthusian thesis of the right to individual pleasure.

They will draw from it the conclusion that whatever has the nature of procuring this pleasure is permitted, and whatever is an obstacle to it must be set aside. The neo-Malthusian current, then, is going to contribute powerfully to acclimatizing the idea that, in the conjugal union, it is proper to disassociate as effectively as possible pleasure from procreation.[4] In this way neo-Malthusianism is going to incite people to free love and, by that very fact, destroy the family. For this notion, marriage in effect involves a commitment to fidelity that compromises the total freedom which each partner must enjoy at every moment, whatever situation may arise.

Joining Socialism to Liberalism

At the present time, the socialist and liberal ideologies, together with their underlying philosophical references, continue to furnish the principal arguments for "justifying" disdain for human life. *The two ideologies in question have even coalesced in producing this very result; that is what explains the violence, without precedent in history, that has been unleashed against human life.* This union of the two ideologies is accompanied by the reinforcement of characteristic themes of which we will mention but a few.

The theme of internationalism reappears under the rubric of the "New World Order," which leads to the questioning of the right of nations to decide matters themselves, and hence of their sovereignty. This "one worldism," or "globalism," goes hand in hand with a new conception of the market: it must be worldwide. Everything must be subordinate to it, including both politics as well as the productivity of man. In this market individuals are given a simple function.[5]

Class struggle is found again under the form of opposition between the strong and the weak, the productive and the unproductive, the healthy and the sick, the rich and the poor, the north and the south.

Penury, seen first of all as concerning food resources, is now generalized to include all resources and the whole encompassing environment. This trend leads straight away to a redefinition of the right to living space, eventually to the profit of a privileged few.

The messianism exercised by an "enlightened" minority is claimed by a new caste of international functionaries who certainly posses, in all vital matters, a knowledge inaccessible to the majority.

The neo-Malthusian position on the right of individuals to pleasure is amplified, generalized and exported to poor countries where it is first used to hide the unmentionable motivations that compel the rich to want to control the life of the poor.

The theme of generic humanity, which has already proven its effectiveness in racist and segregationist systems, reappears in the new moralities of the human species with a racist connotation that is not admitted. The biomedical techniques presently available permit, in turn, the programing of scientific eugenics.[6] It is necessary to avoid the soiling of "noble blood" with "impure blood"; human society needs the former. Inferior individuals must be diverted from the transmission of life, and neither the learned nor public powers — we are assured — must avoid the responsibility that falls to them in this domain.

Especially worrisome is the perverse use that can be made of state-of-the-art biology which explores the human genome. By abusing its resources, eugenics will be able to spread and, with it, new criteria of segregation, eventually dressed up with the title "quality of life."

THE IDEOLOGY OF GENDER

The combined influence of the socialist and liberal traditions is especially striking in the two principal anti-life ideologies presently so active: the ideology of "gender"[7] and the ideology of the "new paradigm." While owing so much to neo-Malthusian liberalism, the ideology of "gender" is strongly influenced by Marx and Engels. It actually pervades most of the international organizations that deal with controlling life.[8] As for the ideology of the "new paradigm," it is also pervaded by the socialist tradition. It is, however, closer to the pure and firm liberal tradition of portraying health as a product in service of the market.[9]

Class Struggle Reactivated

For Engels, the oppression of women is the expression par excellence of class struggle under its original form.[10] In the era of tribal communism, a matriarchal system predominated, in which children belonged to the mother's clan and drew their inheritance from it. Once men became responsible for the growth of productivity, and as they accumulated goods of increasing value, they made children their own heirs, and thus the patriarchal system was born. Mothers were deprived of their rights over children: such was the first form of alienation. Issued from this revolution, the new condition of women signaled the emergence of the prototype of class opposition.

"The first opposition of classes manifest in history coincides with the antagonism between man and woman in conjugal marriage," writes Engels. Woman was the "first servant of man," the ideological "vulgate" assures us; this was translated into multiple pregnancies, household chores, and social marginalization. Also the father of the family wanted to transmit his private property, via inheritance, to his children.

According to Marx and Engels, communism will overcome this situation. Woman and man are equal *in this sense:* They will both have the same status as workers in a society in which they will *be* a function. More precisely, the woman, liberated from familial, maternal, and household "servitude," will contribute to industrial production. Should this happen, maternal housekeeping and other tasks performed in the private sphere of the family, would be raised to the rank of "production" in and for society. Legitimate or natural, the children would benefit from the education provided by society. This affords the woman a twofold "benefit": she will be able to make her contribution as a worker in industry; she will multiply and diversify her sexual partners, for society will take care of the eventual outcome by assuming charge of the children.

In summary, the first division of work which affects men and women results from having children. The antagonism between the two is the primordial antagonism appearing in history; it expresses in the monogamous marriage the oppression of woman by man. Communism will put this situation in good order by permitting the woman to be an industrial worker, by making monogamous marriage disappear, by destroying the traditional family, by introducing totally free love, and by extolling the equality between man and woman to the point of considering them interchangeable.

Beginning with the revolution of October 1917, many measures were taken in this regard in the USSR, and they figure again in the code of 1926. While invoking the reference of liberalism, it is toward this outcome that the ideology of gender eventually leads. The family must disappear, for it has no place for complementarity, rather only opposition. And with it will disappear the relationships of kinship, maternity, and paternity. The human being will be reduced to the condition of a mere individual, an ephemeral moment belonging to the State or the market.

The Influence of Structuralism

A very active feminist current, deriving from the ideology of *gender*, encompasses these themes of Marx and Engels. It distinguishes, on the one hand, sexual differences of biology (sex) and, on the other, the roles attributed by society to man and woman (gender). According to this trend, the differences between our human genders are not *natural*; they appeared in the course of history and were constructed by society: Therefore they are *cultural*.

The influence of French structuralism is very perceptible here. It is no longer a question of talking about human nature, these *gender* ideologies continue. Henceforth, the human should be an object of science; he is a structure, an ensemble of "elements such that any modification of one of them involves a modification of all the others."[11] As a structure, the human evolves and this evolution, furthermore, allows us to go back to the profound roots of the human himself: to the forms of animal and vegetable life and, finally, to matter. Whence the revival of interest, among the ideologues of gender, for Darwinian evolutionism and for ethnology which aims at clarifying human behavior by relating it to animal behavior.

Now human societies, in constant evolution, acquire rules for functioning, codes of communication and rules of conduct which are called culture. This latter, together with the rules it entails, is then in constant evolution.[12] The human being is himself inserted into a structured ensemble, economic and social, which is up to him to change radically. He must modify behavioral rules inherited from previous structures, for they are by definition archaic.

As we shall see, these structuralist themes are going to render the influence of Marx and Engels all the more active on the ideologies of gender.

Deconstruct and Reconstruct Society

In effect, according to these ideologies, it is advisable to eliminate the sexual classes, and it is the oppressed class, that is women, who will effect this revolution. In the current portrayal of the Marxist ideology it falls to the proletariat to play the role of the revolution's motor. According to the gender ideology, this role falls to women.

In the new dialectic inspired by Marxism, women will take up the baton from the proletariat: they will reappropriate their own bodies; they will control their fertility and use the new biomedical techniques for this purpose. The final goal sought is not simply the elimination of masculine privileges; it is the total abolition of all class distinction — a goal not to be attained except by the abolition of all differences between men and women. Terms like "marriage," "family," and "mother" must, then, be eliminated, for they no longer correspond to any of the realities admitted by this ideology. Instead, they evoke past historical situations that the ideology must denounce and destroy.[13]

This ideology of gender, therefore, combines themes originating from socialist ideology in its Marxist form, and from liberal ideology in its neo-Malthusian form. It takes as its point of departure a reinterpretation of class struggle, and this reinterpretation ands in disastrous consequences.

The first of these consequences recalls certain gnostic currents: such as that the differences between man and woman must be abolished, and the masculinity or femininity inherent in each human individual no longer expresses anything about the person. On the level of the *individual*, the body is simply an instrument for various pleasures: heterosexuality, homosexuality, indubitably solitary pleasure, contraception, abortion, etc. And therewith gender ideology joins the neo-Malthusian ideology of Margaret Sanger (1883-1966).

This ideology also leads to the destruction of the *family*. In effect, neither heterosexuality, nor procreation to which it is bound, can claim to be "natural"; they are "biologicized" cultural products. It is society that invented masculine and feminine roles and what follows from that, namely, the family. We must, then, establish a culture that denies any importance whatsoever to gender differences. With the disappearance of these differences, marriage, maternity and the biologically rooted family will disappear.[14]

Finally, this ideology also has repercussions on the level of *society* by demanding that public powers restructure society in line with gender ideology. We must deconstruct gender, for belonging to a gender indicates that we are clinging to a past moment of history, that of inequality and oppression. It follows, then, that we must reconstruct society in line with gender ideology, abolish the role that ancient society assigned respectively to man and woman. It is not a question simply of adding new "rights," and especially of "new rights for women." It is more profoundly a matter of enforcing a reinterpretation radically different from the historical precedent.

Gender at the U.N.

Developed in radical feminist circles, and disseminated by a group of non-governmental organizations, gender ideology has been welcomed with complacency in international assemblies, especially at Cairo (1994) and Beijing (1995). The U.N. itself, and several of its agencies, lost their credibility by indiscriminately accepting it and giving it its support.[15] The European Union itself followed suit.

An example will show the influence exercised by gender ideology on these institutions. The concept of family was emptied of its traditional meaning when the term began to be used to designate interchangeably heterosexual, homosexual and single-parent unions. Strong pressure has been applied for these new understandings to be included in law. On the eve of the fiftieth anniversary of the Universal Declaration of the Rights of Man (1948-1998), diverse means were used to adulterate its content, even to the point of proposing a new redaction.[16]

As we can see in the old discussion about the innate and the acquired, the natural and the cultural, gender ideology denies all realism with regard to the innate and natural. Between masculine and feminine there is no room for distinction, rather the median or equidistant point between the two is occupied by hermaphroditism. The very idea of natural differences is horrifying and it follows that these differences *must* be abolished. Hence the result is that there is no one more antifeminist than these radical feminists who want to destroy what is uniquely feminine and reduce all behavior to *roles* for which the actors could be interchangeable like the intermingling cogs in the functioning of a machine — to use the Leninist metaphor.

The ideologues of gender deny the blinding evidence, such as the mutual attraction between man and woman, and the fact that human maternity, far from being reduced to a biological function, is part of a woman's vocation and is constitutive of her identity. Furthermore, the immense majority of men and women do not feel bothered by the presence of their differences, and they are not altogether ignorant, of the bearing of historical precedent.

Moreover, it is inadmissible that the U.N. and its agencies, having become active accomplices of an ideological dictatorship, presume philosophical and moral competence, as well as political authority, in accepting the dictates of a minority of radical feminists of dubious representative qualities against the immense majority of people having common, good sense.

---

[1] See, for example, James Kurth, "Hacia el mundo posmoderno," *Facetas*, 2 (1993) 8-13; this article first appeared in English in *The National Interest*, Summer (1992).

[2] Cf. *The Republic* V, 459d-460b; *Laws* V, 737 ce; 739a-741a. These texts can be found in French in *Oeuvres complètes de Platon*, Leon Robin (Paris: Gallimard, 1950).

[3] In its March 1991 issue, the review *Integration Journal* (Tokyo) published, with regard to the People's Republic of China, a special report of great clarity on family planning in the latter country. See in particular the contributions of Peng Peiyun, Minister in charge of the National Commission on Family Planning, "A Long Way to Go," (pp.2-5), and of Duan Yixin, staff reporter for *China Population News*, entitled "Valuing International Assistance," 32 f. The eugenic aspects of the Chinese

policy have been exposed in "Ordering up 'Better' Babies," in *Time* (May 2, 1994) 48 f. A critical analysis of this same policy has been done by one of the best world specialists, John S. Aird, *Foreign Assistance to Coercive Family Planning in China. Response to Recent Population Policy in China* [by Terence Hull] (Canberra, 1992); the same specialist returned to this question in his communication to the Meeting on Family and Demography in Asia and Oceania, Taipei: Sept. 18-20, 1995; this communication in manuscript form has as its title *Family Planning, Women and Human Rights in the Peoples' Republic of China*, pp.34 which provides a first class bibliography. Furthermore, on death by abandoning care, see by the same author, *Death by Default. A Policy of Fatal Neglect in China's State Orphanages* (New York: Human Rights Watch, 1996). For France see Anne Carol, *Histoire de l'eugénism en France. Les médicins et la procréation, XIXe-XXe siècle* (Paris: Le Seuil, 1995).

[4] See Chapter I, *Life Dried Up in its Source*.

[5] We analyze "globalism" in *EPA, DTL* and *BPCV*.

[6] Sometimes covered with considerations about the "quality of life," eugenics is very much active right now. See Pierre-André Taguieff, "Sur l'eugénisme: du fantasme au débat," *Pouvoirs* (Paris)n.56 (1991) 23-64; Anne Carol, *op.cit.*; Daniel J. Kevles, *Au nom de l'eugénisme. Génétique et politique dans le monde anglo-saxon* (Paris: PUF, 1995); Ellen Brantlinger, *Sterilization of People With Mental Disabilities* (Westport, CT: Auburn House, 1995), esp. Ch. I: "Historical and Theological Overview of the Eugenics Movement," 3-16. Let us also mention the disputed work of Charles Murray and Richard Herrnstein, *The Bell Curve. Intelligence and Clan Structure in American Life* (New York: Free Press, 1994).

[7] The bibliography on this subject is abundant but scattered. We limit ourselves to mentioning here just a few works to introduce the reader to this ideology. Judith Lorber and Susan A. Farrell (ed.), *The Social Construction of Gender* (Newbury Park, CA: Sage Publications, 1991), providing numerous bibliographical references; H.T. Wilson, *Sex and Gender. Making Cultural Sense of Civilization* (Leyden: Brill, 1989); Henrietta L. Moore, *A Passion for Difference. Essays in Anthropology and Gender* (Cambridge, UK: Polity Press, 1994). A critical study of great value was made by Dale O'Leary, *Gender: The Deconstruction of Women*, in manuscript form (P.O. Box 41294, Providence, RI 02940, CompuServe 74747, 2241).

[8] Betty Friedan, Kate Millett, Bela Abzug, etc., are among the precursors of gender ideology.

[9] See the following Chapter III.

[10] Friedrich Engels' theses are laid out in *L'Origine de la famille, de la propriété privée et de l'Etat* [1884] (Paris: Editions Sociales, 1954); see Engels and Marx, *L'Idéologie allemande* [1846] (Paris: Editions Sociales, 1968), 47, 58, 61, 70,92, etc.; composed in Brussels, this work was not published until 1932 in Moscow and in Germany see also the *Manifeste du Parti communiste* [1848] Part II (Paris: Costes, 1953) 89-31.

[11] The work most often cited is that of Michael Foucault, *Histoire de la sexualité* (Paris: Gallimard, I: *La volonté de savoir*, 1976; II: *Le Souci de soi*, 1984. But one should note the influence of Claude Lévi-Strauss, especially of his *Anthropologie structurale* (Paris: Plon, 1958) 306; and of Louis Althusser, *Lire le Capital* (Paris: Maspero, 1966).

[12] These themes were already put forth in the works of precursors like Durkheim and Lévy-Bruhl.

[13] We cite here a few works that are especially significant for understanding the ideology of gender: Heidi I. Hartman, "Capitalism, Patriarchy and Job Segregations by Sex," in M. Blaxall and B. B. Reagan (eds.), *Women in the Workplace. The Implications of Occupational Segregation* (Chicago: Chicago University Press, 1976) 137-169; by the same author, "The Unhappy Marriage of Marxism and Feminism Toward a More Progressive Union," in L. Sargent (ed.), *Women and Revolution* (London: Pluto Press, 1981) 40-53; Shulamith Firestone, *The Dialectic of Sex. The Case of Feminist Revolution* (New York: Bantam, 1971); Anne Fausto-Sterling, "The Five Sexes. Why

Male and Female Are Not Enough," in The Sciences (March-April 1993) 20-24; Adrienne Rich, *On Woman Born* (New York: W. W. Norton, 1976); by the same author, "Compulsory Heterosexuality and Lesbian Existence," text of 1980 reprinted in Blood, Bread and Poetry. Selected Prose (New York: W. W. Norton, 1986); Alison M. Jagger, *Feminist Politics and Human Nature* (Totowa, NJ: Rowland & Allanheld, 1983).

[14] On maternity as a cultural invention, see Elizabeth Badinter, *L'Amour en plus* (Paris; Flammarion, 1980).

[15] See two considerable examples: first, *Programme of Action of the United Nations International Conference on Population and Development*, held at Cairo, September 5-13, 1994 especially pp. 6-9; 17-23; 45, etc.; then the *Beijing Declaration and Platform for Action* held at Beijing, September 4-15, 1995; see especially "Strategic Objective": A.4 (nos. 69-81); H.2, 3 (nos. 209-229); K.2 (nos. 256-258), etc. See also Josette L. Murray, *Gender Issues in World Bank Lending* (Washington; The World Bank, 1995).

[16] See Chapter V.

CHAPTER III
THE NEW PARADIGM OF WHO

From the time he assumed the directorship of WHO. Dr. Hiroshi Nakajima has given absolute priority to the concept, albeit strange at first view, of the "new paradigm of health." A "holistic" vision of health is intimately associated with this concept. In this Chapter we will examine in detail what these expressions mean. But, for the present, let us just say very schematically that the "new paradigm" refers to a new way of conceiving health for WHO, and that the term "holistic" alludes to the integration of different parameters in the definition and treatment of health matters. The new paradigm was presented as necessary to attain the objective that Dr. Halfdan Mahler, predecessor of Dr. Nakajima as director general of WHO from 1973 to 1988, had assigned to WHO: "health for all from now till 2000."[1] It is within the new paradigm frame of reference that, on the international level, health priorities must be defined which allow for the attainment, they say, of the objective previously set by Dr. Mahler.

We will begin by briefly tracing the path taken by WHO and witness the emergence of the "new paradigm" and of "holism" during recent years.

WHO AND THE WORLD BANK

Political and Economic Dimensions of Health

Since 1949:

> ...under the auspices of UNESCO and WHO, the Council of International Organizations of Medical Sciences (CIOMS) was created,... a nongovernmental organization whose headquarters are in Geneva, the very seat of WHO. Since 1957 the CIOMS has

organized a series of round table discussions aimed at, not only bringing to light the scientific bases of the new developments that have occurred in the domains of biology and medicine, but also analyzing their social, ethical, administrative and juridical repercussions. In collaboration with WHO, a long term program is presently being developed... whose objective is the formulation of principles governing the establishment of procedures for the examination of ethical principles applicable to research activities performed on human subjects. At the request of WHO, a series of medical ethical principles is also elaborated relating to the fundamental rights of prisoners and other detainees in matters of health. Also adopted in 1981 are some international directives regarding biomedical research involving experimentation on human subjects.[2]

For many years, WHO thus entrusted to CIOMS the task of reflecting on ethical questions concerning its field of action, without preventing WHO itself from making pronouncements on ethical questions.

Thus in 1968 Dr. Marcolino Candau, then director general of WHO, emphasized that

Health is an integral part of economic and social development of which the human being is the sole true motor. Without man there would be no reason for development, and without health development would not find its reason for being.[3]

In this text from 1978, C. H. Vigne, then director of juridical services for WHO, declared:

The right to health for all forcefully limits the health for some.... In reality, it is a question of knowing whether one must assure, at great expense, technically developed medical care for a privileged minority or meet the essential needs of the entire population.[4]

Such is in fact the central question for which a revolution, led by WHO and the World Bank, is in the process of putting into effect. In reality, WHO has been looking into the costs of health ever since the 1950s.[5]

Quite a turning point was reached in 1978 at the conference held at Alma-Ata (today Almaty, Kazakhstan):

The conference of Alma-Ata, held under the aegis of WHO and FISE from September 6th to the 12th of 1978, marks the beginning of a *new era: that of the "political science" of health,* no longer founded on the notion of society with its ills and illnesses identified in the community, but rather on the "public," on the entire population, in its mental, physical, social, economic and political aspects. Consequently, health becomes the common responsibility of all the individuals, of the collective, of the government; it is, then, a political question."[6]

Along with setting in relief the *political* dimension of health, they have also set in relief its *economic* dimensions:

Taking into consideration the flimsiness of material means which developing countries can dispose of and the need to assure greater protection to most vulnerable and less favored groups, WHO, for some years has developed an approach according to risk, especially in the area of care for integrated maternal and child care. The evaluation of the individual and collective risks must permit the formulation of objectives for distributing the resources.[7]

The Thrust of the Cairo Conference

In 1991, at the World Assembly of WHO, Dr. Nakajima declared that the "new paradigm for health must consist in a vision of the world in which health is at the center of development and of the quality of life."[8] According to him, the role of WHO does not consist only in offering technical aid to governments; it is also *normative* in the sense that it must propose a new vision of the world. The World Assembly of Health adopted this "new paradigm" in 1992.

At the same time, WHO realized that health care had to permeate all sectors of society. According to Dr. A. Hammad, executive director of WHO for health policies in development, this is the reason why WHO, in order to ensure their leadership role in the world, decided in 1994 to create a task force whose mandate would expire in 1997. This task force was charged with studying the lack of resources, the central role of health in the entire process of development and, above all, how to reconcile equality in both health and in the marketplace.

Also in 1994, the Cairo conference took place under the title "Population and Development." Central to this frame of reference, was the theme "reproductive health" and it received the highest priority in the "new paradigm" of WHO.[9] It entails, among other things, that people are able to have a responsible, satisfying and assured sexual life, that they have the ability to reproduce, the liberty to determine the moment and choose the means of conception. Attached to this theme are "maternity without risk," family planning (including temporary contraceptive methods such as the IUD, or permanent ones such as sterilization), the regulation of fertility (including the interruption of an undesirable pregnancy), the struggle against risky abortion, etc.[10] In the end, the whole network of health services — hospitals, clinics, centers of research, dispensaries, even school or industrial infirmaries — would be obliged to align their activities with this priority of priorities.[11]

According to Dr. Hammad, the emphasis given at Cairo to "reproductive health" (and to related themes) moved the director general of WHO to broaden the mandate "which we had before" from WHO itself. As a consequence, a divisional restructuring occurred in 1995 and gave birth to the Division for Family and Reproductive Health, directed by Madame Tomris Turmen, a Turkish doctor. This new division was charged especially with *integrating the programs* which were previously independent of one another and *integrating the services* designed to meet the needs of women. Thus, the division came to deal with children, adolescents, women and reproductive matters.

The year 1995 was also marked by a combination of important events. In January Dr. Nakajima announced the formation of informal round table discussions on the question of discovering how WHO could "ameliorate the integration of ethics into the general policies and practices of public health as well as in international cooperation in health matters." These discussions took place twice in Geneva: from August 30th to September 1st and from November 20th to the 22nd in 1995. We will examine later in a detailed fashion the tenor of these discussions.[12]

The meeting of the executive committee of WHO, in its 97th session, held at Geneva, January 15-24, 1996, was destined to be the occasion for reaffirming the will, already indicated above, to integrate programs and services . It was also devoted to WHO's financial difficulties, as well as to the redetermination of its "strategy of health for all," and to "fairness" in health matters.[13] Also discussed was a project for revising WHO's constitution and in particular its functions. In a frankly worldwide perspective, Dr. Nakajima did not hesitate to speak of a "contract between WHO and all the people of the world." This contract, he added, calls for new forms of partnership implying that WHO "will be open to all sectors of society, including nongovernmental organizations and the private sector."

Toward a Reform of the U.N.?

We are, then, in the presence of a multifaceted project for the reform of WHO: revision of its constitution, its program, and its modes of action.[14] We should properly note that this project of WHO's reform is itself consistent with the vast project for the reform of the U.N. To examine this latter project in detail would go beyond the scope of the present work, but some indications are nevertheless indispensable.

Let us first of all state that the U.N. established four task forces to put into effect the resolutions of the Cairo Conference (1994), of the Copenhagen and Beijing Conferences (1995) and that of Istanbul (1996). The supervision of these groups was entrusted to Gustave Speth, who directs the U.N. Program for Development (UNPD).

According to Ado Vaher, director of the U.N. Interagency Affairs of UNICEF, the new vision of the U.N. system must give priority to programs rather than projects. The *projects* are not integrated in the overall plan; they are *ad hoc*, for example, to build a hospital. The *programs*, on the other hand, are integrated in the overall vision and imply a five-year plan. Again, according to Ado Vaher, for the execution of these programs — inspired by the new paradigm and the holistic vision which is tied to it — WHO in particular and the U.N. in general can count on a new generation of managers to take up the torch from those familiar with diplomatic and political interplays.

The World Bank and the Burden of Global Morbidity

Within the framework of this new vision, the collaboration between WHO and the World Bank will be very close. It will fall to the latter to decide on the practical aspects of specific programs, and on the technical and financial feasibility to execute them. Furthermore, one must remember that the World Bank is the most important contributor toward the development of health programs — including birth control — in countries of weak and moderate means. More precisely, a genuine partnership exists between WHO and the World Bank for examining the resources available in each country, for determining priorities in health matters, for analyzing the cost-benefit ratio, for risk analysis and, in short, for putting into effect the analytical techniques which will form the basis upon which priorities and allocation of resources will be decided.[15] All actuarial science is mobilized in the service of the "new paradigm."

In the determination of priorities in medical care and research, WHO will be able to use a new guideline, the "concept of date of birth corrected by the factor of disability (DBCD)."

Here is what the World Bank says:

According to the cases of premature death, a considerable part of the burden of morbidity involves disability, whether it be the fact of paralysis caused by poliomyelitis, by blindness or suffering that follows serious psychoses. To measure the burden of morbidity, the present Report utilizes the concept of date of birth corrected by the factor of disability (DBCD), a measurement that takes into account both the years of full life which a premature death causes to be lost and those that are lost because of disability.

The losses of DBCD by persons vary enormously according to regions, variations that result principally from differences in premature death; losses of DBCD because of disability vary much less. We will call the burden of global morbidity (BGM) the total of DBCD lost.[16]

The DBCD and BGM guidelines, then, allow one to determine the months and years that are lost when a person dies prematurely, that is before having attained the median age he can hope to reach in the country where he lives. One can see immediately what kind of policy these indicators could serve in a society in which man would be considered just one product among others — whose value would be determined in terms of production, consumption and solvency — and where illness is treated in terms of cost-benefit and probability of cure.[17] Research would be slowed down or interrupted for some illnesses. In many countries of the Third-World, life expectancy is rather low and the principal cause of it is morbidity, in the occurrence of a great number of illnesses that afflict many inhabitants.[18] Hence, these people tend to die prematurely. By subtracting the age of premature death from the age of life expectancy one obtains the number of years or months lost. Whence this merciless conclusion: there is no sense in caring for people afflicted with incurable diseases or which leave incapacitating sequelae because, if one cared for them, he would prolong an existence useless to and burdensome for society. All the more reason, they will say, we should not encourage research on these diseases. Few diseases would be considered as justifying research: only those which one can treat at reduced cost and from which one can hope for a quick return to good health for the worker. The whole question, then, revolves around the cost-risk-benefit ratio.

"Public" Health? Health "for All"?

Putting this guideline into effect goes hand in hand with a profound change in meaning of the expressions "Public health" and "health for all." Traditionally, including some documents of WHO, public health included everything that dealt with the protection and promotion of hygiene, physical well-being, sanitary conditions, and preventive medicine in society. Previously, public health had been organized to serve the health of people. Now with the new guidelines, the meaning of this expression changes: the health of society, of the *social organism*, takes precedence over the health of the individual. And since people are unequally useful to society, they will have to resign themselves to being cared for according to their utility in the eyes of the social organism. "Health for all" will be adjusted according to the same criterion: *fairness* will require that what is due to each will be estimated according to the usefulness of each to the social organism. In brief, what is sabotaged here is the very idea of the equal dignity of all human beings, of their *universality*.

Let us note right away that this establishment of a hierarchy among people according to their usefulness to the social organism of which they are simple "members" can also be found at the level of nations, according to their varying utility to the social organism, which in this case is world society.

In summary, the ambiguity now involved in expressions like "public health" or "health for all" is too generalized to be an accident of language. It is a deceptive snare that must be denounced.

A Deceitful Indicator

Furthermore, the guideline "Date of Birth Corrected by the factor of Disability" (DBCD) and its corollary, the "Burden of Global Morbidity" (BGM) are both equally deceitful. Both of them have been invented in order to visualize (see Illustration 3) and even dramatize the health situation of the Third-World. It is a question, for WHO and its sponsors — especially the World Bank — to "legitimize" discriminatory programs vis-à-vis poor countries. One is astonished at this reduction of morbidity to mortality, while highlighting the differences between demographic factors. But one is the more astonished at the warped reading of the World Bank regarding the situation of rich countries. Why increase the impact made by disability and morbidity on the economic life of poor countries and, at the same time, conceal the impact of aging on the economic life of rich countries? For the World Bank, this evasion of the relationships of dependence cannot be an error: it can only be a farce.[19]

Since one knows that WHO and the World Bank collaborate closely, one cannot avoid foreseeing that the concept DBCD-BGM of the World Bank will be used by WHO to determine priorities which will then vary according to particular countries. When it is available, the genetic identity card of every individual will allow a still further enlargement of the field for applying these priorities.

Illustration 3

Burden of morbidity attributable to premature deaths and to disability by demographic region, 1990 DBCD lost in thousands of people

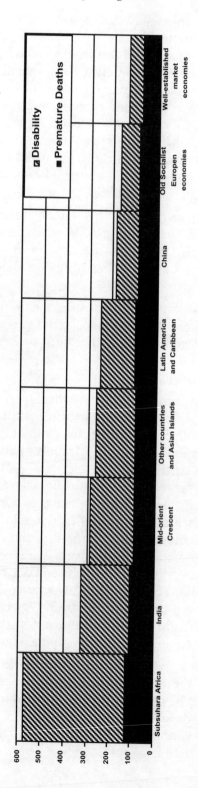

Source: World Bank, *Report on development in the World* (Washington, 1993) 3.

What are the most dramatic consequences of the use of a priority scale based on DBCD? First of all, the suffering caused by diseases left without care. Then, a low life expectancy. Furthermore, research on certain diseases afflicting patients who cannot pay will be neglected. And, for good measure, we can foresee the exodus to rich countries of the few Third World researchers, who could have studied the diseases of poverty which make the DBCD-BGM climb so high.

AXES OF A NEW ETHIC

It clearly follows, then, that, with the assistance of CIOMS and in connection with the World Bank, WHO is assigned the role of a melting pot in the elaboration of a new ethic in health matters on a worldwide level.[20] We are going to examine more closely the principal axes of this new ethic which appear in two categories of recent documents: first, the *reports* of the first and second sessions of the informal discussions of 1995 which we have already mentioned;[21] secondly, the *Report by the Directory-General* (January 1996)[22] as well as different interviews assembled and distributed by Interactive Information Services.[23] We will now peruse these interviews as follows.

Hippocrates Surpassed?

The First Report of the informal discussion in Geneva (the session for August 30 to September 1, 1995) first establishes the principle that "'ethical' doctrine has no meaning if the 'values' affirmed in it are not put into practice." "Ethical debate has no meaning unless it is accompanied by a strategy for transforming the concrete practices of persons and institutions." Such propositions "refer to an ethical debate... on the place and role of health at the heart of social and international relations."[24] "It is not specific health questions that surface but rather the application to health and to international organizations of fundamental questions of ethics, directives and governing...." "It is a question of applying to the domain of health fundamental questions which have been raised by the evolution of today's world," especially the "contradiction between the doctrines of the 'rights of man', 'social rights' and 'fairness,' on one side, and the reality of a 'dualism' increasingly advanced at the very heart of societies, A tacit acceptance of development at 'two speeds,' etc.,"

Just as "the ethical debate must be situated," "traditional ethical references regarding medical practice (e.g., the Hippocratic oath) no longer suffice as the foundation of such practice, as power to act and the ensuing responsibilities have changed."

Furthermore, just as "the ethical debate is necessarily global," "the analysis and solution... must take into consideration the collective logic of institutions, cultures, and economic and social processes."

Born "at the time of crisis," the ethical debate "is situated on different levels" and touches on models of development, medical models, WHO, and the whole system of the U.N. This ethical debate involves a critical reflection on the notions of progress and development. It must recognize in advance "the quality of viewpoints," "but one can agree with what needs to be done without agreeing with the reasons for doing it. The essential thing is... endeavor to act together for the better — or for the lesser evil — for the sake of all."

The criterion, then, must be... the seeking out of convergences.... The first ethical value will be honesty and frankness about the real conditions for determining and putting into effect the policies and programs of WHO; for example, the pressure from funding sponsors on the priorities of programs and — as in the case of family planning — the resistance of developing countries to what they resent as interference."

According to this report, "medical practice... must be related to a health strategy to which it is subordinated and which itself is integrated into broader social strategies." "Rather than represent economic spokesmen as devils, we must dialogue with them." It is even made clear that health arises from the medical field in two ways: "It would be necessary to evaluate the social integration of persons and not only the rates of morbidity or mortality"; moreover, "the criteria for practice varies among those of the medical corps as well as among administrators."

Without doubt, medicine and health are sources of confrontation between society and various small circles. Nevertheless, "in these confrontations... one of the key notions should be: *support autonomy*."

The report again indicates the role of WHO as a *think tank* and of united reflection: "Ethics is not a list of values but the management of contradictions among these values.... The world is sorely lacking in open debate and the evaluation of technologies and their effects. A function of WHO must be to ensure the organization of this possibility...."

The Hippocratic Oath, which reflects an "individual ethic, is surpassed by the introduction of sophisticated technical systems," and with "increasingly making the management of life and death artificial...." "What is to be determined is a new ethic in the medical milieu which starts with its relationships with society and proposes models of behavior for each of its members...." "With the development of technical possibilities, the ideology of the rights of mankind and to personal freedom, pushed to the extreme and without any effort at arranging a hierarchy of these rights, leads to an impasse."

In the evaluation of health policies, a twofold broadening is called for: "a) one cannot stay on a national level, for many decisive actions are played out on a world scale...; b) the evaluation cannot be limited to the field of competence of the countries' health ministers.... Health policies have to be determined such as seeking after alliances between forces that have interests that are in part contradictory but which all have an impact on health." It will even be necessary for WHO to propose "some regulations including health... in international exchanges."

Doubting neither its representative character nor its responsibility, WHO considers that its legitimacy and vocation "will find a new form and force in its ability to acquire the means of responding to the expectations of all the citizens of the world and of facing the questions and challenges of tomorrow...." "The [ethical] debate and reflection must move toward the very foundations of legitimacy," all the more so since "there is in the world a very great need for WHO and because there is also an immense need for regulation...."

Whence the question: "Is it up to WHO to take care of this need?... The answer is that WHO is, on this level and in the domain of public health, the sole instrument available, the sole competent authority." "Assigning ethics to WHO goes back to the urgent need of having a fully functioning international organism of reference." This organism, however, will not be able to work in isolation; "It is necessary to build partnerships with countries, with nongovernmental organizations, with the private sector, as well as with industry."

Ethics and Fairness

The same themes are reaffirmed, and made more explicit and clear in the *Second Report* from the second session of discussions (Geneva, November 20-22, 1995). Let us limit ourselves to pinpointing a few: "How can the rights and responsibilities of the person and those of the collective be balanced?..." "From now on, health policies and ethical choices attached to them must be seen and evaluated by taking into account those forces and agents which are located outside the medical sector...." "Faced with the advances of biomedical technologies, the very vision of the human being, his definition and his biological limitations, are all called into question." "The [ethical] debate in the outside world [that is to say, counting all the people involved and the sectors concerned] cannot be managed without the ability of convoking WHO, and without its full mobilization as a world forum...." WHO will be made the "instrument of animation of a world democratic debate on ethical questions raised by health policies." But when is there a question of ethics? When, "in concrete situations, values are in contradiction...." "The basic assumption is that the ethics of dialogue, of action and of cooperation in the domain of health as elsewhere, must be based on notions of *respect* for the human being and cultures, and of *responsibility*[25] that is, for oneself and for others...." "Hence, one must be wary of the temptation of stopping short a priori at lists of values proclaimed as universal."

Then there arises the unavoidable question of *fairness*. "It is possible... to achieve unanimity in favor of the principle of fairness in having access to care or on the validity of research on the quality of care. That being so, it still remains to determine the actual situation: what one understands by fairness; up to what limit in the quality of available care is it still possible to speak of fairness — from country to country, and between sectors of the population."

It is still necessary to ask oneself "if the quality [of care] must be related to the kind of technology employed, or rather to the therapeutic result, or further, to the quality of the relationship between care-providers and patients."

The "Special Event" in 1998

At midterm, that is to say, during 1998, WHO especially plans "to elaborate a deontology of dialogue and partnership for international cooperation in health matters; bring up to date, if necessary, the dispositions of WHO's constitution in order to provide greater place for ethical concerns." The first report even foresees a "special event" in 1998 to reformulate "the role and global strategy of WHO in the light of the contribution of ethical reflection." This points out the importance of the informal discussions. It is already established that the "special event of 1998" will concern the rights of man,[26] and it is being prepared by several agencies of the U.N. (e.g. UNFPA) and or several nongovernmental organizations (e.g. IPPF).

WHO further plans to "facilitate the dialogue and coordination between WHO and the nongovernmental organizations, on the one hand... and on the other, among the nongovernmental organizations themselves ;... to establish within the U.N. itself interagency groups to ensure in a permanent way a common ethical reflection and coordination of approaches to themes proposed that cut across lines.

In the long run, that is, some time in 2001, WHO intends, among other things, to "help countries and people to organize their development by relying on their own potential and in solidarity with others."

AUTHORIZED CONFIRMATIONS

That the two reports we have just examined faithfully reflect the projects of the present direction of WHO, WHO and its director general themselves furnish the proof.[27] Without doubt, despite their clarity, the reports in question are expressed with an understandable prudence. But some of the responsible higher echelons of WHO, including the director general, were not bound by the same circumspection, if one is to believe the statements they made in 1996, that is to say, a little after the publication of the two reports. These assertions, and those made much before 1996, remove all possible doubt about the intentions of WHO and the meaning of the two reports.

The statements in question are found in two types of declarations. We come upon them first in the *Report by the Director General* presented by Dr. Hiroshi Nakajima to the 97th session of the Executive Committee of WHO (January 1996). We meet them again with even greater clarity in many interviews granted to Marguerite A. Peeters, beginning in 1996, by high functionaries of WHO.[28]

Health: A Product Subordinated to the Economy

Two expressions frequently come up in the statements of WHO and especially in those of its director general, Dr. Hiroshi Nakajima.[29] These two expressions are "new paradigm" and "holistic."

These two key expressions we will examine on two levels. First of all, we will define them according to statements emanating from WHO. However, the ultimate meaning of the expression will not appear except as a subhead in the following Chapter IV where we will examine the kinship between WHO's themes and certain contemporary trends.

The expression "new paradigm" used by WHO is somewhat surprising at first. In reality it conceals a new ideology of scientism, well on its way to dissemination and implementation. To understand what this expression signifies, we must go back to the definition of health such as it appears in WHO's constitution: "Health is a state of complete physical, mental and social well-being, and does not consist merely in the absence of disease or infirmity."[30] This definition of health is "holistic," that is to say, very encompassing and even very ambitious. It is evident that WHO has for some years been subjected to the pressures of its principal financial donors. They pressure the organization into proceeding to selective choices reconcilable, on the one hand, with the encompassing definition of health and, on the other, with the need to observe budgetary economies.

What sort of criteria must govern these choices? Priorities are chosen "according to the resources available at the time and the probability of success." In each case, one will have to weigh the relative costs and benefits. The "paradigm of health," is thus presented, first of all, as a model of conduct in health matters — a model not in the sense of an "example" (the verb to love, a model of joint effort), nor of a "type" (a Peugeot 306), but rather a model in the sense of a global program matching a plan of action which one considers worthy of execution.

Dr. Nakajima certainly takes into account the fact that the objectives researched by health personnel are in conflict with those of economists. Nevertheless, by reason of the economic crisis affecting the world today, he recommends that the "new paradigm" and its priorities be accepted at least provisionally. The Hippocratic medical ethic, of the old and also original paradigm of WHO, must, then, be frozen and eradicated when confronted by the new health ethic, that of the new paradigm. This ethic considers health as a product subordinated to economic imperatives. One manufactures it, one sells it, one consumes it according to the criteria of rarity and ability to pay, that is, according to the laws of the marketplace.

And so it is by means of paradox that WHO proclaims that it is about to put into effect a "new strategy of health for all."

The accessibility of health care is *relative* to these new criteria. And from that will flow those priorities which have been retained.

Criteria of Priority

First of all, one will have to take into account the resources available to the society under consideration. The scale of priorities will vary among societies and even within the same society. The criteria according to which one will provide care or refuse it will vary case by case.

The scale of priority will vary according to the individual. Discrimination will be enforced between those people who are active, and, those people who are inactive. The criterion observed here, then, is of the utility of the individual within society and for society.

It would be useful next to evaluate the probability of success. A new nomenclature of diseases, of treatments and medications, adapted to the new paradigm, will have to be prepared. Some maladies such as malaria can be taken care of, but they have their handicaps; they should no longer be considered as having priority. Other diseases, regarded as incurable, will no longer be treated, or won't be treated except within the framework of market logic.

Illnesses of old age — like Parkinson's and Alzheimer's Disease — will no longer be considered as having priority; according to the specific situation, they will not receive treatment and research subsidies will be reduced or suppressed. And it is here that the issue of euthanasia appears: it flows from the very logic of the "new paradigm."

Thus it follows that a new balance has to be found between public and individual health.

In some way "public health" is considered as a matter of right and it takes precedence over individual health. Medicine must care for the social entity before dreaming of caring for the individual. From the viewpoint of public health, absolute priority is afforded "reproductive health," by which we must understand — despite the euphemisms — the possibility of controlling the transmission of life quantitatively and qualitatively. Control of the number of births and eugenics are necessary in virtue of the "higher interest" of the social entity.

The new health paradigm developed by WHO, then, responds to the requirements of globalization which we previously analyzed in detail.[31] The world market and the developing global society, they believe, need this holistic model.

Nevertheless, we must observe that this new paradigm is incompatible with the morality derived from the Hippocratic and Judeo-Christian tradition. The "economicist" imperatives of globalization do not require simply a redetermination of health activity; they necessitate an entirely new "ethic" to form the basis of the new "rights."

The "New Paradigm" and the Logic of Evil

In concluding this analysis of the "new paradigm" and its ethic, we must say that it comes across like a mosaic of rehashed, ill-fitting themes. The various ideas comprised under this label are easily discernible in current trends. That the "new paradigm" has at its source modern trends, or that one cites analogies between them, is ultimately of secondary importance. It is not even necessary that there exist an association between the "new paradigm" and the different trends which we are going to review, in order for a genuinely intrinsic logic which leads to evil to be evident. After all, the existence of the devil is proved *a posteriori* from his works just as, in metaphysics, we also prove the existence of God by proceeding from effect to cause.

Sources or Analogies?

The "new ethic," resulting in the criteria we've just enumerated, demonstrates fundamentally Marxist roots: health becomes the stake in a struggle to death, not only between individuals and societies, but also among societies themselves. The "economicist" determinism of Marx is hence reinterpreted. All individuals and all societies must become workers in order to deserve to be cared for, to be cured, and in effect, to live. Human society is an immense organism composed of members having unequal usefulness; we must therefore remove the inactive ones.

Here we find again the utilitarianism common to both Marxist and liberal traditions. A la Bentham, the costs and benefits are weighed; the "least sickness" or the "greatest profit" is calculated — depending on the situation. Nevertheless, while the ideology of gender reinterprets in its own way — that is to say, from the radical feminist viewpoint — the "proletarian" reading of the master-slave dialectic, the "new paradigm" reactivates the "lordly" reading of the same dialectic. The struggle for life occurs to the advantage of the "lords" who will manage the health, scientific and economic resources according to their own interests and will put them at the service of a program of an artificial selection in the best traditions of Galton and Binding.[32]

One equally observes a kinship with *structuralism*, which was discussed with regard to gender.[33] Ethics is a product totally relative to history and cultures. Here we are plunged into full moral relativism: there are no ethics that are not completely situated in and relative to constantly changing situations. Thus the immediate application: according to this trend, the Judeo-Christian and Hippocratic morality has seen its day. It must disappear and yield its place to the new ethic of the "new paradigm" — a verdict made more emphatic by the end of the millennium, as we approach the year 2000. Since this morality corresponds, they say, to an antiquated culture, it forms an obstacle to the emergence of a new society in a new age.

Also, a well known theory is that the care of the social body — appearing as "public health" — must take precedence over the care of individuals. It appears in the works of Galton, John Stuart Mill, Binding and their followers. More recently it has been developed by Pierre Simon, who demonstrates its link with the themes of struggle, selection and the new ethic.[34] Since the same Dr. Simon explains with great detail that this new ethic has been developed in the French Masonic lodges, we are not precluded from considering that the "new paradigm" of WHO is no stranger to works on the question, which have been in progress for a long time in the workshops of the French Masons.[35] The methods of dissemination, by "networks" and by "osmosis," also remind one of the methods to which the Masons have recourse.

Ethics and Responsibility

Here we find the ethic of responsibility as opposed to the ethic of conviction. According to Max Weber, the ethic of *conviction* requires, for example, that "the Christian do his duty and rely on God for the outcome of his action"; when all is said and done this is the ethic of the prophets, of heroes and the saints who seek to do good and avoid evil, even if they must lose their life. As for the ethic of *responsibility*, this is the ethic of the politician: working in a violent world, he will not burden himself with considerations of good or evil in order to save his life or affirm his supremacy. He will inevitably have recourse to methods unacceptable to those holding to the ethic of conviction. He must face the consequences of his actions. Contrary to what happens in the ethic of conviction, the ethic or responsibility makes no reference to good or evil actions. According to Max Weber:

> No ethic exists in the world that can neglect this: in order to attain "good" ends, we are obliged most of the time to reckon, on the one hand, with morally dishonest means or with the least dangerous one, and, on the other hand, the possibility or even the eventuality of unfortunate consequences. Neither can any ethic in the world tell us when and in what measure a morally good end justifies morally dangerous means and consequences.[36]

Procedural Justice

The ethic of responsibility has strongly influenced the thought of John Rawls, known for his conception of procedural justice which ends up reducing justice to fairness and loyalty. This concept of fairness is also basic to the "new paradigm." The latter ignores the categories of good and evil belonging to the ethic of conviction that provide the norms of conduct. According to the new ethic — that of the new paradigm — the moral norm must be sought in agreement, in fairness: loyal openness to the ideas of others, tolerance for all opinions. Ethics will be procedural: what is right or wrong will result from a consensual conventional decision, resulting — if necessary — from a vote. A democratic decision will be a decision resulting from a majority vote.

Here, then, we find once again the influence of the utilitarian trend (balance of cost and benefit); of an agnosticism before all metaphysical anthropology; a structuralism with a permanent questioning of the rules proper only to a culture.[37] There remains, then, an ethic perpetually relative to cases, to situations and to the voluntary determinations of those who formulate it. For, opposed to equality, which is rigorous, the concept of fairness has something changeable about it: it lends itself to all sorts of interpretations.[38]

Finally, the "new paradigm" also echoes the attacks currently brought against the sovereignty of nations. This is exemplified in two ways. First, the "holistic" vision of the world, essential to the new paradigm, subordinates sovereign nations to the programs of the ideologues of globalization, The principle of subsidiarity is thus perverted: individual nations are reduced to being cogs in the global society. Then, the partnership among intergovernmental organizations (WHO) and the nongovernmental organizations, obviously chosen for their allegiance to the "new paradigm," are going to reinforce the power of the United Nations' apparatus and augment its capacity for putting pressure on States and thus eroding their sovereignty.

---

[1] Dr. Mahler's concept of WHO was explained in a document entitled *Global Strategy for Health for all by the Year 2000. The Spiritual Dimension*, EB 73/15 (Oct. 21, 1983).

[2] Maurice Torelli, *Le Médecin et les droits de l'homme* (Paris: Berger-Levrault, 1983) 58.

[3] *Ibid.* 9.

[4] *Ibid.* 53 f.

[5] See for example C. E. A. Winslow, *Le Coût de la maladie et le prix de la santé* (Geneva: WHO, 1952); mentioned by Torelli, *op.cit.* 74.

[6] M. Torelli, *op.cit.* 52, emphasis in text.

[7] *Ibid.* 176.

[8] See the documents published by the Interactive Information Service (IIS), especially the *Reports* no. 17 published by Marguerite Peeters in 1996.

[9] This is what appears already in the collection published by WHO under the title *Reproductive Health Priorities.. Safe Motherhood. The Mother-Baby Package*. Distributed in 1995, this collection contains in particular a volume cofinanced by the

Rockefeller Foundation entitled *Mother-Baby Package: Implementing Safe Motherhood in Countries. Practical Guide* (Geneva: WHO, 1995); as well as a brochure *Achieving Reproductive Health for All. The Role of WHO*.

[10] See *Technical Definitions and Commentary* prepared by the Division of Family Health and the Special Programme of Research and Research Training in Human Reproduction, organs of WHO, for the Cairo Conference in 1994.

[11] Once again, India appears to be one of the principal laboratories of the "new medical ethic." See "Reproductive Health Care in India: A New Paradigm," *Population Briefs* (New York: Population Council) 2, (2), (Spring 1996) 5.

[12] See *infra*, **The Axes of a New Ethic**.

[13] See *infra*, *Ethics and Fairness*, and Chapter V.

[14] On this reform and on the "new ethic" which is its epicenter, WHO has already expressed itself with clarity. See for example WHO, *Achieving Reproductive Health for All. The Role of WHO*, Document WHO/FHE/95.6 (Geneva: WHO, 1995); WHO, *WHO's Reproductive Health Programme*, Document WHO/FHE/RHT/HRP/97.1 (Geneva: WHO, 1997).

[15] Let us mention at least two publications especially revealing of the present tendencies of the World Bank: *The World Bank Research Program 1995*. Abstracts of Current Studies (Washington, 1995); Rodolfo A. Bulatao, *Key Indicators for Family Planning Projects*, Technical Paper No. 297 (Washington; World Bank, 1995); this study concerns the extent of the effectiveness of family planning projects.

[16] World Bank, *Rapport sur le devéloppement dans le monde 1993. Investir dans la santé* (Washington, 1993) 1.

[17] See *DTL* 93-158.

[18] Let us recall that *life expectancy at birth* is the estimate of the number of years that a newborn can hope to live in the region studied, if the rate of mortality by age were identical to those of his birth year. The *rate of mortality* is the relationship between the number of deaths deducted in a year in a determined territory and the mean population of this territory. *Morbidity* designates the frequency and action of disease upon the population. For more details on this subject see our work *Pour comprendre les évolutions démographiques* (Paris: APRD, 1995).

[19] "Dependent" persons are usually defined as those younger than fifteen years of age and those more than sixty-four years old in the countries of the "South," those younger than twenty and those older than sixty-four in countries of the "North." In wealthy countries, those of the "North," there are often more than two dependents to one nondependent.

[20] *World Health. The Magazine of the World Health Organization*, published in Geneva, devoted n.5 of its 49th year (September-October, 1996) to the title "Health, Ethics and Human Rights."

[21] Geneva, August 30 - September 1 and November 20-22, 1995. The reports refer respectively to WHO/DGE/Ethics/95.1 (F) and WHO/DGE/Ethics/95.2 (F).

[22] See WHO/OMS, *Ethics and Health, and Quality in Health Care. Report by the Director-General*, Executive Board, 97th Session (Geneva) document EB 97/16 (January 9, 1996). This report had not been discussed at the World Assembly of Health in May of 1996 as it should have been.

[23] See *supra*, note 13, and *infra*, note 2.

[24] Emphasis in the text.

[25] Emphasis in the text.

[26] This "event" will probably take place at the launching of a *Global Health Charter*. This appeared particularly in what seems to be a very "holistic" charter presented by John H. Bryant, president of the CIOMS, at the meeting of the Advisory Committee on Health Research, Geneva, October 15-19, 1996, under the title *WHO's Re-*

newal of the Health for All Strategy — Implications for Ethics and Human Rights. This charter can be used for the purpose of making null and void the *Universal Declaration* of 1948.

[27] The reader may refer to several documents of WHO, Geneva, among which we cite: *Towards a Paradigm for Health*, DGO/91.1, June 19, 1991; *Allocution* of Dr. Hiroshi Nakajima before the executive council of the World Assembly for Health, January 14, 1991; A44/DIV/4; *Idem, Allocution* January 21, 1992, A45/DIV/4; *Idem, Allocution* May 3, 1994, A47/DIV/4. Especially interesting is the Press Release NHO/3 published on January 16, 1995 by WHO/OMS. This text takes up again the proposals made by Dr. Nakajima at the opening of the 95th meeting of the executive board; it's title is *WHO Director-General Warns of "Time Bomb" in Global Health Inequities*.

[28] See IIS, *Reports* nos. 18 to 24, 1996. We follow closely these documents respecting the literal statement of those interviewed.

[29] We recommend to the skeptics that they become acquainted with Dr. Nakajima's projects by referring to *Ethique de la santé au niveau mondial. Rôle et contribution de l'oms*, Geneva, EB95/Inf. Doc.20, January 23, 1995. This document gives a chronology of Dr. Nakajima's initiative on health and ethics and indicates how he "now is considering broadening the role and approach of WHO in this domain on a worldwide scale and in the context of international cooperation."

[30] WHO published a collection of *Documents fondamentaux* 40th ed. (Geneva, 1994). Its definition of health appears at the beginning of the Constitution, p.1.

[31] See especially *EPA, DTL, BPCV*.

[32] See *supra, Eugenics and Neomalthusianism*, in Ch. II.

[33] See *supra, The Influence of Structuralism*, in Ch. II.

[34] See Pierre Simon, *De la vie avant toute chose* (Paris: Mazarine, 1979); see also *EPA* 104.

[35] The CIOMS closely collaborates with WHO on ethical questions. Is it not possible that this nongovernmental organization has been used by some of its members as a bridge between the lodges — French and/or Anglo Saxon — and WHO?

[36] See Max Weber, *Le Savant et le Politique* (Paris: Le Monde, 1995) 172-175. The quotation is found on p. 173.

[37] See *supra, The Influence of Structuralism* in Ch. II.

[38] See *supra, From Equality to Fairness* in Ch. V.

CHAPTER IV
THE NEW AGE: ITS PARADIGM AND NETWORKS

That the New Age has strongly influenced the "new paradigm" of WHO, that its influence is perceptible in the projects for WHO's reform and detectable in the anti-life movements — all appears with crystal clarity in its vocabulary and can be inferred from an internal analysis of its theories.

THE NEW AGE IN ITSELF

One of the reference works on the New Age, entitled *Les Enfants du Verseau* (The Children of Aquarius), bears on the cover the subtitle *Pour un nouveau paradigme* (Toward a New Paradigm).[1] It abounds in references to the *holistic* vision of the world.[2]

Let us follow attentively a few of Marilyn Ferguson's propositions:

> Humanity has known many spectacular revolutions in its interpretation of reality, great leaps, sudden liberations. . . .In order to describe such discoveries correctly one speaks of "change of paradigm," a term introduced by the philosopher and historian of science Thomas Kuhn, in his book *La Structure des révolutions scientifiques* (The Structure of Scientific Revolutions) published in 1962.[3]

But what should we understand here by "paradigm"? We can advance in our comprehension of the term. The meaning of this word is close to that which is given by Bachelard to "epistemological break" — the progress of science is discontinuous or spiral — or that given by Foucault to *épistèmè*. Cultures are sustained by a determined structure which conditions knowledge.⁴ This structure, or épistèmè, must be disputed; one must break with it in order to give birth to a new epistemology, which in turn will condition new knowledge.⁵ Moreover, Foucault speaks of an epistemological break with regard to medicine itself.⁶

Now according to Marilyn Ferguson,

A paradigm is a framework of thought (from the Greek *paradeigma*, "example"). A paradigm is a sort of intellectual structure that allows for the understanding and explanation of certain aspects of reality.... A change of paradigm is, unequivocally, a new way of thinking about old problems. For example, for more than two centuries top rate thinkers acknowledged... the paradigm of Isaac Newton.... But to the extent that scientific men pushed their investigations..., certain data appeared intermittently which refused to fit in with Newton's conception. That happens to every paradigm. Finally, observations accumulated outside the old framework of explanation and, becoming too numerous, put it to the test. It is habitually at this point of crisis that an individual has a great heretical idea, a new and powerful awareness that comes to explain the apparent contradictions.... The problem is that one cannot accept the new paradigm until he has abandoned the old one.⁷

How is the new paradigm presented?

For the first time in history, humanity has access to the control panel of change, to the understanding of the manner in which transformations are produced.... The paradigm of the Aquarian Conspiracy conceives humanity as rooted in nature and encourages the autonomous individual in a decentralized society by considering us as stewards of all our resources, interior and exterior. It sees us as heirs of evolution's riches, capable of imagination, invention and experiences which we have but still only glimpsed.⁸

These extensive quotations from one of the New Age classics are necessary in order to understand what is in preparation at the U.N. and to comprehend the role of the think tank which WHO has assigned to itself.

The whole approach is as follows. The Renaissance and above all the Reformation saw man affirm his independence for the first time. Man as issue of the Reformation no longer needs the Church: he enters into direct relationship with God; he no longer needs moral norms: he obeys only his conscience. This evolution — which we haven't time to trace in detail here — is continued by the "great minds" of the seventeenth century and the "philosophers" of the Age of Enlightenment.

The New Age is the phase following this evolution and it intends to consummate the break already initiated by the Reformation vis-à-vis the old paradigm,[9] that of the Age of the Fish, in short, Christianity. The New Age, then, proclaims the complete independence of man. In essence, man is now a superhuman who, by means of appropriated methods and techniques, is going to explore the heretofore undreamt of resources of his body, his psyche and the universe itself. In this respect, the New Age is a new expression of *Pelagianism*, the doctrine according to which man can save himself by his own power through having recourse to various psychological or magical practices.

We thus perceive in *holism*, also central to the New Age, Feuerbachian overtones. Freed from the old paradigm, liberated from God and the oppression He exercises through the Church, in sum "freed from alienation," man can finally take charge of his own life and death and exercise his power over everything. He can and must transcend himself, autotranscend himself in some way. Whence the interest in the "brain," its left and right hemispheres, its hidden potential and its latent powers which must be liberated.

Marilyn Ferguson, who does not skimp on references to Teilhard de Chardin, specifies what the new paradigm implies in political and economic life and in the life of women. In a long chapter, she explains what the new paradigm of health is.[10] She salutes the neoparadigmatic nature of the definition of health given by WHO and she follows closely behind with: "Well-being comes from a matrix: the body-psyche *continuum*."[11]

Undoubtedly, the superman will continue to be limited by the horizon of suffering and death. However, he will not be turned away from seeking pleasure, the drug experience and, in any case, immersion in the great cosmic whole. Belief in reincarnation will excuse the violence of abortion or war. Previous life continues through today by means of obscure energies; reincarnation in a later life removes any importance from the forms of violence plaguing our present existence.

In this pantheistic vision, the entire world is penetrated by a universal energy that recalls the *pneuma* of the Stoics. Every individual is divine. The New Age wouldn't have any difficulty, then, in subscribing to the *natural contract* between man and nature advocated by Michel Serres in 1990.[12] But the social body is also divine, and its health — public health[13] — is more important than the health of individuals. Now in this holistic vision, Mother-Earth, Gaia, is also divine. When all is said and done, man must resign himself to submit, even sacrifice himself to the determinism of the cosmos. Too many human beings, especially poor ones, threaten the ecosystem. To protect it, it is necessary to exercise strict vigilance over demographic evolution. From that one will conclude that respect for the ecosystem requires two complementary measures. On the one hand, it will be necessary to reinforce all the means which allow us to control population growth; this measure above all aims at poor populations accused of poorly managing their environment. On the other hand, it will be necessary to screen the knowledge and techniques, even simple ones, that would permit poor people to take care of the most frequent diseases; in that way, the mortality rate, especially infant mortality, will be maintained at a *high* level.[14] With this, the New Age brings its "legitimation" to the level of priorities elaborated by WHO with the aid of the World Bank.[15]

The "Gentle Conspiracy" and Its Network

Since there can be no new paradigm without action, Marilyn Ferguson explains for us how the Aquarian Conspiracy will work. The definition of the "conspiracy" is explicitly attributed to Teilhard de Chardin: "A conspiracy of men and women whose new perspective is capable of launching the crucial contagion of change."[16] She explains further: "The Aquarian Conspiracy is a different form of revolution with revolutionaries of a new style. It aims at the overthrow of conscience in a critical number of individuals sufficient to provoke a renewal of society."[17] Her book starts with a reference to this Conspiracy and its opening and tone remind one of the beginning of Karl Marx' *Manifeste du parti communiste*:

> A powerful network without directors is in the process of producing a radical change in the United States. Its members have gotten rid of certain key elements of Western thought; they could have even broken the continuity of history. This network is the Aquarian Conspiracy. It is a conspiracy without political doctrine, without a manifesto. . . . More extensive than a reform, more profound than a revolution, this gentle conspiracy for a new program for man has launched the most rapid cultural realignment of history.[18]

We learn how this "gentle conspiracy" is spread: by the "powerful network" mentioned at the beginning of the very first sentence of the book. One will be able to count on "an invisible but powerful organizing principle inherent in nature" (p.45). "Our major challenge is to create a consensus around the idea that a fundamental change is possible" (p.36).

Groups of "self-organized" individuals will constitute the units of action. It will be the minority that "will influence people, not by simple rational arguments, but by a change of heart" (p.211).

More precisely, the unit of action will be the *network*, that is to say, "a tool for the phase following human evolution." And the author continues:

> Enlarged by electronic communications, freed from the old constraints of family and culture, the network is the antidote to alienation. It generates sufficient power to remake society. It offers to the individual an affective, intellectual, spiritual and economic support. It is a place of invisible welcome, a powerful means of modifying the course of institutions, especially the government.[19]

These networks are, so to speak, imperceptible and yet present everywhere, active everywhere, penetrating the heart of individuals, the most diverse circles, institutions and even religions themselves.[20] Everything being grist for the mill, one is reminded of secred societies and sects whose members are invited to become part of the network. It even seems that someone can find himself inserted into a network without clearly realizing the situation in which he finds himself or the influences to which he is subjected.

An "integrated segmented polycentric network" (SPIN) " draws its energy from coalitions, from the combination and recombination of talents, tools, strategy and contacts." While bureaucracies are fragile and vulnerable, the network is malleable like the brain in which other sections "can replace damaged cells." "In a network many people can assume the functions of others" (p.220).

> [A network] is a source of power never yet exploited in history: many self-sufficient social movements bound together in view of the ensemble of goals and whose realization would have to transform every aspect of contemporary life. . . . Networks often adopt the same action without conferring with one another simply because they share the same assumptions. In fact, it's this common reserve which is the collusive force.

> In effect, the Aquarian Conspiracy is a network of numerous networks whose calling is social transformation. . . . Its center is everywhere. Although numerous social movements and groups of mutual aid are represented within its union, its life does not

depend on any of them. It cannot dry up, for it is a manifestation of change among people.[21]

Toward a World Directorate

The reference to the "new paradigm" is common to all the networks. It explains the convergence of their action. It also explains why there is no contradiction between the holism inherent in the paradigm and the "decentralization" mentioned by Ferguson. Decentralization refers to the units which can act in an autonomous fashion without ever losing sight of a "radical center." In any case, the groups constituting the networks have been awakened in the extreme. They have recourse to the famous "salami tactic," which consists in obtaining slice by slice what cannot be obtained all at once. They practice *infiltration* in institutions with a plan of action directly derived from the new paradigm. With some candor, Ferguson herself gives an example of great clarity:

> There exists an informal coalition of conspirators in the agencies and circles of Congress. Within the Departments of Health, Education, and Welfare the innovators have created informal action groups in order to divide up their strategies of inoculating with new ideas a system that resists them and of morally supporting each other.
>
> Projects which would otherwise appear unrealizable can, solely through a program of federal subsidies, attain official recognition. The governmental apparatus that grants accreditation determines what is fashionable in the field of research. This aura of officialdom is what the conspirators try to obtain for various projects.[22]

This means that the networks can act like pressure groups or lobbies, infiltrating the vision of the holistic new paradigm into national or international institutions, public or private. There is no need to complicate the task by founding new institutions. Existing institutions marvelously play the role of launchpads for the new paradigm.

We shouldn't be surprised, then, to find that the "new paradigm" advocated in the New Age movement leads to a reinterpretation of *North American messianism*. America, we are assured, is "the matrix of the transformation."

> One understands better American history [when] one sees it as a millenarian movement, based on a spiritual vision of change. . ., one observes a constant: "the fundamental belief that freedom and responsibility will lead, not only the individual, but the whole world to perfection." This sense of a collective and sacred

objective, which has sometimes led to aggression in the past, is changed into a sense of the mystical unity of humanity and of the vital power of harmony between human beings and nature.[23]

Even inside the United States,

the innovation is peculiar to California. California is a foretaste of our future changes of national paradigms as well as of our quirks and manners... a phenomenon existing "solely in California" can be nonetheless of capital importance.[24]

Supported by gleaming California, the New Age is presented as the heir of "many great North American revolutionaries" who have

belonged to a tradition of mystical fraternity (Rosicrucian, Masonic and Hermetic). This sense of fraternity and spiritual liberation played an important role in the ardor of the revolutionaries and their commitment to bring about a democracy. This American experience was consciously conceived as a capital phase in the evolution of the human race. "The cause of America is in great measure the cause for all humanity," wrote Thomas Paine in his incendiary pamphlet *Common Sense*.[25]

It is in California that the Esalen Institute began at Big Sur, a melting pot for the "movement of human potential." The Aquarian Conspiracy bloomed in the California environment:

... the Aquarian Conspiracy draws its substance from California as from a substratum. Its "agents," come from all the states of the Union, assemble there from time to time to sustain themselves and mutually encourage one another.[26]

THE GREATEST MENACE SINCE ARIANISM

After the analyses of the three preceding chapters, we must state that questions related to sexuality and human life henceforth have to be seen by taking into account the ideology of gender and the holistic ideology of the new paradigm. The influence of these two ideologies and the coverage given them by the media are too important to simply dismiss. It is in no way a question of yielding to a fear of a plot. It must be admitted, however, that here we are dealing with two complex trends presenting a common goal: they forbid us from considering the question of life as, so to speak, a problem limited to its relationship to morality, penal law, medical deontology, etc. *The very manner of posing the question of the right to life has undergone a profound change.*[27] The question of life is at the very heart of a new ethical project, discussed in international networks and infiltrating existing organizations, while inspiring multiple activities but all converging on the world level.

In order for this new ethic to be accepted, one must start with a clean slate and eradicate the old paradigm to which — for good measures — they attribute all the evils, real or supposed, of our century: underdevelopment, hunger, disease, "destruction of the environment," "overpopulation," etc.

The Return of Gnosticism

The New Age, then, disseminates a *gnosis*, a knowledge more or less esoteric which is reserved for the initiated. Spread by contagion, this knowledge will ensure its own salvation and render faith in Jesus useless.[28] We are dealing here with an immanentist naturalism, close to pantheism, impregnated with cosmic determinism, and rejecting any linear conception of time in favor of a cyclic one. There is no longer any place for the history of salvation. Hence, one kills all hope, and, with reincarnation, these doctrines consolidate the tendency toward a resigned and demobilizing fatalism.

The world forms a whole of which man is a part, of which he is a member, without truly emerging from it to the title of a reasoning and free creature, made in the image of God, called to the supernatural life and eternal salvation. The same may be said for society: every intermediary body, beginning with the nation and family, are called to be dissolved in favor of the *holistic, global* project encircling the entire planet. In brief, little by little one arrives at a cosmovision and an anthropology which have flourished in pagan cultures, in which man was seen as an ephemeral being, fundamentally and definitively mortal. Individuals will believe what they retain from their experience and will be imperceptibly disposed to find their security in a leader or directorate requiring, in the name of a superior knowledge, total submission.

The recent discussions and international conferences — Rio de Janeiro (1992), Cairo (1994), Copenhagen, Beijing (1995) and Istanbul (1996) — permit us to observe the profound influence of these themes on the world technocratic establishment.

Disparate Components

However, it is necessary to observe that the "new paradigm" is presented as a vast *patchwork* whose component parts are disparate, whose ultimate foundations are elusive and whose coherence is intentionally blurred.[29] We are here confronted with a new gnosis, a "superior knowledge" being transmitted by osmosis to its initiates. It is distressing to discover that this "knowledge" pretends to explain everything, when all is said and done, by reference to the unconscious, the invisible, the unknown powers of the brain, the voiceless energies that work within the universe, etc. In the best *illuminist* tradition, the "old paradigm" is liquidated after the most summary process. As such, it has brought into play an intelligence, a reason, a will and a human sensibility that have inspired actions whose fruits are objectively verifiable.

How, for example, can the genesis and fruitfulness of the *Universal Declaration on the Rights of Man* (1948) be ignored? From Aristotle to Bachelard, the epistemologist of the old paradigm have not waited for the New Age to pose questions about the opacity of the real. In the same manner it is rapidly relegating to total silence the history of Revelation — while dispensing from the discussion its historicity and objectivity. It will be necessary, therefore, to erase all memory of the paradigm of the Age of the Fish. Improvising as an ethicist, Mr. Nakajima goes so far as to declare that "monotheistic ethics will not perhaps any longer be able to be applied as such to the future."[30]

Now to the old paradigm the "new paradigm" opposes what we must surely call a considerable bluff. The "new paradigm" is first of all presented as a syncretistic hodgepodge. The incoherent mention of anthropologists, psychologists, economists, politicians, sociologists, doctors and gurus are hurled and entangled without any principle of discernment being provided. Man has nothing else to do but abdicate his ability to discern the real and from the imagined, the true from the false, the good from the evil. The "new paradigm" is a scientism of baubles which presumes the privilege of giving an account of the whole universe and imposing itself on everybody for the sole reason that it embodies the supreme stage of human evolution, personal as well as collective.

To look at it more closely, the "new paradigm" is derived from the domain of *virtual reality*. Pieces of the real are buried in a nebula indefinitely expanding. An amalgam in which astrological nonsense abounds, the "new paradigm" has in the end no authority to impose itself except what it arrogates to itself. This "tautological" demonstration of its pertinence would be but a mental game if the paradigm in question didn't have the ambition and plan to *occupy* every brain. It is the spearhead of a project without precedent for generalized mental colonization — of a delirious imperialism requiring the submission of minds to the authority of those who produce it.[31] From the anthropological viewpoint, it is the biggest enterprise of alienation in history. From the political viewpoint, it is the most formidable danger confronting democracies. With the New Age and its networks, we enter a total war without precedent, in which psychological weapons dominate and in which all the resources of politics, law, biomedical sciences, and the most diverse disciplines are concentrated on the same target: the destruction of the "old paradigm."[32] From the Christian viewpoint, it is the greatest danger that has threatened the Church since the Arian crisis.[33]

A Millenarian Pantheism

This pantheism brings to its point of incandescence the classical millenarianisms,[34] the rantings and ravings of Jakob Böhme, Paracelsus and other indefatigable sculptors of the philosopher's stone. In this sense, Ferguson's work is perfectly in place in a collection in which *The Lama Child* and *The Jaguar Woman* are joined to tell their "secret adventure."

There we would have but a harmless game for a fecund imagination if the "new paradigm" were not presented as an ideological cover, useful to those who produce it as well as to those who wish to use it in order to dominate the world.

The new paradigm, with its networks, its taking diversity into account ("decentralization"), its globalist aim ("holism"), is a new rehash of the organisms which appeared in previous eras. The universe is presented as an organism composed of different members exercising different functions. In this pantheistic system there is place for beings whose utility is unequal. Men themselves are "cerebrally" different and unequal. The salvation of humanity is in the hands of a minority of Conspirators — an enlightened and active minority, indispensable to any ideology. Nonetheless, "the minority doesn't have to persuade the majority. . . . The new vision will propagate itself."[35]

Networks and Hermetic Freemasonry

All the indications available lead us to believe that, with its new vision of the world, its new ethic, its networks, its objective, its modes of action, and its barely perceptible structures, the New Age movement is the objectively ideal ally for the great Masonic allegiances whose trails the press sporadically reveals.[36] More precisely, the New Age is the ideal ally of *operative* Freemasonry which, in order to seduce public opinion, gives glimpses of its rites, its symbols, its degrees, its lodges, its temples, its attire, its initiation rites, etc. However, the New Age appears above all to be the objective ally of *hermetic* Freemasonry. The description of the New Age networks presents numerous similarities to what we know of hermetic Freemasonry.[37] Freemasonry par excellence, the latter finds its principal weapon in its very secrecy. It doesn't have any of the decorum of operative Freemasonry but acts through intermediary persons; it never lowers the mask, does not have temples, and it infiltrates operative masonry itself and uses its members. This Masonry acts by way of contagion across existing networks or those remaining to be created, without ever losing sight of its supreme goal: the destruction of the old paradigm and the establishment of the new.

"New Paradigm" and "holism": it is difficult to imagine that the use of these expressions by the New Age and by Dr. Nakajima, director general of WHO, could be the result of sheer coincidence. One will hesitate, perhaps, in stating that there is connivance and fortuitous non-similitude. In any case, confirmed or dubious, an absolutely proven link would seem to matter little. On the other hand, that one finds again and again, on both sides the same way of depicting situations, similar modes of action and goals that completely converge is what permits us to affirm that we find in the New Age movement as well as in WHO the same logic of evil, the same will to destroy the "old paradigm" — the primary target of the project and the will to enthrone superman. Superman? It is he who, in the insane dream to take control of his own evolution, works at destroying in himself the image of God, his very condition as a creature — and so much of the intolerable residue of the old paradigm.

The real question, then, is very simple: who is pulling the strings — at WHO and in the big international institutions, public or "private" — and who is taking charge of population control? At the end of 1998 will Mr. Nakajuma be judged effective enough to have his functions renewed?

---

[1] Marilyn Ferguson, *Les Enfants du Verseau. Pour un nouveau paradigme* (Paris: J'ai Lu, 1995). The first American edition had the title *The Aquarian Conspiracy* and was dated 1980. The French translation was first published by Calmann-Lévy in Paris, 1981.

[2] Historically speaking, the pioneer of *holism* is a South African, Jan Christian Smuts (1870-1950). Lawyer, Prime Minister and self-taught evolutionary philosopher, Smuts was an ardent defender of the Commonwealth and a pioneer of the Society of Nations. In 1926 he published *Holism and Evolution* (New York) with many later editions. The *Encyclopedia Britannica* asked him for the article "Holism" for its 1929 edition. He also published in London, 1929, *Plans for a Better World*. Smuts participated in the conference in San Francisco and played a significant role in the writ-

ing of the United Nations' Charter in 1945. Leonard Monteath Thompson, who devoted an article of four columns to him in the *Encyclopedia Britannica* (Chicago, 1969), concluded by writing: "For him [Smuts], the world order had to be based on the continuation of the leadership of the white nations."—Other authors should also be mentioned here: the German Hans Driesch (1867-1941) and his organic evolutionism, the South African Conwy Lloyd Morgan (1852-1936) and his emerging evolutionism, the Australian Samuel Alexander (1859-1938) and his ethical evolutionism, etc.

[3] Ferguson, *op.cit.* 19f.

[4] On the influence of structuralism, see *supra* Chapter II.

[5] According to Ferguson herself, Thomas S. Kuhn is the principal epistemologist of the New Age. His most famous work, *La Structure des révolutions scientifiques*, was published in the United States in 1962; a revised edition appeared in 1970. This last edition was translated into French and published in Paris by Flammarion in 1983; it was republished by Flammarion in 1995.

[6] See Michel Foucault, *Naissance de la clinique* (Paris: PUF, 1963). See also *supra*, Chapter III, *Health: A Product Subordinated to the Economy*.

[7] Ferguson, *op.cit.*20, f.

[8] *Ibid.* 24.

[9] *Ibid.* 374 f.

[10] *Ibid.* 238-281.

[11] *Ibid.* 248.

[12] Michel Serres, *Le Contrat naturel* (Paris: Flammarion, 1990).

[13] See *supra*, Chapter III: *Public Health? Health for All?*

[14] This type of "ecofascism" was theorized about, among others, by Maurice King in "Health is a Sustainable Atate," in *The Lancet*, n.8716 (Sept. 15, 1990) 666 f.

[15] See *supra*, Chapter II: *Public Health? Health for All?*

[16] Feguson *op.cit.* 18.

[17] *Ibid.* 19.

[18] *Ibid.* 15.

[19] *Ibid.* 216.

[20] The influence of the New Age shows through the *Manifeste pour une éthique planétaire. La declaration du Parlement des religions du monde*, edited with commentary by Hans Küng and Karl Joseph Kuschel and translated into French by Edouard Boné, S.J. (Paris: Cerf, 1995).

[21] Ferguson, *op.cit.* 220 f.

[22] *Ibid.* 235; on the infiltration by the New Age see also pp.16 ff.

23 *Ibid.* 128.

[24] *Ibid.* 131.

[25] *Ibid.* 123 f.

[26] *Ibid.* 123. On April 9, 1996 Warren Christopher gave a striking speech at Stanford University. The Secretary of State redefined there the fundamental axes of North American messianism by bringing them up to date. He related it to the theme of security, free commerce, the environment, resources, globalism, population, etc. The perspective of this speech is clearly "holistic" and the central themes of the New Age are paraded by. See *American Diplomacy and the Global Environment Challenges of the 21s Century* (Palo Alto CA.: US State Department, Office of the Spokesman, 1996).

[27] We broached this problem regarding "La securité démographique, stade totalitaire de l'impérialisme" in *L'Enjeu politique de l'avortement*, pp. 157-176 in the 1990 edition; pp. 189-208 in the 1991 edition.

[28] See the work of Jean Vernette, *Le Nouvel Âge. À l'aube de l'ère du Verseau* (Paris: Tequi, 1990). This can be completed by reading the article by the same specialist, "Sectes, noveaux mouvements religieux et nouvelles croyances," in *Esprit et Vie* (Langres) n.35 (Sept. 7, 1995) 481-491. See also the pastoral letter of Cardinal Godfried Danneels, *Le Christ ou le Verseaux*? (Malines) 1990, as well as the instruction of Most Rev. Noberto Rivera, Archbishop of Mexico City, *Instruccion pastoral sobre el New Age*, 1996.

[29] See Ferguson *op.cit.* 186.

[30] See IIS, *Report* n. 19, March 1, 1996.

[31] See *DTL* 22, 212 f.

[32] On total war, see Michel Schooyans, *Destin du Brésil* 50 f., 60 and *passim*.

[33] Arius, a priest of Alexandria (+ c.336), developed a heresy that denied the divinity of Christ, considering him as subordinate to the Father. He received the support of many emperors. There resulted a religious and political crisis that long divided the Church. The heresy was condemned at the Councils of Nicea (325) and Constantinople (381).

[34] On this subject, see the monumental work of Henri du Lubac, *La Postérité spirituelle de Joachim de Flore* (Paris: Lethielleux, I *De Joachim à Schelling*, 1978; II, *De Saint-Simon à nos jours*, 1980).

[35] Ferguson *op.cit.* 212.

[36] See Xose Figueroa Custodio, "La Francmasoneria hermetica," in *Excelsior* (Mexico City) Dec/7, 1991, 11 M.

[37] By definition we know very little about hermetic Freemasonry. One often refers this back to the enigmatic Jacques de Molay (c.1243-1314). After numerous confrontations with ecclesiastical authorities of the time, Philip the Fair had him burned at the stake. See the *Encyclopedia Britannica* (Chicago, 1969).

CHAPTER V
DANGERS TO THE RIGHTS OF MAN

The year 1998 marked the fiftieth anniversary of the Universal Declaration on the Rights of Man. Historically speaking, this declaration was not the first. Many nations have provided themselves with documents proclaiming the rights of man or some of them, and these documents are beacons of primary importance in the political and cultural history of the nations in question. Let us think, for example, of the *Magna Carta* of 1215 in England, of the Declaration of Independence of the United States in 1776, of the Declaration of the Rights of Man and of the Citizen in 1789. Although rooted in a particular national context, these texts have often inspired other analogous texts within the framework of other nations.

THE UNIVERSAL DECLARATION OF 1948

Originality

The peculiarity, and even originality, of the Declaration of 1948 is that it is *universal*. It proclaims that every human being is the subject of these rights. These rights flow from each person's belonging to the human race. From the fact that a being is human, these rights must be recognized as his. This universality extends and consolidates the *fraternity* already affirmed in documents prior to 1948. It gives fraternity a universal scope. Human sociability is a sociability among brothers and sisters. All have the same dignity and rights; all are equal. This *equality* means that, over and above whatever distinguishes them (origin, religion, intelligence, race), all men have the same rights from the sole fact that they are human.

Just as the rights of man had been proclaimed within the particular framework of certain nations and for the use of their internal politics, so equality has often been affirmed in different particular traditions, religions, philosophical, cultural, or otherwise.

Here again, the peculiarity and originality of the Declaration of 1948 is that, in strict coherence with its universal scope, it proclaims that all men are equal in dignity and rights. This equality flows from each man's objectively belonging to the human race.[1]

We know that the Declaration distinguishes two categories of human rights. In the first place there are civil and political rights: the right to life, to liberty, free movement, liberty to find a home, the right to property, freedom of thought, of expression, of association and political participation (arts.2 to 21). In second place come the economic, social and cultural rights "declared" for the first time: the right to work, to union activity, to health, to food, to housing, etc. The Declaration also emphasizes the importance of the social and international context, so that men may effectively enjoy their rights. (arts.22 to 30).

Fruitfulness

The productiveness of this Declaration is illustrated, not only by the very effective use to which it was put to denounce torture, oppression, injustice, abuses of power, etc., but also by the effective juridical instruments it inspired sporadically throughout world. These rights have been regulated and protected. Many conferences have been devoted to this text; the Vienna conferences in 1993 resulted in a final declaration of great importance.[2]

THREATS TO THE DECLARATION

The Half-Open Door

At the time of the Vienna Conference on the Rights of Man (1993) Boutros Boutros-Ghali seems partially to open the door to a revision of the Declaration of 1948:[3]

> As a process of synthesis, the rights of man are, in essence, rights in motion. I mean by that that they have at once the object of formulating immutable commandments and expressing a moment of historical awareness. They are, then, altogether both absolute and situated.

This is, at the very least an ambiguous text, since one could be tempted to interpret "situated" as meaning "relative to different situations."

More worrisome was another passage which, if it were to be taken literally, would risk radically overturning the concept in of the rights of man explained in 1948:

> The 1966 agreements... permit us to affirm — and we must strongly say this again — that the civil and political rights, on the one hand, and the economic, social and cultural rights on the other, are on the same level of importance and dignity.

A text like that risks being exploited by those who want to subordinate the right of individuals to the right of development[4] or the rights of individuals to those of the social body.

It is, then, advisable to reaffirm that the first right of man, of this *free* being who is man, is the right to life, and that this right is opposed to the action of all other men; without this right all others vanish. Economic and social rights only make sense when they explicate and make more precise this fundamental right.

Two examples show this clearly. To declare the right of all to health is obviously not simply to express a wish that everybody be well — "and too bad for those who don't have this chance." This right implies a concerted action to allow each person to preserve his health, his life — and to exercise his liberty. The same goes for the right to work: if it appears in the Declaration it is because, in order to live, man must work. Human work not only provides for the biological needs of man; it is also one of the conditions for exercising his liberty: by carrying out his work man realizes himself; through his work he can choose what he desires to do.

The same can be said for the right to property, to food, to housing, etc. All the rights of man have their source and support in the primordial right to life, which, for this very reason, is considered as the most fundamental right par excellence.[5]

The proposals of Boutros Boutros-Ghali are, therefore, worrisome to the degree that he "strongly" affirms that civil and political right, on the one hand, and economic and social rights, on the other, are "on the same level of importance and dignity." That is to ignore the fact that economic, social and cultural rights express the indispensable conditions for safeguarding the fundamental right of human individuals to live and to live in freedom.

The Inclusion of "New Rights"

Several other converging indications prove that this Declaration is threatened. The gravest threats do not come from circles desiring to rewrite the Declaration of 1948[6] or from those nongovernmental organizations that have launched trial balloons about rewriting or replacing the Declaration of 1948, e.g., that of CLADEM.[7]

The threats come first of all from the clearly affirmed desire to broaden the list of human rights declared in 1948 to include some "new rights": to "sexual and reproductive health" — including the right to abortion, to different models of the family, to recognizing the status of homosexuals. Among other organizations, the International Federation for Family Planning (IPPF) and Family Care International[8] are devoting themselves to spreading this new approach.[9] But the offensive in this direction comes above all from the European Union. At the conferences of Cairo (1994) and Beijing (1995), representatives of the Union were the principal propagators of these "new rights."[10] Invoked since the eighties, these new rights will very likely lead to the global Charter of Health in 1998.[11] The content of the universal Declaration of 1948 would then be little by little eroded and would remain but a decorative facade for purely rhetorical usage.

But, alas, we have to assert that the Universal Declaration of the Rights of Man, and especially the right it proclaims to life, is threatened by other more or less crafty conduct, for which the list would be very long. These threats come from diverse subrepticious procedures: more or less "authorized" interpretations given to the Declaration, concealment of key words, shifting of emphasis, distortion of meaning, relativization, etc.

Before taking up the most devastating procedures, let us pause an instant over two proven tactics.

The Tactic of Derogation

The tactic of derogation is a well-known process.[12] It consists in solemnly proclaiming a principle as good, and subsequently supplying a list of conditions and circumstances in which the law determines that the principle doesn't apply. A typical example, rather a caricature, is furnished by Article I of the Veil-Pelletier law in France: "The law guarantees respect for every human being from the very beginning of life. This principle may not be threatened except in cases of necessity as determined by this law." Pretense! This tactic distorts the right completely. It subordinates the inalienable right of man to life to the will of the legislator. This tactic has the effect, then, of weakening the rights of man in their very foundation.

From Consensus to Law

Another tactic is already widely used in international assemblies and conferences. What is sought in these meetings is a consensus.[13]

As in the case of Cairo and Beijing, reservations, divergences, and disagreements are mentioned with extreme discretion, even practically skirted. Why? Simply because consensus, invoked at the opportune moment, will broadly open the way to international agreements, which, once ratified, will have the force of law in the countries concerned. Here consensus leads to an indirect legislative procedure, so to speak, which ensnares the imprudent.

DISTORTIONS OF MEANING

We will consider here two particularly serious examples of distortion of meaning whose victims are the concept of equality and the family.

From Equality to Fairness

In Western philosophical, political and juridical tradition equality is a concept technically well assured. Equality does not mean sameness; it signifies that we are all different but have the right to the same respect.[14]

The fight for the recognition of the equal dignity of all men has been the motive behind all social struggles and revolutions. Equality is one of the pillars of every State based on right. Now, under the influence of various trends which we have already touched on, equality tends to be supplanted by fairness.[15] This is especially flagrant in the *Beijing Declaration and Platform for Action*. Fairness is a soft concept that in no way postulates prior recognition of the same dignity in all men that is essential to the idea of equality. Dispensing with this objective anthropological reference, fairness is dependent on the subjectivity of those who give it meaning, a meaning that is always changing, and thus causing a fluctuating account of what is just and leaving it at the mercy of a pragmatic consensus and compromise.

The subreptitious introduction of fairness risks, then, engulfing equality which is, after all, the focal point of the 1948 Declaration. Interpreted as the reduction of equality to fairness, this Declaration is emptied of its meaning, since instead of attesting to an objective equality, it would make the content of fairness depend upon the consenting wills of those who are engaged in making the decision.

At present, it goes without saying that all those who have never been for equality are delighted to be able to invoke fairness. One considers, for example, countries that discriminate against women or that are immersed in the caste system. Fairness, in effect, is entirely compatible with discrimination.

In the end, the risk is that, thus reinterpreted, the 1948 Declaration will yield to more and more divergent exegesis, with the foreseeable consequence that international society will be more and more *Babelized*.

We find ourselves, then, in a situation which is reminiscent of the time when Naziism, Fascism and Communism were at their peak. In order for the "new paradigm" and a sophist interpretation of the 1948 Declaration to be imposed, one has to begin by rejecting any anthropology that affirms the equal dignity of all men and women. The true motive for the rejection of this notion is the same that makes people reject the ethics of the "old paradigm." Rooted in the monotheistic tradition, the latter stands as an obstacle, Dr. Nakajima assures us — to the "new paradigm of health." On this point WHO's director general is joined by Anthony Piel, who explicitly identifies equality with the monotheistic tradition.[16]

The "Polymorphous" Family

A second example is the family. As the preparatory facts demonstrate, the Declaration gives to the word family its traditional meaning: the enduring union of a man and woman to found a home and have children. "The family is the natural and fundamental element of society and has the right to protection on the part of society and the State" (art.16).

For many years, though, certain agencies of the U.N. have given various meanings to this word. There is the classical heterosexual family, but also the lesbian, homosexual, and one parent "family." Since the family has become polymorphous, the work is marked by *polysemy*! A family could have a biological "father" or "nonparent", a biological "mother" or "nonparent," and eventually children corresponding to every concoction imaginable.[17]

Still more definitions of the family are circulating. For example: "The family is an enlarged environment in which decisions about health are taken."[18]

This totally equivocal use of the word family will wind up by seriously eroding the 1948 Declaration. It will ruin, as a consequence, economic, social and cultural rights to the extent in which they directly affect the well-being of the members of the family community.

THE RELATIVIZATION OF RIGHTS

Even the fundamental rights proclaimed in the Declaration can still be "relativized." Interpretations will eventually lead to having man's rights considered as dependent on the domain or situations in which they are exercised; they are conditioned, even limited, by circumstances and situations. We will give four examples of relativization: with regard to woman, to the quality of life, to cultures and to time.

Relativization According to Women's Status

If one recognizes the universal application of the principle that all human beings are equal in dignity, and that this dignity is inalienable, then one must admit that every person presents a singularity, a uniqueness, that deserves respect and that gives rise to rights. A right doesn't become a right unless it is accompanied by an obligation with inherent due respect.

For many years now international conferences have had the tendency to reserve a special treatment for the rights of woman. The Vienna conference, for example, devoted some interesting paragraphs to the "equality of condition and fundamental rights of the woman" (arts.36-44). As for the Beijing conference on women (Sept. 4-15, 1995), it produced, besides the Beijing Declaration, a long document entitled *Platform for Action*. Strongly influenced by radical feminist trends, this document is entirely devoted to the specific rights of women and to a program of action for reinforcing them. From beginning to end, these documents use argumentation which favor the rights of women expressed in terms of fairness.

Together with many others, this document reveals the tendency to distinguish the treatment reserved for the specific rights of women from the treatment accorded generically to the rights of man. One of the problems that consequently appears and that was perceptible well before Beijing, is that a conflict arises between the specific rights of woman and the generic right to life of the child she is carrying. By dint of exalting the specificity of the rights of woman, the woman may derive justification from her specific rights for the disposal of her child's life, boy or *girl*. It follows that the right of every human individual to life is found relativized in the name of the woman's specific rights. Fairness is, then, invoked to increase the rights of woman in the name of her femininity. *They play fairness off against equality.*

This type of relativization could be extended to other particular categories of individuals. By emphasizing their unique attributes, some categories of human beings would finish by being declared excluded from the human family. The Declaration would, *for them*, be inapplicable.

What the radical feminists have not sufficiently faced is that the process which they are turning in their favor could be turned against them. In fact, by virtue of insisting on the specific distinctiveness of the feminine condition, the risk is great that it may one day be invoked to object that the rights of man proclaimed in the Universal Declaration be extended to women as well as to men. In the name of her specificity, the woman could be partially omitted from the inclusion in the rights of man. Her "dignity" could be broken down into "specific" rights, set up hierarchically according to the criteria of function and usefulness in the social body. There would thus be the rights of woman, then the rights of the mother, then the rights of the young girl, then the rights of the adolescent, then those of the child before and after her birth.[19] In the name of fairness, woman, the first concerned with "reproductive health," could be pressured into conforming her sexual conduct to WHO's "new paradigm." Her reproductive behavior would be subjected to the control of technocrats charged with seeing that its definitive priorities are respected.[20]

But why use the hypothetical? Situations such as those we've just envisaged are witnessed today and are even frequent. Documentary films and reports are available to show that some women are forced to abort, are sterilized as if on an assembly line, "hormonized" by means of long-term implants, treated as inferior beings by male operators who appraise them with disdain. The supreme refinement of "reproductive health" and the height of contempt are reached when the technocrat transfers to the woman herself the power of destroying her infant: the horror attaining its height when, having been prematurely aroused to sexual consummation, an adolescent girl is immediately vaccinated against the infant she could be carrying!

Since all of that is done in the name of fairness, one must observe that the word fairness has sometimes become a new name for slavery and contempt.

To cut short similar trends, we must maintain that feminine specificity — and with it any other type of specificity — defines the particular manner of the woman's belonging to the human community. The rights which flow from this distinction have no meaning except insofar as they clarify the fundamental rights common to all human beings anterior to any specification. It is because she lives her *human condition* in the feminine mode that recognition of the dignity of woman is demanded. But this requirement could not be invoked by women in order to refuse to other categories of human beings a specificity of the same rank as the one invoked — justly — to ground their claims.

In short, specificity should not to be placed on the same level as universality and hence can never be opposed to it. It is clear again that we must maintain the strict equality of woman and man with regard to what we could call human rights, an expression that is perhaps less open to the twisted interpretations to which the French expression of the rights of man is exposed. In effect, to speak of fairness regarding woman and her rights would permit the introduction of discrimination which is totally incompatible with equality.

Relativization According to the "Quality of Life"

Not long ago, the quality of life, signified minimal requirements that had to be established for man to be able to live decently: food, clothing, housing, health, education, etc. The notion quality of life was close to the notion of condition of life and the common good. General conditions in a given society permit a life of such a quality. In Western Europe in the eighteenth century, for example, conditions were not as good as they are today. The differences are concretely demonstrated in measurable demographic indicators such as infant mortality and life expectancy. The improvement observed over time is not only due to material progress and to scientific and technical discoveries; it is also due to moral, juridical and administrative progress, and to a more astute sense of social justice and the common good. What was being established was a whole ensemble of conditions of existence, a human environment, allowing each man to realize his abilities better, and to the benefit of the community, with the irreplaceable contribution that each can offer.

Today, however, the notion of quality life is increasingly disconnected from the notions of a general condition of life and the common good. The quality of life is now related to subjective criteria with which one assesses whether a life is worth living or not. Such an assessment will naturally fluctuate according to established criteria of priorities.[21]

Therefore it follows that the seriously handicapped, those with cancer or AIDS, infants in the womb of their mother, mongoloids, the elderly, those with sleeping sickness or malaria, the immense number of poor people, etc. — without speaking of those who belong to such and such an ethnic group or race — are all exposed to being told that their life isn't worth living, that they are too great a cost to society, that they are an unbearable emotional burden to others, etc. They must, then, expect the end, or death, which corresponds to their "lack" of quality of life.

In sum, the quality of life is reduced to a question of economic and social usefulness, of interest or of convenience. Presently, the quality of life criterion is presented as giving way to a right that surpasses the most fundamental right to life itself and to integrity. There we have the kind of aberration to which can lead placing the fundamental rights of individuals on the same level with economic, social and cultural rights.[22]

Relativization According to Cultures

Another procedure used to weaken the Declaration consists in relativizing it according to cultures. In Muslim territories orthodox circles often invoke Islamic specificity in order to apply charia or to keep women in a state of submission. In various African countries female clitoral excision continues to be performed in the name of traditional cultures.

Now the rights of man are not deduced on the basis of cultures, much less of any particular culture: they are universal. Their implementation must certainly give rise to legislation proper to each society; that is but an application of the principle of subsidiarity. But the Declaration considers that at the source of every cultural differentiation there are free and equal human beings who especially have the right to physical integrity. The U.N. and the 1948 Declaration were born precisely to act as a safeguard against this abusive relativization. As a consequence, the very existence of this Declaration has enabled many women — in Islamic lands and/or Africa, for example, to obtain recognition of their dignity and equality with men.

Relativization of Time

This is one of the most subtle and widespread procedures. The individual is regarded as an ephemeral moment, a simple link between the past and the future. He navigates in an odyssey of time and space. The social body is anterior to him in time and superior to him in rights; health is "public."[23] The individual must, then, adapt himself to the collective body into which he is inserted. This "body" will at times be the State, other times, the Market, or the Global Village, or even Gaia, Mother Earth. Dead, the individual "will survive" by reinserting himself into the whole out of which he was issued.[24] Some will make it clear that the body belongs to society as well as to the individual. It is therefore "disposable"; its integrity must not be protected by rights. Situated in time and space, the body must be administered to by those who enjoy a superior knowledge, a scientific knowledge of the sense of history and the determinisms whose imperatives cannot be ignored.

WHAT KIND OF SOVEREIGNTY? WHAT KIND OF DEVELOPMENT?

Flexible Sovereignty

To put the emphasis on equality rather than fairness is not only essential for the defense of man's rights in general and the individual's socio-economico rights in particular; it is essential for the defense of nations. The transition from equality to fairness entails grave consequences for the relationships among nations. The most solid basis for protecting sovereignty and, at the same time, for promoting interdependence is not to be sought in fairness but in equality. In both cases, reference to equality is absolutely essential. The whole edifice of the U.N. has been built on the sovereignty of member nations. All the member nations are, in principle, equal in dignity.

However, the evolution of defining equality as fairness risks precipitating a questioning of national sovereignty. Furthermore, from the onset the sovereignty of the majority of the member nations of the U.N. was breached by giving the right of veto to a few great powers. Moreover, this sovereignty is already poorly handled in actuality by reason of the enormous diversity that exists among nations.

More serious still is that in corrupting the meaning of equality into fairness, one risks precipitating the contesting of the very principle of national sovereignty; many theoreticians are already applying themselves to doing just that.[25]

In effect, by virtue of talking about fairness among nations, as is frequently done in our day, one empties sovereignty of its content. Justice in the relationships among nations is abandoned to the judgment of authorities who are in a position to impose what they understand by "fair relations among nations." The sovereignty of nations, then, becomes flexible: it is limited. And this limitation is imposed in an attractive manner. This means that fairness, which is compatible with discriminatory practices among men, is also compatible with discriminatory practices among nations.

The Excessive Role of Some Nongovernmental Organizations

Sovereignty is also flexible and limited by the growing role of some nongovernmental organizations. It is well known that some of them have long played a considerable role in the execution of programs controlling life as well as in the big international conferences devoted to this subject. They act sometimes as sensitizing agents, sometimes as executors, sometimes as pressure groups, and in some cases as lobbyists. However, since the Beijing conference the tendency is becoming more blatant to entrust some nongovernmental organizations with yet more important tasks. Carefully selected because they are "ideologically correct," some nongovernmental organizations like IPPF are being given assignments in the public domain. They receive a delegation from UNFPA or the World Bank to collaborate in executing fixed plans of action at international conferences. A significant change of direction has been initiated since the Beijing conference, since it is foreseen that individually selected nongovernmental organizations, acting in concert with public international agencies, will intervene directly in local communities.

This manner of action does not honor the demands of solidarity, and furthermore it constitutes a flagrant attack on the sovereignty of States. The just authority of the latter over their particular national communities risks being short-circuited by the interjection of these organizations totally lacking in legitimacy. What is more, these organizations depend on a "delegation" emanating from international agencies which still do not have the authority to delegate powers which they themselves do not possess.

It is inadmissible that the just sovereignty of States be sacrificed on the altar of a holistic, globalist project that dissolves the sovereign nations' identity, in which the diversity of the human community is expressed.

What Kind of "Right to Development"?

We have previously recalled that the 1948 Declaration included two points: one devoted to individual rights, the other to economic, social and cultural rights.[26] to the rights of the second type Group 77 (G77) intends to add the right to development.[27] This group regularly insists on giving priority to development in less developed countries. For them what matters urgently is to reach a stage of development that will permit the honoring of economic, social and cultural rights. It is only after that, we are assured, that one will be able to honor individual civil and political rights.

This manner of interpreting the rights of man is unfortunately disastrous for developing countries themselves. It was a mistaken idea for them to see in the 1948 Declaration a means of the colonizing West to render its domineering yoke more cumbersome by imposing its "particular" conception of man's rights on the whole of human society.

This reading, attributed to some Third World leaders, of the 1948 Declaration was often inspired by a theory of dependence, and was so perverse that it seems to come from imperialist cenacles rather than from the elite leaders of poor countries. In fact, from its genesis, the Declaration drew lessons from the Second World War and found that those ideologies which caused the war — Naziism, first and foremost — held the rights of man in contempt. By proclaiming these rights, the Declaration intended above all to prevent the return of any sort of totalitarianism, while also contesting in advance every attack on human rights. For the rest, many fashioners of decolonization have understood from the outset how they could use this Declaration to their advantage to legitimize, in an *ad hominem* way, arguments against colonizing nations. In effect, how will the poor nations be motivated to fight for their development unless a consciousness of their dignity is awakened in every citizen?

It was, then, a proper approach for the leaders of decolonization to appeal to the first principles of the Declaration, for the very idea of universality, that is to say, the equal dignity of all men, even if it emerged slowly in the West, is no more a monopoly of the West than fire is the monopoly of those who discovered it.

Now by virtue of giving priority to the "right of development" and equivocating on the promotion of individual rights, the wealthy countries and even international organizations use the *ad hominem* argument for the "right to development" against the Third-World whose leaders sometimes imprudently promote. This astonishing reversal is observable in many ways.

First of all, in a general way, "the right to development" invoked by the Third-World offers rich countries the perfect occasion for "aiding" the poor countries and maintaining them in chronic dependence. Aid, very often conditioned, thus becomes an addictive drug.

Then, it is easy for the international establishment to "recognize the right of poor countries to development" and to pretend to "help them to exercise their right to development." But, in the very name of these formidable declarations, rich countries manipulate their advantage by pressuring the poor countries to strictly calibrate their individual rights to the requirements of development as the rich countries define them. This is the very pretext under which rich nations and international organizations program anti-birth policies, which are then "welcomed" by the Third-World leaders and put into practice with their support! China provides a caricature of this kind of situation.[28]

Besides, the wealthy countries have no reason to relent while they're doing so well. For if, in the name of the "right to development," the governments of poor countries feel themselves justified in deferring without end the promotion of the individual rights of their citizens, why shouldn't the world powers maintain their control over the Third-World countries in the name of the New World Order requirements?

An Audit of the U.N.

Much is spoken of an imminent reform of the U.N., but information on this subject is given out with parsimony. In order to reform itself, the U.N. must above all, renew the double goal which defined its origin: to promote the rights of man and to work toward development.

The analyses which we have been conducting reveal that the U.N. has not slowed its drift toward objectives contrary to its origins.

The U.N. has become a very heavy apparatus, badly administered, and urgently in need of a cost-benefit analysis — the very sort of inquiry to which it is all too ready to subject its members. Through many of its agencies, along with its preferred nongovernmental organizations, the U.N. has become a supranational machine and a financial abyss used by "paying" nations to exercise a generalized mastery over human life. At present, the U.N. and its agencies have become, not without a certain arrogance and definitely without any legitimacy, an apparatus of supranational government at the service of the New World Order, which the Masonic lodges ardently desire and which the New Age disseminates through its networks.

For the U.N. and its satellites, an independent audit is urgently required.

In the meantime, member nations must question the appropriateness of paying their contributions and the ends for which they are used. It is also necessary for developing countries to analyze in depth the "aid" which they receive through U.N. channels, and to ask themselves what benefits they really derive from it; to question *what such aid is costing them*, and what it eventually yields for the rich countries.

Europe in the Globalist Nebula

As for Western Europe, it would be well advised not to embark on the ship of the "new paradigm" or to imperil the 1948 Declaration. The attitude adopted by the European Union at the time of the

Cairo, Beijing and Istanbul conferences, is as astonishing as it is inadmissible. First of all, in matters that concern both their own identity and their future, the European nations have voluntarily renounced exercising their sovereignty in these international assemblies. On this point, the Treaty of Maastricht has tied their hands. Under the pretext of "union," these nations have alloted themselves a sole spokesman, renouncing, by this very abdication, their claim to be heard as well as their legitimate authority.

Whence the question: what good does it do for Europe to speak with one voice if what it has to offer to the world is but a renunciation of its own foundational principles? By what right should the spokesman at the service of a nonrepresentative entity be entrusted with serving the European political body, when it has no power over him? Would not these political bodies have understood that by weakening the 1948 Declaration one would remove the barriers designed to check the return of despotism? Would they not have comprehended that, due to their behavior, foregoing their rights will onlly ruin the safeguards against tyranny? How could they not have seen that in disavowing the signatories of the 1948 Declaration they would reduce their rights to the state in which they were before the onslaught of Naziism?[29] More precisely, would not the European States have noticed that, by their attitude, they restored the rule of a juridical positivism which is analogous to that which cleared the way for nascent Naziism?

One can hardly believe that such stakes would have escaped the notice of European authorities and their spokesmen. And one shudders at the idea that they could be in connivance with the authors of the "globalist" plans which we have analyzed.

Europe has renounced the idea of universality essential to the 1948 Declaration. This is how scandal has arisen, for by its attitude the European Union betrayed its own heritage and betrayed as well the Third-World. It even remains ambivalent when confronted by its own demographic collapse — a nevertheless dramatic example of what may be imminent justice.

Finally, the conferences which we have mentioned have provoked an underlying debate concerning two dominant conceptions of rights, which it will suffice to outline: the one considers that positive rights must respect the "unwritten" laws (Cicero); the other considers that positive rights proceed from the will of the legislator. During recent international conferences the European Union has clearly distanced itself from the first conception. The consequences of abandoning it — if we must to confirm them — now appear in the degree to which the weakest people can no longer count on the right of protection of their rights.

The European nations have not understood, or won't admit, that they have just consented to the erosion of their most precious acquired political and juridical morality: the *equality of all men*, the mother cell of all democracy. These nations cannot consent to the dissolution of their sovereignty in the globalist nebula. In doing so, Europe is about to lose the Third World War, a war of a totally new type in which Europe is seduced into abandoning equality in favor of a Californian fairness.

With the complicity of numerous Europeans, Europe has become the victim of a project of ideological colonization without precedent. It is subjected to a process of deprograming-reprograming aimed at making it accept a package, a parcel, comprising a new Ethic, a new juridical order, a New World Order

PERVERSION OF HUMAN ACTIVITY

At the end of the assessment sketched in the preceding chapters, the Catholic Church, under the personal impetus of John Paul II, appears more and more as the last refuge for the unconditional defense of human rights beginning with the right to life.[30]

Despite her efforts, we must unfortunately observe how nefarious is the influence of the anti-life ideologies and the dramas provoked by the practices that are their concrete expression. These ideologies and practices entail a perversion that embeds itself in the most diverse levels of human activity.

Perversion of political life: in a nation which admits, even legalizes, practices attacking human life in its integrity, the weakest are without protection. They are exposed to the discretionary power of the strongest, and cannot count on the protection which every State professing justice has the duty of offering. In this case, the State has abandoned the care of the common good; it exercises its authority in favor of only certain members of the political society and to the detriment of others. The power which is exercised in such a State loses its legitimacy; even if it keeps the structures of a democratic society, this State tends toward totalitarian despotism. Must we add that, with due proportion, these remarks also apply to international organizations?

Perversion of rights: the powerful of this world always have the tendency of turning their will into the force of law. As the work of K.

Binding illustrates, juridical positivism, which one finds in all authoritarian regimes, always consecrated the will of the strongest. When the law is not directed toward the good of all and tries to conceal unjust actions, it loses all authority and one must refuse to obey it.[31]

Perversion of economic life: contempt for human life often appears both as the condition and the consequence of a hyperindividualistic conception of the market. It appears as a condition in the sense that those who are neither productive nor self-sufficient must be set aside preventively so that they won't be obstacles to the market's proper functioning. It appears as a consequence in the sense that men are set aside if they become non-productive and non-self-supportive.

Perversion of medicine — to which we must add biology. Medicine has drawn all its nobility from the service it offers without any discrimination to men weakened by disease. But it must be recognized that we are witnessing a radical change in the practice of medicine. Some doctors place their technique at the service of the strongest, the wealthiest, and even the "social body." Thus they revive a lugubrious tradition which has seen doctors devote their knowledge to programs of extermination, repression and torture.

Demography can also be implicated in programs that show contempt for human life. Together with agronomy, and basically with any scientific discipline, it can be placed at the service of groups and special interests; it can also be led to favor one approach to population problems over others and to provide statistical arguments for the enemies of life.[32]

As has been demonstrated, all scientific disciplines that affect man closely can be transformed into disciplines of combat, and their effectiveness can be formidable. All of them can, in the name of dehumanizing scientism, espouse insupportable claims to control life.

Nevertheless, what is most serious is the *perversion of moral conscience*, both on the level of individuals as well as on that of societies. When evil is declared good and subjectively perceived as such, when sterilization, abortion and death are presented as good, as "rights" and perceived as such, this signifies that the most fundamental moral references are shattered.

The real victims of this evolution are, most certainly, the unborn infants, women and the poor of the Third-World, but also the young whose moral conscience risks being profoundly perverted by an irresponsible sexual education.

The conclusion which can thus be drawn is that our society is obsessed with a culture of death. This culture of death is translated into a self-preserving mentality. Fearing death, men assure their own security at any price. They see others as rivals and potential or actual enemies. Rather than share, they accumulate, protect and defend their possessions. Couples say the same thing as rich societies: "The fewer children we have the more will we be able to enjoy life!" "The fewer men on the earth the richer shall we be!"

In short, contempt for human life reveals what one may cite as the structures of sin. These are not only observed in the economic domain, but are also found and derived from the most diverse areas of human activity and in the entirety of social relationships.

Thus the entire dimension of respect human life is indissolubly social, conjugal and personal. It is already clear how foolish it is to seek happiness in the cult of death!

---

[1] Of the abundant literature on this question we draw attention to two classic works: Albert Verdoodt, *Naissance et signification de la Déclaration universelle des Droits d'Homme*, (Louvain-Paris: Nauwelaerts, 1963); Philippe de la Chapelle, *La Déclaration universelle des Droits d'Homme et le catholicisme* (Paris: Librairie générale de droit et de jurisprudence, 1967).

[2] See *Déclaration et Programme d'action de Vienne, June 1933* (New York: U.N., 1995). On this conference see the important article of Antonio Augusto Cancado Trindade, "Memoria de Conferencia Mundial de Direitos Humano, Viena 1993," *Revista brasileira de Estudos Politicos* (Belo Horizonte) n.80 (January 1995) 149-224.

[3] The booklet *Déclaration et Programme... op.cit.* is preceded by the *Déclaration liminaire* of Boutros Boutros-Ghali; we have quoted from pp.8 and 12.

[4] See *infra*, this Chapter, *What Right to Development?*

[5] See Joaquim Carlos Salgado, "Os Direitos Fundamentais," *Revista brasileira de Estudos Politicos* (Belo Horizonte) n.82 (January 1996) 15-69; esp. 26 and 56 f.

[6] According to G. Magazzeni, special assistant to the high commissioner for human rights, neither a new declaration nor a rewriting of the 1948 one was foreseen for 1998. Regarding this subject see the "Interview with Gianni Magazzeni" by Marguerite Peeters in *Report IIS*, May 23, 1996.

[7] A *Propuesta para una Declaración Universal de los Derechos Humanos desde una perspectiva de género* was put forth by CLADEM (Lima, Peru) in 1994.

[8] María José Alcalá, *Compromisos para la salud y los derechos sexuales y reproductivos de todos. Marco de acción. Sobre la base de los acuerdos y convenciones internacionales pertinentes, incluidas las conferencias de Beijing, Copenhague, El Cairo y Viena* (New York: Family Care International, 1995).

[9] See, for example, IPPF, *Le Droit humain à la planification familiale et à la santé reproductive* (London, 1996(; IPPF, *Declaracion de derechos* (no available location or date).

[10] See the astonishing manual of Simon Stanley and Sara Hyde (eds.), *Handbook on European Union Support for Population and Reproductive Health Programs* (New York: UNFPA, 1995).

[11] In Chapter IV, note 26, we allude to the *Global Health Charter* prepared by WHO.

[12] See *BPCV*, questions 3, 31, 59, 61 f., 65.

[13] On consensus see above Chapter II, *Procedural Justice*; BPCV, q.42.
[14] See *supra*, this Chapter, *Originality*.
[15] See *supra*, Chapter III, *Procedural Justice*.
[16] See Marguerite Peeters' interview with Anthony Piel in *Report IIS* August 5, 1996.
[17] See what is said about the family with regard to gender, *supra*, Chapter II, *The Ideology of Gender*.
[18] "Family for me means an extended environment where decisions about health are taken." Original enough, this definition is owed to Dr. Tomris Türmen and appears in his interview given to Marguerite Peeters on January 17, 1996, distributed by *Report IIS*; see above Chapter III, note 8.
[19] On this subject see the interview cited above in *Ibid*.
[20] See *supra*, Chapter III.
[21] See *infra*, Chapter VII, **Some "Indications" that Carry No Weight**.
[22] See *supra*, Chapter IV, *The Return of Gnosticism*, etc.
[23] See *supra*, Chapter III, *Public Health? Health for All?* And f.
[24] See *BPCV* q. 142; see also Chapter IV.
[25] See James Kurth, "Toward the Post-Modern World," *The National Interest* Summer 1992.
[26] See *supra*, this Chapter, *Originality*.
[27] G77 each month publishes the *Journal of the Group of 77*, P.O. Box 20, New York, NY 10017.
[28] See the works of John Aird, *supra*, Chapter II, note 3.
[29] See above **THREATS TO THE DECLARATION**; also *BPCV* q.72.
[30] This is clearly demonstrated by Mary Ann Glendon, professor at Harvard Law School, who led the Vatican delegation at the Beijing conference. See "Women's World: Beijing and Beyond," *Church* (New York) Summer of 1996, pp.19-24.
[31] One of the most stimulating works for studying the relationship between rights and politics is by to Mary Ann Glendon, cited in the previous note. To this famous Harvard professor is owed the book, *Rights Talk. The Impoverishment of Political Discourse* (New York: Free Press, 1991).
[32] On this subject see Gerard-François Dumont, "La science peut-elle être neutre? Le cas de la démographie," *La Famille: des sciences à l'éthique* (Paris: Bayard/Centurion, 1995) 27-40.

CHAPTER VI

TO LOVE IS HAPPINESS

From our very first chapter it has been apparent that contempt for human life is not a superficial phenomenon. Such contempt proceeds from a morose conception of human existence. How can a conception of man that places its trust in suspicion, resentment, jealousy, anxiety, fear and even hate lead to happiness? How could a lugubrious ideology that recommends, as the price of unbridled pansexualism, sterilization, abortion, systematic contraception and even euthanasia provide men with the joy of living and the joy of loving? Neither this conception of man nor this ideology are compatible with the highest aspirations of the human heart. It is nevertheless on the road of happiness that we can indeed make our way.

SOME REASSURING FACTS

Faced with an assault of discouraging proposals and anti-life recommendations, it would be fitting to recall some reassuring facts.

First of all, nearly everywhere in the world life expectancy has never been so long (see Illustration 4). In almost all regions we observe a drop in infant mortality (see Illustration 5) as well as in maternal mortality.[1]

At the same time, the world population continues to grow, yet the rate of increase is diminishing (see Illustration 6). This growth is explained by birth rates which remain relatively high in poor countries, and above all, by the fall of of mortality rates and the increase in life expectancy.[2]

The prolonging of human life, the diminishing of mortality rates and the growth of world population are the foremost result of *scien-*

84 The Gospel Confronting World Disorder

Illustration 4

Life Expectancy

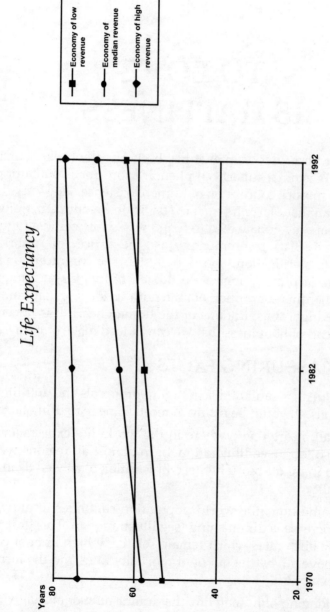

Source: World Bank, *World Development Report 1994*, Oxford University Press, p.160

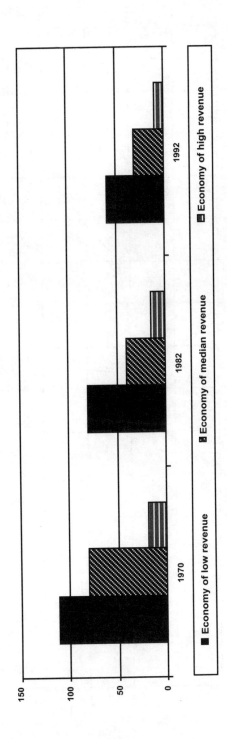

Illustration 5

Infant Mortality

Deaths per 1,000 live births

Source: World Bank, *World Development Report 1994*, Oxford University Press, p.160

Illustration 6

Change in the Rate of Increase in World Population

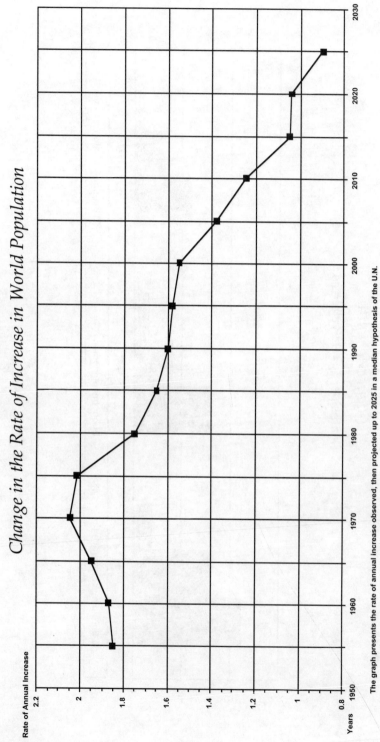

The graph presents the rate of annual increase observed, then projected up to 2025 in a median hypothesis of the U.N.

Source: G-F. Dumont, *Le Monde et les hommes. Les grandes évolutions démographiques* (Paris: Litec, 1995) p.16.

tific and especially *medical* progress. Such progress is primarily due to *preventive* as well as curative medicine. Equal mention must be made of better management of medical resources. This success of medicine, without precedent in the history of humanity, deserves to be hailed. We will never know how much suffering, how many tears, and how much grief have been avoided through such progress.

Similar observations must also be made with regard to *agriculture*, breeding and the production of foodstuffs in general. Technically speaking, never has the capacity for food production been so high on a worldwide scale nor the availability of such advanced techniques.

Educational networks have also been expanded throughout the world. The growth of primary education has unfortunately spread too slowly, and too many men, above all women, do not always have access to it. On the other hand, a growing proportion of young people have access to professional and higher education.

These positive results are the fruit of numerous coordinated efforts by personal and collective initiatives as well as the action of public and private organizations.

In this regard, one must also praise the action undertaken since the end of the Second World War by some international organizations working for a better world. The U.N. and its specialized agencies have done a remarkable job in the field of human rights, peace, development, education, health, nutrition and the environment. Other international organizations have made substantial advances by introducing greater strictness in the management of international monetary resources.

Also worthy of mention is the very important work performed by numerous nongovernmental organizations, particularly those of Christian origin, in all areas related to human rights and development. Often working with very limited resources, these organizations prove that intermediary bodies can indeed be creative and effective when the dignity of the human being is at stake.

Finally, a further reason for confidence is the victory which has been won by men striving for freedom and justice over the major contemporary totalitarian regimes: Communism, Fascism, and Naziism.

All these achievements attest to the *inventive capacity* of man in every domain when he is confronted with the challenges that arise from nature or society. They attest to the will of man not to yield to any fatalism, and they further attest to his refusal to surrender himself to impotent moroseness.

The attacks against human life appear as a countercurrent to this constructive dynamic. Their emergence points to the *return to the warlike tradition of destruction and death*. These attacks benefit from the complicity of man's heart and mind. But it is also from the heart and mind of man that proceed the positive achievements showing that man, today as yesterday, is always capable of transcending himself when he is summoned by his fellow men toward a positive goal.

HEART OF GOD, HEART OF MAN

The root of these attacks on human life is a false conception of happiness. Most people today, especially young people, are beginning to realize that neither money, nor consumerism, nor technical prowess, nor even knowledge, suffices to insure happiness. All those things which men crave can even create obstacles in the great quest for happiness, and provoke jealousy, hostility and divisions among men. From the most tender age to the most advanced, men know that happiness cannot ultimately be found except in tenderness, affection and love. What moves man's heart, and what motivates his actions are love and the desire to be loved.

It is enough to see what is transpiring in today's world in order to realize the supreme power of love. Men must relearn the ability to stand in awe before the love of a man for his fiancee, of a mother for her child, of a son for his elderly father, or before the quality of attention an artist brings to his work, the doctor to his patient, or the professor to his students, in order to realize that true joy comes from loving and being loved.

Why is love anchored in the heart of human existence; why does love and love alone satisfy the human heart? Very simply it is because we are created in the image and likeness of God who, according to St. John's definition, *is* love.[3] God made the heart of man according to the image of His own heart, and although sin has wounded this likeness, it has never been able to destroy it totally. Now, since God loves us, He also desires our happiness. That is why, since our heart is modeled on the image of God's heart, in order to love, we in turn must desire the happiness of others. The fundamental truth is that we have been created to love and be loved. From the beginning till the very end of our existence there is love. For man, to be called to life and to call to life is to call to love and to be loved, follows from God's creating us so that we may love.

The truth of this fundamental fact is meant to fill our whole existence with great joy: the joy of knowing ourselves to be loved by God, to be called to love Him freely, to be called to love others freely, and to be loved by them, because we are all living images of the same God-Love.

We are also filled with joy to learn that *love is stronger that death* (Ct of Ct 8:6) and that after our corporal death, we are all called to see God face to face, to love Him and to be loved by Him eternally. This hope liberates the believer from the fear of death and renders it a servant of truth (see Rm 6:21-23).

This primacy of love lies at the very heart of our existence as a simple truth, accessible to every man who is even remotely attentive to daily life. What confirms this in actual experience is that the meaning of my life is always revealed to me by an other. I do not recognize myself except through others, because I am loved and I love. In order to be myself I need to be recognized by others and to be loved by them. And reciprocally, so that others, may be themselves, I must acknowledge and love them. Thus to refuse to welcome another, to acknowledge him, to love him is already to destroy him. But to wound and to destroy the other is also to wound myself.

This basic recognition of ourselves comes to us first of all from God, and that is what St. John affirms when he states that "God loved us first" (1 Jn 4:10, 19). In his finite and sinful condition man is capable of refusing this twofold vocation to love: the love of God and the love of other men. And when he puts this twofold refusal to love at the heart of his existence, man mutilates himself and ends up destroying himself. The death of love, the refusal of the other and the destruction of myself are the fatal components of one and the same drama.

Confronting this drama, the Church announces news so marvelous that man doesn't always dare to believe it: it is because he is made in the image of God that, despite the weight of sin, man is capable of loving, and of loving with his heart of flesh.

THE BODY, THE PLACE OF LIBERTY

Man in his corporal condition bears the image of God, and this is precisely what makes for his originality. He is capable of knowing the truth about his existence because of the intelligence God has given him. God is not only love; He is also Light (1 Jn 1:5). If He has made us capable of loving, He has also made us capable of comprehending our concrete existence as well as the world in which we live. God, who has not left us ignorant of our origin, has neither left us ignorant of the end for which we were made.

However, God our Father does not in any way wish to constrict His children and intends to respect their liberty. He counts on their initiative to find their way to happiness here below. The twofold capacity offered to man of knowing the truth and freely conforming his conduct to it causes him to surpass the created world in which he is nevertheless solidly rooted. This twofold capacity permeates man up to and including his corporal condition. It is because of this twofold capacity that man cannot be reduced to an animal.

Utilitarian and hedonist ethics tend to reduce man to his purely corporal even animal condition. This is why, rather than relying on the resources which his reason and will offer man, they rely on instinctive determinisms and are prepared to satisfy them. Now it is in his concrete corporal condition, *and not in spite of it*, that man is invited to live his liberty. Without doubt, in this condition, he feels the pull of his instincts. But the sign that man is not irremediably tied to the determinisms that program the life of the animals, the sign that he transcends all of them, is his ignorance of his future, the necessity he finds himself in of creating his future. Except for being blinded by the weight of not knowing his future, man perceives with great clarity that his future is open, that it is not predetermined, and that he must discover it. The future has to be built, because love is a creative discovery and because happiness itself must be earned.

It is precisely to guide, in a responsible way, his undetermined future that man needs to know the meaning of his life. This meaning is already revealed to him by the natural light of his intelligence, but it is above all offered to him through the light of revelation. The coming of the Word of God among us by His incarnation in the womb of the Virgin Mary, imparted dignity and, so to speak, "deification" to our human condition. Henceforth, knowing through the assent of his reason the meaning of his life, man can determine his conduct.

Thus can we more fully perceive the link between man's corporal nature and his free will. Knowing the meaning of his earthly existence, man can invest the corporal dimension of his being and behavior with a repository of freedom, which would remain inaccessible to him should he prefer to yield to the domination of his passions.

Therefore, knowledge of this meaning and of grace reveals that it is in the body itself that man is not only open to freedom but called to it, and that he is open to happiness and called to it. His future need not be determined according to primal impulses; rather he must open himself to it with a hope that it is not vain,[4] since he is called to give, reasonably and freely, a concrete historical content to the call to happiness, that is, to the full realization of his life.

A NEW ANTHROPOLOGICAL ERROR

How can conduct hostile to life insure happiness? Such conduct proceeds from a being closed within a timid conception of his existence, a conception that exalts man's withdrawal into himself, exalts possessiveness and as complete a mastery as possible over the world and over others. This conception of existence can evolve into the expreme paradox of considering mastery over death as the supreme affirmation of mastery over others and oneself.

For two centuries now, anthropologies of this type have already produced bitter fruits reflected in political regimes of a totalitarian character. How can an existence doomed to definitive death lead to anything else but revolt, to lordly arrogance, to nihilism and, in essence, the most radical kind of pessimism? "The fundamental error of socialism," said John Paul II in his encyclical *Centesimus Annus* (CA 13), "is that it is anthropological in nature." It follows that the fundamental error of the anti-life ideology is also of an anthropological character. The criticism directed against Communism, Fascism, and Naziism must be equally directed at the anti-life ideology and to the organisms that derive their inspiration from it. Let us quote John Paul II again: "When society deprives certain categories of men of the right to life (those to be born or those who are moribund), one falls back into the totalitarian practices of our century."

More precisely, the anthropology that is reflected in the anti-life ideology is inadmissible on essential points. It is based on a reductive conception of reason limited to the capacity of measuring, calculating and comparing. Questions that bear on the origin and meaning of human life are declared a priori to be without interest. Whatever the individual subject cannot know directly is said to belong to the world of prejudice. That is the triumph of "free examination." Any truth offered on the basis of testimony is declared inadmissible; only observation and individual experience count. The will from that point on needs to conform to nothing else but itself: the subject chooses his subjective truths according to his likes of the moment. He enters into agreement with other subjects, not on the basis of assent to the same known truths, but on the condition that there be a concurrence of interest in a given situation. That is the triumph of a purely contractual relationship of which people are always the most at risk of becoming the victims.

The anti-life movements proceed from this nontranscendent rationalism which chooses to ignore the fact that, by definition, both the reason and the will have been impoverished in their nature, hampered in their field of action and ultimately wounded by sin. For such a rationalism literally everything can become the object of a contract, a convention, a consensus — and be covered by the authority of positive law. This rationalism has inspired most of the capitalist, nationalist, racist, and imperialist adventures of the 19th and 20th centuries. In its contemporary forms this nontranscendent rationalism always results in violence and death.

Therefore, the Church highlights some natural truths for men, whose perception has been clouded by ignorance and sin. She recalls, among other things, that the human body constitutes an integral part of the human person, that man's liberty is inherent to the integrity of his corporal condition, and that, as a consequence, the body is not disposable: it may not be the object of contracts and transactions. Organ donations themselves cannot be made except under precise conditions.[5]

Faced with movements hostile to life, the good news that the Church reminds us about today involves an enhanced value of the body and human sexuality. The body is a constitutive dimension of the person and, in its sexual dimension, it is a means of interpersonal communion.

DEATH AS HORIZON

The anthropology inspiring anti-life movements is not only inadmissible by reason of its subjectivist rationalism. More fundamentally still, it is unacceptable because both its guiding principle and the end result are the death of the concrete man. Subjectivist anthropology leads the individual to seek his happiness in himself. And thus this anthropology entails the loss of the meaning of love.

From the Love of Death to the Death of Love

However, this anthropology is itself surpassed by those who hold that, to affirm oneself as an individual, one must deny God, deny the world as given, deny other individuals and even be disposed — paradoxically — to deny himself. Everything that conditions human existence is perceived as putting a strain on man's autonomy; they assert that this autonomy must be total in order to have liberty. *To be free, man must be able* to cause death and even cause his own death, gratuitously, without having to render an account to anyone else. If the mortality of man is said to be relative, if for example the perspective of personal survival beyond death is affirmed, the individual's liberty is mortgaged and compromised by this fact, by this perspective, by this hope. To be master of his own life and that of others, the individual must, then, be master of his and their death.

This anthropology excludes, not only the perspective of personal survival, but also the possibility of any reference to the existence of God. If God existed, it argues, He would be an obstacle to the liberty of man. To be total, man's liberty postulates the death of God. Feuerbach's influence is very clear here. What constitutes the measure of man is his pride, the unconditional affirmation of himself in the struggle for life, by challenging to death or having the wisdom to resign himself to it. Man realizes himself as being definitively mortal in and by death.

One will not be surprised to see that this totally atheistic and pitiless anthropology entails the very negation of all parental and filial love as well as of all sociability. If they hold to this anthropology, parents perceive the child to come as a lessening of their being and, if he successfully reaches life, as a lessening of their possessions as well; they have some interest, then, in destroying it. The eventual presence of an infant is perceived by the parents as an encroachment on their own existence. From this perspective, the parents intolerably find that the child signifies their own death. What they give to the child they deprive themselves of; what it is, they are not. The child is perceived as an essential limitation to their finite being, as the sign of their total finiteness.

This lordly anthropology is a prelude to abortion and infanticide, and also obviously foreshadows, for the same reasons, the euthanasia of elderly parents by their children as they become adults. For the life of the parents and what they have impede the autonomy and even the life of the children who now become autonomous. We've fatally come full circle: to be free man must control life from beginning to end. Must we add that this death-obsessed anthropology resounds dramatically on the life of the *couple*? In principle the very idea of *fidelity* is compromised and with it marriage is destroyed. For he who advocates fidelity advocates freely consented dependence vis-à-vis someone from whom one expects an enduring contribution to his realization. From this destruction flows other well known consequences: stripping sexuality of its meaning while making it multirelational and free of any responsibility toward the transmission of life.

At the end of this anthropology, man doesn't see himself as needing anything from anybody: neither from others nor from God. He has not received the existence he shares with other creatures from a Creator. He is confined within his individual solitude and his horizon is nothing but pure and simple oblivion into total and definitive death. He believes that he is affirming himself and has the illusion of creating himself by this perverse and pathetic expression of liberty which is in reality destruction.

Warlike Order

This anthropology, which pushes modern subjectivist rationalism to its paroxysm, is going to engender disastrous political consequences.

Being doomed to total disappearance after death, the individual can entertain[6] himself with the idea that happiness is found in the State, society or the market. He can try to console himself with the idea whatever is universal in a particular individual's action survives in the State.

Nevertheless, on this social level we again find the spectre of death. The individual who believes himself justified in causing death in order to affirm his liberty also believes himself justified in causing death for a higher reason; e.g., when the State or the economy is threatened with destruction. For the State and the economy are perceived and presented as the sole benefactors able to entertain, console and protect the finite individual facing his definitive death. War, then, is justified inasmuch as it causes death so that the State, society or the economy can remain free with a liberty that cannot bear the slightest conditioning. Consequently, just as this anthropology involved the rejection of love, so this aggressive conception of society and the market brings with it the rejectionion of any "order" other than that imposed by the supremacy of the strongest in society.

Here we arrive at the source of all contemporary totalitarianism, and it is from this source that the contemporary contempt for human life proceeds.The claim to total autonomy on the part of individuals results in death being made the absolute end to life. This claim can also be assumed at intervals by the State, society, or the marketplace. Eventually, it is to them that individuals transfer the mastery over life and death which they had previously claimed for themselves.

"THE STING OF DEATH IS SIN"

When we scrutinize more closely the anthropology that underlies anti-life movements, we understand still better why it is *despairing*. In effect, definitive death is held as an inexorable law of nature. Since there is no longer place for a loving Providence, the individual's wisdom consists in accepting the immanent order of the world, and this order requires that man seeks his highest self-realization in accepting death.

The Era of Sin

Such an anthropology inherently implies all principles of segregation, exclusion, and extermination. The individual cannot affirm himself except by coveting what the other has, knowledge and ability included, and, more radically, what the other *is*, in the strong sense of this verb.

This anthropology, then, is at once despairing — for after death there is nothing — and *violent*, because the naked force of masters is completely unbridled and at the service of their liberty. And the perspective of "survival" in the state, or in generic humanity, or in the market is also entirely despairing and incites violence, for the individual, wholly ephemeral, is in every way doomed to disappear totally. In brief, total mastery over the life and death of individuals is a necessity of the system. The same today as yesterday, the partisans of this anthropology have no alternative to propose but this morbid culture of death, to impose it or defy it, and its obligatory corollary: sterility.

This anthropology, then, makes way for the reformulation of the old lordly ethic that, in turn, involves the promise of a violent exterminating imperialism. Partisans of the culture of death have strictly nothing else to propose.

In a striking formula, St. Paul explained the culture of death when he wrote: "The sting of death is sin" (1 Cor 15:56; see Hos 13:14). It is through the fascination exercised by sin that death incites to action (see Rm 6:20-23). The prospect of death gives man a sort of vertigo which prompts him, not to "redeem the present time" (see Eph 5:16), but to consume and use up his time of living in the lusts that bewitch him (see 1 Jn 2:16; Rom 7:7; Heb 3:13) thereby pushing him to let himself be gripped by nothingness. Since death is seen as an absolute end, the time of life is the time of sin. It is the time of "the concupiscence of the flesh, the concupiscence of the eyes and the pride of life" (see 1 Jn 2:16) and of proud trust in themselves (see Rm 7:5; 8:5 f.). Rejection of the divine promise of life means that man had already been seduced, that is, led astray by sin. Through his sin and his pride man shows that instead of choosing the life, to which God calls him, he prefers death (see Dt 30:15, 19). Here we behold the drama of our origin (see Gn 3:13) that continues despite the triumph of life over death the morning of Easter.[7]

The Deification of Violence

The option for or against life is not, then, simply an expression of a moral choice. It expresses a fundamental religious attitude of welcoming or rejecting the God of life. The choice against life proceeds, in the final analysis, from a declaration of war against Him who is the God of the living not the dead (see Mt 22:32). All the anti-life ideologies sink their roots deeply into this atheistic humanism, which had already borne the fruit of contemporary totalitarianism.

From the moment that man, in order to affirm himself, believes he must deny God, anything becomes possible. Nothing can impede the flood of violence. The man who affirms himself as master of life and death installs himself as the mortal god; he makes it impossible to discover the image of God in himself and others. *The major source of all the anti-life currents is to be sought in this rejection by man of his reference to God.* As this existential reference is denied, practically and/or theoretically, there is no further place for the common divine paternity nor, consequently, for fraternity among sons of the same Father. Furthermore, even on the simple human plane, the ideas of paternity, fraternity and filiation are ruined and, with them, the idea of the family, since parents, like brothers and sons, are natural facts from which the individual must liberate himself in order to be himself.

Thence it follows that a hedonist morality, making utility, interest and pleasure the goal of life, rapidly ends by producing a lordly morality whose force nothing can moderate. On the contrary, it will be left to society to insure the quest for power that the citizen has undertaken in his particular condition as an individual doomed to death. Society brings to its completion the warlike compulsion of individuals by sweeping away every bothersome entity solely because it is perceived as an obstacle to the liberty of the masters.

Thus the culture of death finishes by deifying violence under all its forms: that which opposes both individuals and society, and that which opposes society. This violence is necessarily total and results in a war that is also total.

AT THE SERVICE OF MAN'S HAPPINESS

Once God is chased by man from the political horizon, the bell tolls for the death of man himself. The perversion of the meaning of the State, in the modern era, proceeds from an unrestrained affirmation of the individual's claims.[8] Thus results a completely unacceptable conception of democracy.

Pluralism and Agnosticism

If by democracy one means a society which is organized for the happiness of all its members, it goes without saying that such a society cannot be morally neutral, indifferent, agnostic or atheistic (see CA 46 f.). Political pluralism does not signify that a democratic society can be built upon any ethic whatsoever or without an ethic. A political regime always puts into practice a certain anthropology consisting of certain principles that oversee the quality of the social tissue. Authentic political pluralism is always defined in conjunction with the common good and the subsidiary role of the public authorities. This pluralism cannot, therefore, mean that political society may profess an agnosticism or atheism, or moral and religious indifference. Experience shows that where such is the case, political society becomes intolerant and tyrannical: intolerant because, before the anthropological and moral void it itself has decreed, political society establishes a civil religion, that is, the cult of a "mortal god" incarnate in either the State, the party, the race or economy; tyrannical because the exclusive source of law is found in the will of the majority which, illegitimately claims itself to be infallible.[9]

Love, the Future of Man

Faced with the ideologies that invoke the rule of a majority which includes the culture of death in its institutions, the Church reminds us, following Aristotle, that the law, as such, cannot suffice: the law must be good, that is, in accord with reason, and justice. But the Church wishes above all to be at the service of man's joy (see 2 Cor 1:23 f.). Certainly she doesn't ignore the reality of sin that divides and separates; but neither does she ignore the fact that, despite sin, man aspires to live in peace with his fellow men, and the fact that he is capable of loving.

On this subject the Church also reminds men of some elementary truths to which they have access through the light of their intelligence alone.[10] These truths do not proceed from gloomy systems; they are not only discoveries of human intelligence, but are also the fruit of the historical experience of men who draw from history lessons for life.

With the greater part of the moral traditions of humanity, the Church, following Jesus, affirms that we must not do to others what we would not have them do to us and, all the more that we must do to others what we would have them do to us (see Mt 7:12; Lk 6:31). If the tradition of human wisdom has called this maxim the "golden rule," that is because on respect for it depends whether men will live in good conviviality and peace or not.

On the political level, this maxim has inspired the development of laws in all systems aspiring to greater justice. The law cannot be the expression of mere will or the particular interests of the strongest; it must be ordained to the common good. As for the ruler, he must protect the weak against the ever-threatening rapacity of the strongest.

Wherever these basic truths are rejected or simply threatened, peace and harmony can no longer flourish among men or among nations. These truths and principles involve — do we have to say it? — the prohibiting of killing, which has been evident in the great moral traditions of mankind. Inversely, every time human societies have given in to violence, they have found the road to recovery by remembering these very principles. Such was the case for the Universal Declaration on Man's Rights proclaimed in 1948.[11]

What makes civilizations progress is not first of all prodigious material achievements; it's increasing realization that all men deserve to be respected and loved. Love is the future of the human community, for the heart of man is made for love. The Church says that this irrepressible longing for happiness is the sign of moral health for humanity. It shows that, despite the passions and pressures to which he is subjected, man persists in seeking happiness by knowing the truth about himself.

The persistent aspiration for happiness is, then, the best rock upon which to build the efforts to overcome the present threats to human life. The anthropologies that make the individual the exclusive source of all morality eventually lead to seeking happiness in death. The Church must obviously take a position in this controversy about man's happiness. The Church proclaims to men that Jesus came into the world to reveal man to himself, to inform men, by His very incarnation, of the price God places on man in his incarnate condition.[12]

LIBERTY THROUGH DEATH?

The Disintegration of the Person

What is so tragic in the anti-life ideology is that it postulates man's absolute rejection of all forms of dependence in order that to be total master of himself and others. But to love is to be dependent, it is to accept being dependent, and it is to welcome and be welcomed. The anthropology that inspires anti-life currents necessarily leads to the death of love and to death period. Pessimism cannot be pushed any further: here, the horizon of man's life is the winter and death of the heart.

This anthropology is condemned to see the body as nothing but a pure instrument, a pure object for serving the proud affirmation of the individual.[13] The body loses its meaning as a constitutive dimension of the person, a vehicle through which a person is part of the world and of time for the purpose of living out his freedom in the truth of his total being. When the body is reduced to a thing, the person disintegrates, as it does in the gnostic tradition; it totally evades any rule whatsoever. The body becomes, not only the place of absolute amorality, but also totally disposable.[14] I can use my body for sexual pleasure, I can mutilate it if such mutilation is useful to me. I can even dispose of my corporal life by means of a "testament of life" which will make euthanasia a "procured suicide." Now if I can dispose of this given which is my body, I can dispose, for a greater reason, of the bodies of others, for the pleasure that would bring me or the usefulness I can derive from it. An even greater reason, let us add, to destroy another's body would be that it is an obstacle from which I must liberate myself to be myself. Another's death is the price of my life and the condition of my liberty.

Compromised: Fidelity and Fecundity

This disintegration of the person, this divorce of the body from the soul, kills human love and conjugal happiness, for it reduces love to individual pleasure. And this reductive and mutilated concept of love produces two consequences.

It compromises *fidelity*, which becomes strictly conditional and translates into a decline of marriage and the banalization of divorce. Contrary to what the heart of man spontaneously expects, it is now forbidden for the word love to be considered as forever (*amour cannot rhyme with toujours*). Here love is circumspect, calculating, suspicious even: "I love you conditionally and as long as my desire to love you endures." Love as a lasting reception and giving between two persons is stripped of its meaning by a sort of avarice of the heart. Fidelity is dispensed parsimoniously and always precariously. The other is not loved for what he is, in his difference and singularity; the love which one bears is subordinated to the pleasure the other brings, and to the use he serves. The very idea of transparence no longer has a place here, for to keep the future open it is no longer in the interest of the partners truly to let themselves be known.

This disintegration of the person also compromises fertility for the same reasons. The partner is perceived as he "who gives pleasure," and as he in whom it would not be wise to place complete trust. The idea of a common project, of a common enduring work has no place here. The same thing goes for both spouse (partner) *and* child: if I want to remain master of myself, I must not tie myself to either one. Furthermore, to be free, I must necessarily reserve to myself the declaration that love is dead. My liberty presupposes not only the right to disentangle myself, but also requires that every engagement on my part be compromised as conditional.

That is exactly what we call free love, which, if it involves marriage, has divorce as both consequence and cause. It but certifies the impasse in which false love ends, depending upon the extent to which, from its inception, a *conditional* notion of death overshadows it.

Machismo and Feminism

Extreme machismo and feminism are the corollaries of this truncated conception of love and corporeity. The *macho* man is really denying his personal integration; he doesn't see his body as the place of interpersonal relationships but as an instrument of pleasure. He is psychologically mutilated because his utilitarianism inhibits his capacity to give of himself. The *feminist* also denies her personal integration for the same reasons as the macho persona. She is equally as psychologically mutilated in her ability to welcome others and to give of herself. Instead of emphasizing her rights to her feminine specificity, she thinks rather of the equality of the sexes in terms of dissolution of identity.[15] It follows that, as man no longer assumes his virility nor woman her femininity, man and woman in some way anticipate their own death by refusing paternity and maternity. And since man and woman are made to love each other in all truthfulness, they wind up hating and despising each other when they refuse to be themselves.

Obligation of Purpose

This truncated conception of love finds still another of its expressions in *systematic contraception*. The latter has as its objective to prevent the existence of a "given," the child. In effect, a love that has conditional duration is a love doomed to be infertile. Already infertile in the heart, it is likewise infertile in the flesh.

In fact, the child is perceived as a threat to the liberty of the partners. And since, in order to affirm oneself, this liberty can go all the way to causing death, the existence of the unborn child will always be left hanging on the eventual — totally free — decision to abort it. From before its birth, the human being is perceived as something that I must have the power to put to death so that I can be free. Moreover, what will reinforce this desire to dominate is the fact that the child will be perceived as further unbearable in that it will reflect the image of the other partner who is only loved conditionally.

Contraception, then, is not claimed simply as a "right" which the progress of science would impose. It is claimed in the name of a truncated vision of love. In this vision, fidelity, and fertility are always matched with a "reprieve," by reason of which the dynamic which began with contraception is expanded to include divorce, sterilization and abortion. In effect, since man "is not sure" of loving his partner and loving him/her enduringly, he must match his conjugal relationship with the following condition: that his partner be at least temporarily infertile. This condition is imposed even in the name of an *obligation of purpose*: the reasons imposing this infertility are so compelling that, in case of failure, the partners will be justified — so they think — in having recourse to a remedial abortion! For the rest, it is the same logic that demands the inverse attitude of openness to fertility. The child can be admitted to existence but only on condition of being wanted, of giving pleasure. And here, in the opposite direction, the imperatives will have the same importance which, in the first case, justified the child's elimination: it can be called into existence by any means whatsoever — especially artificial and in vitro fertilization — with efficacy alone counting.

Abortion: Prototype of Gratuitous Violence

This truncated conception of love also leads to *definitive sterility*. This simply means that even the possibility of fertility is set aside. The sterilized person is denied and destroyed in one of his or her constitutive dimensions: his or her capacity of transmitting human life. Even when the decision for it is taken by the person concerned, sterilization appears in this situation as a new form of voluntary servitude, since the person sterilized is "accommodated" to the will of the other — partner or public authority.[16] By its irreversible character sterilization is in some way a partial death; it consecrates the subordination of the mutilated one to his or her master, who reserves the ability to remain fertile for himself or herself.

Here again one finds the same logic that explains abortion. It appears as the most total use of freedom by the one who is the strongest. The partners already exercised this absolute liberty vis-à-vis each other in truncated love, compromised fidelity and conditional fertility. But at the end of this escalating matter, the strongest pose as absolute masters over life and death. They "cause" death in order to affirm themselves. However, in this instance they haven't any excuse of legitimate defense, for the victim of their violence is but weakness and fragility. Furthermore, it is precisely this act which reveals the *absolute character of the violence*: the unborn child is but life, without any power to resist a warlike assault, and it is *because* it represents human life in all its disarmed truth that it — so they think — can be put to death.

The unborn child is not put to death above all because it inconveniences its parents. To put the unborn child to death they invoke material "justifications"; economic, social, political, etc. But the primordial justification is found elsewhere: the aborted unborn child is a prototypical victim of violence that is totally gratuitous and to which man has recourse because he imagines it gives him a supreme expression of his liberty. This violence is, by definition, *without any other reason save an arbitrary decision of the executioner*. He has to fully mask his true motivation, by means of ideological considerations, or diverse "justifications," for the murder of the unborn child is the *expression of the desire to destroy life in its pure state; it is the primordial violence which, in the end, will give rise to all the other forms of violence*.

The putting to death of the unborn child thus reveals man's sinfulness. It is pride that pushes man to pose as master of his fellow men and, because such a man states that God is dead, he is able to, and even must, appropriate to himself His attributes.

At the end of so much devastation there remains — need we say it? — no place for the family. The crisis of the family is directly linked to a tragic anthropology from which are derived the theories which converge toward contempt for life and which are diffracted into multiple corollaries concerning fidelity, contraception, sterilization and abortion.

The problem of respect for human life and, above all, for the unborn child, is thus first of all an anthropological problem;[17] it is also a problem of *natural morality*. However, the theologian will be justified in completing this analysis by making it clear that, if the unborn child is the perfect victim of the insane pride of man, it is because men perceive in this innocent child the shining image of God. The violence of man who, to be free, believes he must put God to death, puts God to death a second time by destroying the image of Himself which He offers in the faces of the Holy Innocents.

The Unfaithful Steward

The perverse repercussions of this Caesarlike anthropology are not limited to that. Such an anthropology leads man to reserve for himself, not only mastery over his life and that of others, but he also sees himself as having the ability to do anything, including destroying for the sake of destroying. He no longer sees himself as the steward of creation, the administrator of the gifts given by God to men,[18] but he finds himself able to affirm himself even to the point of destroying his environment.

This anthropology thereby affects, not only relationships among men, but also the relationship of man to nature. There is nothing surprising about this, as our century has seen the dual affirmation, on the one hand, of the total liberty of individuals and, on the other, the marvelous capacity offered to these individuals by science and technology. These abilities have clearly reinforced in man the conviction — a little naive, it is true — that he controls nature. The exploration of space, the discoveries in nuclear physics, the innumerable technological exploits, the interventions into genetic codes, etc.: such feats jostle one another to push man into believing that he can do anything, so much so that neither material nature nor man himself need be respected. He finds that nature can be manipulated toward any end an individual desires. The reason he gives for this, once again, is that man is a mortal god unto himself: he can make of his life whatever he wishes for the one and only reason that it is what he wants.

In summary, man is confronted daily with the experience of death and with his incapacity to postpone its arrival, and thus wants to evade it by controlling it. His life no longer makes sense, except for the meaning he freely fashions. Man no longer possesses the truth to which he could refer himself in the pursuit of happiness. And so, he poses as absolute master of himself and his life, of his death and that of others, as well as master of the world environment. Finally, his technically-oriented reason confirms him in this twofold mastery. How then, with such alienation, could man welcome the capacity which he is offered to become a cooperator with God?

---

[1] The *rate of infant mortality* expresses the relationship between the number of deaths of infants of less than one year old and the number of children born into a given territory during the course of a given year; it is expressed in one percentiles. The *rate of maternal mortality* expresses the number of women who died in the course of a given year, as a result of complications during pregnancy and delivery, per 100,000 live births in the same year.

[2] One of the best works on this subject is that of G.-F. Dumont, *Le Monde et les hommes. Les grandes évolutions démographiques* (Paris: Litec, 1995).

[3] See Gn 1:27; 5:1; I Cor 11:7; Jas 3:9; I Jn 4:8, 16.

[4] See *BPCV* q. 142.

[5] On this subject see Maurice Torelli, *Le Médecin et les droits de l'homme* (Paris: Berger-Levrault, 1983) 264-274. The position of the Church regarding this is summarized in the *Charter of Health Personnel* (Vatican City: Council for the Pastoral of Health Services, 1995), see esp. 83-91.

[6] See Pascal, Pensées n. 171 in the edition of Léon Brunschvicq (Paris: Hachette, 1945).

[7] See also Jas 1:14 f.; Rm 6:16, 21, 23.

[8] Certain problems that we are going to explore have already been encountered in the teaching of Leo XIII about liberalism. See *Quod Apostolici Muneris* (1878); *Diuturnum Illud* (1881); *Immortale Dei* (1885); *Libertas Praestantissmum* (1888).

[9] On the "omnipotence" of the majority, see de Tocqueville, *Democracy in America* (New York: Knopf, 1945) I, Ch. VII, P. 111.

[10] See *supra*, **A NEW ANTHROPOLOGICAL ERROR**.

[11] See *supra*, Ch. V.

[12] One can recognize here the central themes of John Paul II's encyclical *Redemptor Hominis* (1979). We know that this theme runs throughout all the teaching of the Holy Father. This teaching itself is firmly anchored in the Second Vatican Council and especially in the Constitution *Gaudium et Spes*, esp. art.22.

[13] See *supra*, Ch. V regarding the question of gender.

[14] See *BPCV* qq.34-38.

[15] See *supra*, regarding gender in Ch. V And the rights of woman.

[16] See the bibliographical references in *supra*, Ch. I, note 8.

[17] See *supra*, **A NEW ANTHROPOLOGICAL ERROR** and **LIBERTY THROUGH DEATH**.

[18] See Gn 1:28; *Gaudium et Spes* 51 and 57.

CHAPTER VII
WE WERE ALL ONCE A BABY IN THE WOMB

A DEEPLY MOVING DISCOVERY

A mother who is expecting a baby will never spontaneously say, "I am carrying an embryo," or "My fetus is well." She will say, "My family is growing," "I am expecting a child," "My baby is beginning to stir." A mother has no need of learned studies in order to perceive that the life she is carrying derives all its dignity from the fact that it is a human life. What inspires awe with the parents, what fills them with joy, what justifies their pride is that, in their love, they have begotten a being that is part of their flesh and yet which, they already know, will be totally different from them, both physically and psychologically.

The Joy of Expecting

It is marvelous to see young couples sharing with each other and with other people the joy of their new arrival. Everyone is preparing to welcome the baby. Even before his birth, people are aware of him. Where will we put the crib? Will he have enough clothing? Boy or girl? What will his first name be? Who will be the godfather and godmother? All of which confirms the joy which is brought by the expectation of a new human being who progressively manifests his presence among us.

Wonderful images, filmed with perfected techniques, allow us to peer into the prenatal history of this child.[1] Such pictures, often of great beauty, permit us to observe the beginning of human life and to be witnesses of the most awesome event of which we have all been the subject.

Ultrasonography also brings us a moving visualization of the little being in the mother's womb. From the moment of this visual perception of her baby, and then with its movement within her, a unique bond is established between the mother and her "nasciturus" which will become increasingly stronger as the weeks go by. According to the opinion of more than one reputable ultrasound technician, once a mother has seen the first images of her infant, it is very difficult for her to entertain the thought of an abortion.

With greater starkness but with utterly exemplary rigor, different techniques permit other specialized researchers to highlight the individuality of the human being from its most hidden origins.[2] Issue of father and mother, the infant is nonetheless different from them; he has his own genetic patrimony.

These discoveries and techniques invite us to marvel, not only at the newborn, but at his very evolution since his conception without any interruption of continuity.

During the same period, but this time on the part of the adults, an education in love and human sexuality takes place which admirably shows how the heart and body of man are prepared to conceive and welcome this little being and to be enchanted by it.

These discoveries are all the more moving in that they touch us personally, since we must realize that we *have all been like this being* as it is seen with the microscope, the endoscope, the ultrasound. The vision through various lenses touches us, but the vision which nature itself offers is even more awe-inspiring, in a very different way.

Common Ground

Like most mothers throughout the world, the Church with great realism extends her affection to these beings who are advancing toward the light.[3] She doesn't limit her tenderness to their physical dimensions. It is enough for her to know that this little one is there in order to love him for the same reasons as one loves any other person. The realism which the Church displays is curiously the same as that which is found amongst propagators of abortion and those who use fetuses for experimental purposes. Most of these practitioners explicitly acknowledge the human character of the fetus and embryo.[4] Must one point out that this is the only common ground in the matter of abortion between them and the Church?

Despite its being unique, this common ground is nonetheless precious. In effect, it clearly demonstrates the fact that most of the partisans of abortion are fully aware that it involves the execution of a human being. The legislator who legalizes this execution can no longer ignore the fact, not only that he is depriving an infant of the protection of law, but even worse, is that he is supporting the murder of an innocent.

To all these practitioners, and to all those involved in the political process, the Church and those devoted to life ask *in what name do they think they have the power to suppress the weakest of all human lives.*

Moreover, the Church draws our attention to the grave and inevitable consequences in the banalization of evil. A society in which abortion is permitted places the very principle of elementary respect for all men into question. The Church's position is of extreme simplicity: the human being must be recognized and protected from conception in the mother's womb until natural death. This simple position has been defended until quite recently by all codes of medical ethics and by all legislation in those countries which are considered civilized.

Such legislation has had as its first objective the protection of the unborn infant with the relevant punitive measures demonstrating the seriousness of the legislator's determination to protect the infant. Acting in this way, the legislator gave legal form to the "golden rule" as well as to the other fundamental precept of natural morality: "Thou shalt not kill!"

Defending the Man in the Unborn Baby

In many countries, and even in certain Christian milieux, moral conscience has became obscured to the point that some very elementary truths are no longer perceived by everyone. In this case it belongs to the Church to bear witness before all men regarding the equal dignity of all human beings, and the universal right to life. All men are equal in dignity, and it is sufficient to be human in order to merit this respect and to have one's right to life acknowledged. It is this truth which, in the course of history, has made nations and peoples rise up against tyrants. It is also in virtue of this truth that men have maintained that the human body is not disposable.

By proclaiming loudly and clearly that the weakest human being deserves to be honored by reason of his humanity, the Church is but repeating the same truth which has been evoked in the condemnation of slavery, domination and extermination.

It is therefore inexact, and furthermore unjust, to present the Church as the only defender of life before birth. It is *inexact* because the truth concerning respect due to all men is accessible to any reasonable human being. It is unjust because this truth has flourished and continues to flourish in environments totally ignorant of Christianity. This fact alone should trouble the promoters of abortion, since it is not at all clear what progress can be achieved for humanity by rejecting such a truth, which has been espoused throughout the centuries by every civilized community, namely that to defend the infant is to defend man.

LOVE DISARMED

The knowledge of so fundamental a truth as the respect due to every human being has been made easily accessible to each man by the necessary natural light. However, revelation has provided man with further reasons for respecting all human beings.

In the Image of God

The first of these reasons is that man has been created in the image and likeness of God (see Gn 1:26 f; 9:6; Wis 2:23; Jas 3:9; see also I Cor 11:7; Mt 5:48). The New Testament provides the opportunity for theological reflection to clarify this likeness: man resembles the Trinitarian God. He is capable of relationships with other men who also share the existence received from the same Trinitarian God. It is God the Father who brings us into existence through His Son and maintains us therein through the work of the Spirit.

From that flows revelation's insistence on the fundamental unity of the whole human family. From the book of Genesis onward we are told that Eve is the "mother of the living" (Gn 3:20) and that all men take their origin from Adam and Eve (Gn 9:19). In the final analysis, this unity has its source in the reference to God, the one Creator (Lk 3:38).

This fundamental unity, furthermore, is affirmed in regard to the first couple: "Man and woman He created them" (Gn 1:27). From the outset, to be himself man needs woman in whom he recognizes "flesh of his flesh" (Gn 2:23). Man was not created to be alone. He needs the other to be himself.

Christ brings this teaching to its perfection by giving us His "new commandment": "That you love one another ; that as I have loved you do you also love one another" (Jn 13:34). "These things I command you, that you may love one another" (Jn 15:17). The Christian must not simply acknowledge other men as his equals but must love them as Christ loved all men even to the point of forgiveness (Mt 18:21 f.; Lk 23:34; Acts 7:59).

The dignity of every human being from the moment of conception is ultimately sealed by the incarnation of the Son of God in the womb of the Virgin Mary. Jesus wanted to live the very same life that all humans live from conception to death. In so doing, He wished to demonstrate the value He attaches to the human condition even before birth. He also showed that He, the Lord of the world, depended on the *Fiat* of the Virgin Mary in order to be welcomed and loved before His birth (see Lk 1:38). St. Joseph himself confirmed the welcome of Jesus in that he did not call it into question despite his temporary perplexity (see Mt 1:24 f.).

The Good Samaritan

The parable of the Good Samaritan (Lk 10:25-37) embodies in essence the new commandment and illuminates the Church's position regarding every human life, especially that of the unborn infant.

Christ gives the example of the Samaritan because this man took the initiative in approaching the wounded man, and he did so unconditionally. The Samaritan decides to become the neighbor of one who is completely reduced to powerlessness by reason of his wounds. He loves with the same heart of God who took the initiative to love us even when we were sinners (see Rm 5:8). The Samaritan is praised because he shows himself "compassionate as your Father is compassionate" (Lk 6:36); he is perfect "as your heavenly Father is perfect" (Mt 5:48).

The Samaritan's attitude, then, imitates God's attitude, who throughout the Old Testament made multiple covenants with His people, and who offered His love to His people despite their infidelities and inconstancy. More precisely, the Samaritan imitates the attitude of Christ Himself, who took the initiative of coming close to men to restore in them the image of God which was damaged by sin.

The connection between the Samaritan and Christ leads eventually to identification. On the one hand, by his practical conduct, the Samaritan shows that he loves "in deed and truth" (I Jn 3:18), and, probably without being clearly aware of it, he identifies himself with Christ. But, on the other hand, Christ Himself does not hesitate to identify Himself with this "heretic," for, like him, freed from the constraints of the law, He is entirely open to loving.

The parable of the Good Samaritan, then, offers us a theological lesson before furnishing us with a *moral* teaching. Before indicating to us something that we need to imitate — "Go and do likewise" (Lk 10:37) — the parable explains to us that the heart of the disciple must beat and love in unison with the heart of the Master. The parable makes us understand that the Samaritan embodied the ideal of "man in the image of God," and that to behave as he did is to love as God loves. Through the example of the Good Samaritan, Jesus reveals something of the mystery of God.

A further revelation of the mystery of God is found in the figure of the wounded man. In effect, the Samaritan recognizes the image of God in the wounded man; he recognizes one of his brothers. Motives of animosity, even hostility, must be silenced before what is essential. And the condition of being weak from the wounds directs us precisely to what is essential: this wounded man is a human being like me, he had fundamentally the same dignity as I; I must therefore be a neighbor to him.

It even happens that by making himself the neighbor of the wounded man this "heretic" finds the way to God, while the Law hindered the priest and Levite from making this discovery. The Samaritan didn't wait to rationalize; he is facing a concrete situation and acts accordingly. He reads this "sign" of the wounded man; his heart is not blocked by prejudices. In the wounded man he does not see an enemy but a brother. Because he was faithful to this brother, despised by others to the point of being ignored, this "heretic" sees opening before him the path leading to the God of Love. He will soon perceive that this God of Love was already present and acting in his heart, even before he stopped to take care of the bruised man.

The teaching of this parable is also about a theological virtue before being of a moral nature. What saves the "heretic" from his wandering is his *just* conduct toward his neighbor. His attitude of love, totally generous and disinterested, shows that he loves even to the point of forgiving. Love and salvation begin when man is willing to convert: he disarms himself interiorly in order to approach the other.

The parable also illustrates the teaching on the last judgment, in which Jesus identifies Himself with the poor (see Mt 25:31-45), as well as the teaching on persecution, in which Jesus identifies Himself with the victims (Acts 9:5; Lk 10:16). It also illustrates the penetrating warning of St. John: "If anyone say he loves God but hates his brother, he is a liar; for he who does not love his brother whom he sees cannot love God whom he does not see" (I Jn 4:20). And echoing St. John are the words of Jesus related to us by St. Clement of Alexandria: "To see your brother is to see God."[5]

Those who refuse to recognize their neighbor in the unborn infant act like the priest and Levite of the parable. Like those who reason in a rationalizing manner, they engage in hair-splitting about the limits of love of neighbor. They get bogged down in a casuistry regarding the condition the other must meet in order for one to love him. As the confirmed rationalists do, they imprison the other within the limits of their definitions, and it is on the basis of such that they condition love.

Now what can be derived from this parable is that the question of one's neighbor does not arise first on the side of the infant. Like the wounded man, the unborn infant can in *no way* impose himself; he is all weakness. The "problem" of the unborn infant is to be with those stone-hearted people who will not let themselves feel compassion (see Dt 15:7 f.; Col 3:12; I Jn 3:17; Jas 2:15 f.) for this being whose fragile presence is quickly recognizable.

It follows that the abortion of an innocent being is not only a very grave aberration in the justice due to men; it is also a very grave sin against the justice due to God. This double fault, already serious in the order of nature, takes on a special gravity for the one who pretends to be a disciple of the Lord. Abortion reveals, in effect, that man refuses to love in the way God loves; he refuses to adopt the sentiments of the Heart of Jesus (see Phil 2:5). He refuses to see in the unborn child the neighbor who silently implores our attention. He refuses to bring his heart into harmony with the Heart of Mary, who was the first to come close to the fragile being that Jesus was within her womb, and which we all were as well for the first nine months of our life.

Rejection of the Two Commandments

With regard to the Christian faith, the extreme gravity of abortion stems from what it means from the religious viewpoint. *From this viewpoint, abortion is neither more nor less than the rejection, en bloc, of the two great commandments.* Grave sin against God, it is also a grave sin against man. It is also, then, a sin against oneself, in the sense that the one who is involved in an abortion degrades himself. Abortion reveals the ravages caused by the culture of death. Those who commit abortion, by that very fact, fall into irreligion.

Just as the Good Samaritan by his practical attitude drew close to man and God, so do those who, by their practical attitude in committing abortion, declare themselves hostile to man and God. They pose as rivals to both God and man. They suspect the poor infant as a threat to their power, their possessions and their being. Like Herod, they avoid the risk of recognizing in the unborn child the call to go beyond themselves and the call to conversion. For, if in fact he is recognized and welcomed as the image of God, the child does indeed change a life and transform it. Like the Pharisees who rejected the man born blind (see Jn 9), they prefer the security of their position to the beckoning of the poor man. And yet this poor little one, and not their own knowledge, could have placed them on the road to God. And thus they reject God Himself by rejecting the image that could have revealed Him to them.

A PERSON?

The parable of the Good Samaritan also helps us to reduce to their proper proportions the doubts raised by some concerning the question "is the unborn baby a person?"

There is no doubt that, by their very nature and method, experimental sciences cannot determine the presence of a person. But they afford inestimable illumination to the philosophical and theological reflection in this matter. From the start, they are able to discern a new human life with its own individual characteristics. They show that the new being conceived preserves its own recognizable genetic identity card throughout its development. Furthermore, the same experimental sciences show that these human beings have common characteristics which attach them to the human family.

From its conception the human individual has its own patrimony that will permit the affirmation of its personality and its progressive development. If the fruit of human reproduction is a human being, one can hardly see how a human individual could not be a human person. It is even rather annoying to have to recall such a truism.

From this vantage point, birth marks no break in the development of the individual. The entire education process will have as its marvelous task the full blossoming of this infant whom so many parents affectionately call their "treasure." And this treasure is entrusted to the mother for the first nine months. If, with the passage of time, the individual's personality becomes fully developed it is because from his origin, he has been given the capacity of relating to other persons more advanced in their evolution than he. That is why it is necessary to maintain that the equality of dignity remains constant from conception until death, and that it is independent of the degree of physical development.

It is, then, with good reason that the Church states: "The human being must be respected and treated as a person from his conception, and thus, from that moment on, one must acknowledge his rights as a person, among which ranks in the first place the inviolable right of every innocent human being to life" (*Donum Vitae* I, 1).

Moreover, one sees how the story of the Good Samaritan makes the casuistical quibblings about the "prepersonal" or "potentially personal" character of the conceived baby so ridiculous. The parable teaches us that the other, the neighbor, is beyond all confines of definitions. The neighbor is he to whom I am near. The first step in promoting the affirmation and blossoming of the unborn infant's personality depends on us: we must consider him as our neighbor and welcome him. A terrible privilege is held by adults, who can use their liberty to welcome as well as to reject, to love as well as to destroy! What a terrible vulnerability for the coming child, who is left so exposed to the love or hatred of older people!

It is above all before this totally unarmed little being that the Church renews with joy and pride her preferential but not exclusive option for the poor (*CA* 10f., 28, 57). And she makes it her duty to ask all men to allow their hearts be touched (see Lk 10:33, 1 Jn 3:17).

SOME CONVERGING TRADITIONS

About four thousand years old, the Code of Hammurabi (1793-1750 B.C.) condemned abortion, even involuntary or accidental abortion.[6] The Assyrian laws were no less rigorous; they were also more meticulous. They punish involuntary abortion provoked by beating. As for voluntary abortion, resulting from abortive maneuvers, it imposes the penalty of death, with the method being specified: impalement without burial.[7] Through the celebrated Hippocratic Oath the doctor committed himself to provide neither poison nor abortion even if asked to do so.[8]

In Rome, according to Mommsen, abortion "was always regarded as a grave immorality."[9] From the time of Septimus Severus and Caracalla, it had been punished with pecuniary penalties, banishment, even capital punishment. One text reveals the value placed on human life: "Those who are in the womb of their mother are considered as born in almost all civil law."[10]

Among the Greeks, Lycurgus and Solon, as well as the laws of Thebes and Miletus, considered abortion as a crime that had to be punished. Among the Jews, according to Flavius Josephus, abortion was punished by death (Antiquities of the Jews I, 4, C. viii).

One observes the same rigor in Western legislation among the Visigoths, in France, in England, etc. This strictness was reaffirmed from the Renaissance on by Charles V and, in France, by Henry II,

Henry III, Louis XIV, Louis XV, the penal code of 1791 and that of 1810.

In the Christian tradition abortion is condemned in the *Didache* (end of 1st century, See II, 2: V,2), in the Letter of Pseudo-Barnabas (first quarter of the 2nd century, see XIX, 5; XX, 2); in the *Apology* of Athenagoras from the end of the 2nd century (see 35 f.). The same condemnation is found in Clement of Alexandria (end of 2nd century), Tertullian (beginning of the 3rd century), St. Cyprian (+258), St. John Chrysostom (end of 4th century); St. Jerome (+420), and St. Augustine (+430).

This condemnation was also confirmed by various councils and synods: Elvira (c.306), Ancyra (314), Lerida (524), In Trullo (682), etc.

Beginning with the Renaissance, we find the condemnations by Innocent XI (1676-1689), St. Alphonsus Liguori, Pius IX, the 1917 Code of Canon Law, Pius XI, Pius XII, Paul VI, John Paul II, the Second Vatican Council and the 1983 Code of Canon Law (#1398), etc.[11]

In summary, the moral and penal qualification of abortion has experienced modifications, but its condemnation has been constant in the tradition of the Church. This condemnation is, moreover, well anterior to Christianity.

COMMUNION IMPOSSIBLE

For the reasons we have given, and together with all those who, throughout the centuries have recognized a human being in the unborn infant and who, consequently, have wanted to protect it, the Church regards abortion as morally inadmissible. She is strengthened in this position by the discoveries of the biomedical sciences concerning the origins of the human individual as well as by the concessions of many partisans of abortion. This condemnation is but the consequence of the value which the Church, relying on the light of reason, places on human life.

Furthermore, the Church condemns abortion for theological reasons. Here again, the condemnation of abortion is but the consequence of the value the Church, enlightened by revelation, attaches to human life. From this viewpoint, the Church solemnly condemns abortion for a simple and fundamental reason: he who, either in theory or practice, rejects the "new commandment" (Jn 13:34) and the unity of the two commandments — the love of God and neighbor (see Mk 12:28-34) — *places himself outside the Church.*

Salvation in Peril

From this point of view, the excommunication imposed by the Code of Canon Law (c.1398) simply takes note of a factual situation in which some Christians place themselves. This excommunication means that there is no possibility of pretending to be in communion with the Church if, in theory or practice, one rejects the commandment of love to the point of depriving the most innocent human being possible of life.

The excommunication in question also further reveals the value the Church places on all human life (see Gn 9:5; Ex 20:13; Mt 5:21 f.; see also Mt 5:28). For the believer, it is a signal of greatest alarm. Moreover, excommunication is often seen as a just penalty for the "abominable crime" (*Gaudium et Spes* 51,3) that abortion or infanticide is. But more than that, it is a warning of the greatest importance that the Church, "mother and mistress" of life, addresses to people who, by their behavior or thinking, commit abortion. This warning is also addressed to those who, by a grave abuse of their power or competence, authorize or render materially possible the murder of the innocents.

To them, the Church announces solemnly that their salvation is in peril. Their pro-abortion conduct reveals a serious religious fault, since abortion is the very negation of man as the image of God. Again, it is a grave sin against God and man.

That is why John Paul II solemnly declared in his encyclical *Evangelium Vitae* that *"to kill directly and voluntarily an innocent human being is always gravely immoral"* (n.57; see also n.62 emphasis in the text). One can, therefore, consider this affirmation an integral part of the rule of faith for the faithful.

Let no one make groundless accusations against the Church! Her apparent severity here is but the other face of her tenderness toward all men: the unborn infant, first of all, but also the sinner invited to repent and convert his heart.

There is no place in the Church for contesting the dignity of man because he is made in the image of the Trinitarian God and saved by Christ. And, for the same reason, the Church expresses her repugnance for and condemnation of all ideologies and programs of action that show contempt for human life in all its stages. This repugnance also extends to those whose practices attack the integrity and dignity of the human being.[12]

Structures of Sin Approved by Law

Until recently, abortion was neither admitted not tolerated in the positive legislation of civilized countries. Abortion was an act of some men and women who furtively performed it on their own. Threats to human life before birth did not enjoy the support of positive law. The deplorable evolution of much national legislation shows that the respect due to human life is more and more at the mercy of persons and societies.[13] On this latter level, alas, one can observe that the major dangers do not come exclusively, or even primarily, from direct agents, namely, for instance, from the mother or the abortionist in the case of abortion. They arise from the death mentality which has led astray a significant number of medical professionals, politicians, lawmakers, the media, economists, etc.

Already in *Quadragesimo Anno,* Pius XI taught that the solution of social problems did not depend solely on employers but rather on the entirety of the active forces of society. All things considered, society generated the structures of sin which evolved into grave social injustices. All social forces, then, had to intervene in society in order to reform the structures, so that these would be more in accordance with the demands of justice.

The present situation is analogous. Respect for human life does not depend exclusively on agents directly concerned with abortion but on the entirety of the active forces of society. Society at present also engenders structures of sin that involve very grave injustices vis-à-vis the weakest human beings. Hence, all social forces must intervene in society to reform the structures in order to put an end to practices that cry to heaven for vengeance and yet are sometimes protected by law.

SOME "INDICATIONS" THAT CARRY NO WEIGHT

Abortion is always an *unequal* and therefore *dishonorable* combat in which adults always conquer the little ones. It is the same for infanticide and for euthanasia in which it its always the ones who have the upper hand. With regard to the dignity which must be accorded to every man simply because he is a man, none of the habitual "indications" for abortion carry any weight.

It is, then, appropriate to ask how some have failed to understand the right of the unborn infant to life. Of what worth are the "indications" habitually invoked to justify abortion?

First of all, in many well-to-do circles the infant is looked upon as private property. Some claim to have a "right to the child," as one has a right to a car or a television set. Such logic forgets that the human body is not disposable, that slavery has in principle ended in all civilized countries, and that where it still exists, it must be urgently abolished. When the mentality of ownership is so twisted as to make the claim to a "right *to* an infant," this "right" quickly becomes a "right *over* the infant." One believes that the owner must be able to destroy what he possesses when it doesn't meet his expectations.

A Child? Yes, some couples reply, but only if it's *wanted*. The encounter between the morality of individual pleasure and the cult of effective techniques has engendered a contraceptive mentality in countries of high income. The infant whose arrival is heralded can be kept if it is wanted, and if this want itself lasts. If not, it can be eliminated. This is what is called remedial abortion.

An *economic* argument is also invoked, and it takes several forms. Formerly, in rich countries, the child was seen by the parents as the "staff of old age" (Tob 5:23). And the child is still seen as such in poor countries. But currently in rich countries, State welfare or social security has taken the baton from the child, and the latter is even sometimes perceived as an obstacle to the comfort of the parents.

A variant on this argument consists in saying that in those countries which are currently prosperous the child used to be a source of economic wealth and military power. But today both the productivity of enterprises and military power depend much more on technology than on population. The amoral State can then authorize abortion without any serious inconvenience to itself.

Eugenic reasons, in the name of which so many crimes have been committed both in past times and recently, have returned full-force to the front burner.[14] It is not a matter of simply "justifying" the elimination of mongoloids, malformed, handicapped or seriously ill infants under the pretext that "they are a burden on the family and society"; it is a question of changing the parameters of "normalcy." In effect, they insist, the individual has to be competitive in society. For that he will have to be perfect from every point of view: physically, psychologically and intellectually. An examination of the amniotic fluid will determine — they think — whether the unborn infant runs the risk of not being competitive in society. If they do not receive such a guarantee, then the baby will be eliminated.

Prenatal diagnosis allows for medical determinations and early therapeutic interventions. For this we should be glad. The diagnoses and interventions which follow are morally licit whenever their objective is to discover a disorder and remedy it.[15] Nevertheless, experience proves that prenatal diagnosis often leads to a dynamic less therapeutic than abortive. The goal of the diagnosis is, then, less to discover and remedy a disorder than to avoid all risks. One proceeds to an abortion for reasons of "security" — for the parents, naturally.

The argument of *compassion* also figures among the reasons frequently advanced in favor of abortion. It is elaborated three ways. First, the unborn infant is suppressed because, suspected of a malformation, his "quality of life" will be such — one is assured — that his life will not be worth living."[16] Secondly, the unborn infant is suppressed because he will be "unhappy" and will be seen as a "burden" for a family in which there are already too many children. Finally, one further invokes compassion in having an abortion as a means to correct the unwanted consequences of sexual license or as a complement to the massive campaigns for the use of birth control. Abortion in this case is advocated as an indirect incitement to debauchery.

The argument of "pluralism" is also frequently put forward and serves euthanasia as well as abortion. However, a political society must be characterized above all by the esteem in which it holds man. Behind the etiquette of pluralism one finds the notion that all opinions are equally good.[17] This agnosticism, combined with unbridled subjectivism, has given credence to the idea that it is vain to fight for any particular conception of man whatsoever. The necessities of life in society are such that one must reach an accord on practical conduct.[18] And we know what follows: the strongest, and those who have the use of the media, end by imposing their opinion. There is no longer a common truth concerning man around which it is possible to agree on concerted action.

One consequence of this conception of "pluralism," is the *confusion between what is moral and what is legal*. Since there is no longer any truth about man and since each can choose his own truth, there is no longer a good or evil to which one must conform his conduct. Law assumes the role of morality and absorbs it.

The relationship between the environment and population has recently been invoked to justify abortion and euthanasia. Some assure us that the "supportive capacity" of the earth is going to be overwhelmed. The resources will not be sufficient for all men. We must, therefore, eliminate a certain number of them in order to avoid demographic cataclysm.

In conclusion, the "indications" favoring abortion are being multiplied. These "indications" are especially broadened under the influence of the old Malthusian, racist and eugenicist ideologies. They have created a discriminatory mentality vis-à-vis girls before their birth (but sometimes also boys), and vis-à-vis the handicapped, the elderly, the poor, blacks, etc. The criteria for discrimination and extermination vary as do the methods, but the injustice is always fundamentally the same.

What all the attacks against human life reveal is the profound crisis facing the moral conscience of man and societies. The link between truth and moral conscience has been seriously weakened.[19] In some circles, morality is limited to pleasing oneself and giving pleasure. This mentality exerts its influence even in Christian circles. As such, consciousness of sin is diminished. For many, moral guilt is a category without meaning. For these people, the ravaging results of sterilization, abortion or euthanasia have no significance when weighed against individual pleasure and societal whims of pleasure.

---

[1] One recalls especially the marvelous pictures taken by photographers like Lennart Nilsson and Jean-Marie Baufle. See, for example, Lennart Nilsson, *A Child Is Born* (New York: Doubleday, 1989)

[2] One of the greatest geneticists of our century, Prof. Jerome Lejeune, often brought to light the specificity and singularity of the human individual. With his usual brilliance, he discusses this especially in *The Concentration Can. When Does Human life Begin?* (San Francisco: Ignatius Press, 1992). On the individuation of beings, see the works of the best specialists on the topic: Philippe Caspar, *Penser l'embryon d'Hippocrate à nos jours* (Paris: Editions universitaires, 1991).

[3] An important collection of pontifical documents devoted to respect for life has been edited by Giovanni Caprile, *Giovanni Paolo II: Dieci anni per la vita* (n.p.: Centro Documentazione e Solidarietà, 1988). See also the collection of Giorgio Filibeck, *Les Droits de l'homme dans l'enseignement de l'Eglise: de Jean XXIII à Jean-Paul II* (Vatican City: Libreria Editrice Vaticana, 1992).

[4] Even article 1 of the Veil Law (1975), liberalizing abortion, recognizes this human character. See *EPA* 48 f. And 53; See *supra*, Chapter V, *From Consensus to Law*. Already in 1973 Dr. J. Ferin wrote: "In the mind of biologists a part of the human eggs thus obtained (by fertilization in vitro) is destined to be sacrificed." J. Ferin, "Communication," in Charles Robert (ed.), *L'Homme manipulé* (Strasburg: Cerdic, 1974) 25-34.

[5] Quoted in *Vocabulaire de théologie biblique* (Paris: Cerf, 1966); see the picture in col 463.

[6] See *O Codigo de Hammurabi*, trans. By E. Bouzon (Petropolis: Vozes, 1976) 89-90.

[7] See Guillaume Cardascia, *Les Lois assyriennes* (Paris: Cerf, 1969) esp. 57-59, 81 f., 88, 136-138; 239-247.

[8] See Hippocrate de Cos, *De l'Art médical* (Paris: Le livre de Poche, 1994) esp. 81-83.

[9] Theodore Mommsen, *Le Droit penal romain* vol. XVIII of the *Manuel des antiquités romaines* (Paris: Ed. Albert Fontemoing, 1907). See vol. II, 353.

[10] "Qui in utero sunt, in toto pene juri civili intelliguntur in rerum natura esse,"

Digeste de Justinian, Bk.I, title 6: *De statu humonum*. Roman law also knew a *curator ventris*, guardian of the womb, who had to oversee gestation.

[11] We have arranged a nonexhaustive list of recent condemnations in *EPA* 235-238.

[12] In the Church's teaching on the rights of man, the right to life is obviously fundamental. The deepening of her teaching on abortion has fortunately highlighted, with *EV* n.56, a new approach to the question of capital punishment. The Latin "typical" edition of the *Catechism of the Catholic Church* (see 2266 f.) also discusses this. Marie Hendrickx had a pioneering role in this new approach. See her learned article "Le Magistère et la peine de mort. Réflexion sur le Catéchisme et Evangelium Vitae," in *Nouvelle Revue Théologique* (Namur) 118, n.1 (Jan-Feb. 1996) 3-22.

[13] For a comparative study of law concerning abortion, see Mary Ann Glendon, *Abortion and Divorce in Western Law. American Failures, European Challenges* (Cambridge, Ma.: Harvard Univ. Press, 1987)

[14] See *supra*, note 6 of Chapter II.

[15] See *supra*, Chapter I, Some Abusive Medical Practices.

[16] See *supra*, Cardinal Ratzinger's Preface and Chapter V, *Relativization of the Quality of Life*.

[17] On "pluralism and its ambiguities" see *DLC* 66-83.

[18] See supra, Chapter III, *The Ethics of Responsibility* and *Procedural Justice*.

[19] On this subject see the encyclical of John Paul II, *Veritatis Splendor* of 1993 in *DC* n. 2081 of November 7.

CHAPTER VIII
WE WILL ALL PASS THAT WAY, OR DEATH TODAY

That we will all pass away is clear. But human life is now threatened from its most hidden origins and throughout its existence.

In the course of this century, euthanasia has been practiced on a wide scale, has been made commonplace under the Nazi regime. It is highly significant that the 50th anniversary of the Nuremberg Trials (1946-1996) was largely heralded with silence by the international establishment and the media. This is because remembrance of this trial would raise certain questions. With a somewhat sardonic irony one can wonder whether there would not have been a chance to engage in historical revisionism: why in 1946 did they send to the gallows people convicted of genocide, euthanasia, various barbarian practices, and those guilty of imprescriptible crimes against humanity? Without doubt recalling this historical trial would have raised embarrassing comparisons to those today who practice what we have called "intrauterine genocide," and to those who campaign for euthanasia or who want to deprive couples of the control of their fertility.

In fact, since 1946 the sensitivity of moral conscience has so changed that any distinction whatsoever between good and evil is at times regarded as inconsistent, or purely "cultural" or "historical" relative derivatives.

Euthanasia provides a terrible example of this evolution. Reproached by public opinion, condemned at Nuremberg and, punished by ordinary justice, euthanasia is currently being advocated in various circles, and its practice is spreading with little outcry from public opinion, judges, doctors, and historians. After the legalization of abortion, it would seem that euthanasia would be "a precious acquisition for our society." Hence one simply expects legal projects and propositions will eventually reflect current sentiment — as occurred in the case of abortion.

Without mincing words, the analysis which we are going to make will involve two intertwined points: 1) the act of killing another man with his permission, 2) an intentional act directly procuring death, whether by the act of causing it or by the voluntary omission of care.

The study of this very grave problem will lead us to develop two kinds of considerations: one will bear on the practices themselves; the second will be devoted to reflections on these practices.

EUTHANASIA IN PRACTICE

Studying the Arguments

The arguments put forward to justify the practice of euthanasia revolve around three poles: assisted suicide, compassion, and social and economic utility.

In the particular case of *assisted suicide*, let us draw attention first to the fact that the doctor seems to precipitate in the patient the conviction that he is useless, that no one cares for him and that he must "let go" as soon as possible.

According to the experience related by many psychiatrists who have analyzed cases of attempted suicide, it is very commonly understood that "failures in committing suicide" are manifestations of cries of distress, and calls for help. It should be feared, then, that the person who assists another in committing suicide is not aware of this latent but undecoded cry. As a consequence, the request for assistance is not properly interpreted for what it is, namely, a call for help, and a desire from someone in distress for warm acceptance.

Therefore, faced with someone who has made me part of his decision to commit suicide, I can adopt two very different attitudes: either I go buy some rope for him and help him hang himself, or in a more humane way, I discuss the matter with him and try to make him understand that he still has worth in the eyes of many, no matter what his difficulties are and that there are people available who can help him through his problems.

Regarding the argument of *compassion*, we must ask by what right and according to what criteria can we make judgments on behalf of the sick person? There is no criterion available that permits us to quantify the value of human life — not mine, not that of another. When we pretend to yield to compassion, should we not in reality talk about self-commiseration, that is, flight in the face of a situation which bothers us and which we want to avoid, preferring to close our eyes? For those who live well and who are in full possession of their faculties, the sight of a suffering person can be intolerable: they want to spare themselves the spectacle.

But can I resolve a problem presented to me at the expense of another's life, of someone whose psychological and mental state remain unknown to me because he has difficulty in expressing himself in a normal and lucid manner? Isn't it extremely hazardous for me to euthanize another in circumstances in which I *presume* that he shares the repugnance I feel when confronted with the situation he finds himself in?

The arguments put forward for *social and economic* utility are unfortunately beginning to be spread with great intensity and speed. In many circles in wealthy countries as well as in the Third-World man has become a sort of product that one manufactures, and who is admitted to existence or refused existence according to certain utilitarian criteria, especially social and economic utility.

In an interview that appeared in *L'Avenir de la vie* (The Future of Life), Jacques Attali developed some important considerations regarding this matter:

Euthanasia will be one of the essential instruments of future societies in all imaginable domains. With socialist logic, to begin with, the scenario is as follows: socialist logic calls for liberty, with the ultimate freedom being suicide; consequently, the right to direct or indirect suicide is an absolute value in this type of society. In capitalist societies, killing machines and other techniques which permit the elimination of life when it becomes unbearable or economically too costly will arise and become common practice. And so I think that euthanasia, be it a commodity of freedom or merchandise, will eventually become the rule in the future society.[1]

Foreseeable Consequences of the Practice of Euthanasia

Let us look into these different types of argumentation, particularly the latter, and consider some inevitable consequences of euthanasia, especially on the political, juridical and medical fronts.

First on the *political* level, numerous observations can be readily made. All democracies are founded on unconditional respect for innocent human life. Respect for life and its legal protection are essential in a democratic political society. Negatively formulated, this first observation comes down to acknowledging the fact that all war has as its the end the elimination of certain human beings.

We must recognize the fact that secular currents have played an appreciable role in the analysis of this point. In the 18th century in particular, they made the value of human life the theme of solemn declarations. This was true of the Declaration of Independence in the United States and with the Declaration of the Rights of Man and of the Citizen in 1789.[2]

Consequently, it is to be feared that a State claiming authority to legalized euthanasia is engaging in a trend which leads to what one recent author calls "the criminal State."[3] All our Western societies are based on a certain conception of the equal dignity of all men and their inalienable right to life, whatever their physical or psychological state or their racial, social and intellectual status. Therefore, from the moment one invoked majority rule to contest, by the legalization of euthanasia, this pivotal point of every democratic society, one introduces a totalitarian dynamic into the society. To be honest, those societies which we know to have legalized euthanasia, by definition, demonstrate that they are already engaged in a process which will lead to totalitarianism.

What do we observe on the *juridical* level? Regarding euthanasia, it would seem that euthanasia advocates are going to use a tactic which has proven itself in other areas, namely, the *tactic of derogation*?[4] This unfolds in two phases. At the very beginning, a general principle is asserted with much force: for example, "All men have the right to life." And immediately they hasten to undermine the fundamental principle they've just proclaimed by supplying a series of derogations. Therefore, the risk of establishing legalized tyranny is increased. The law loses its inherent specificity, which has been recognized since the time of Solon of antiquity: being a bulwark of the weak against the strong, it is put at the service of the strongest. Here we should remember that *juridical positivism*, that is, law as it appears in the legal codes emanating solely from the will of men and therefore accommodating the arbitrary will of the powerful, always forms the bedrock of authoritarian systems.[5] We know that without difficulty the law was put at the service of Nazi Germany precisely because, in that country, several authors had brought about the triumph of an ultrapositivist conception of law. It was an irony of history that the principal protagonist of this conception, Kelsen, ended up being a victim of the legal theory he had extolled. Once Hitler attained power, the anti-Nazi bulwark that could have been erected by law was shown to be inoperative because the juridical positivism already in place put at Hitler's disposal the legal theoretical bases which could be that harmonized with his project of death.

On the *medical* level, finally, it is to be feared that history will repeat itself and that the credibility of the profession will be profoundly compromised. One can hardly imagine that the doctor can "change hats" in the same morning, first being the servant of life and then the artisan of death. Hasn't Dr. Schwarzenberg himself declared that "For the doctor the sole professional achievement is curing"? Patients cannot live in the constant apprehension that a death sentence will be pronounced and eventually executed by their own doctor. As for the nursing personnel, they risk, not only being compromised, but also being drained by the lack of motivation, division and even despair that have been linked to the practice of euthanasia.

A State that invests doctors with the exorbitant power of choosing who can live and who must die, or one which requires that doctors practice euthanasia, must be denounced for *this supreme abuse of power*. We must recommend especially to young people that they become informed on historical trends by referring them, for example, to the book by R. J. Lifton, *Les médecins nazis* (The Nazi Doctors).[6] A large portion of this work is devoted to euthanasia and to other medical trends that ensued in Nazi Germany, seduced by the complacency and complicity of lawyers and doctors.

Alternate Proposal: Palliative Care

Toward the end of this first part, we cannot recommend enough that the greatest attention be given to palliative care and to the progress that is being continually achieved in the battle against physical pain and psychological suffering.

These methods must in no case be confused, however, with the sort of life-prolonging medications used for Tito in Yugoslavia, Franco in Spain, Boumedien in Algeria or Tancredo Neves in Brazil. Such intensive medication employs technical means that exhaust the patient causing him physical pain and moral suffering in artificially delaying death and uselessly prolonging his agony. This danger is to be avoided, just as the inverse situation mentioned below, namely, the omission of care even at the most elementary level.

Both in its motivation as well as in its application, palliative care is entirely different. This is called for when one sees that care directed at healing will not work and that a cure is impossible. This is when the *very object of therapy changes*: it is no longer aimed at the disease but rather at the pain, and the doctor's task is actively to reduce it. The inability to cure does not mean one can remove all care.

In this context, it is desirable to differentiate between physical pain, which can be cared for with analgesics, and suffering which is of the psychological and moral order. Many of us, without doubt, have witnessed the need of the dying for compassion vis-à-vis the dying. To have compassion means to bear the suffering together. Compassion in this instance is the extraordinary respect that we are able to give to the dying through expressions of tenderness at this decisive moment of their existence.

Briefly, neither false preservation or abandonment is called for; one neither precipitates nor unduly delays death.

Euthanasia: "Active" or "Passive"?

Given what we have covered, precision in terminology appears useful. The distinction between "active" euthanasia and "passive" euthanasia that some use is not advisable because of the confusion it causes.

The euthanasia of which we are speaking results from directly inducing death through either a deliberate act (injection, acceleration of an i.v. drip rate,) or by the deliberate cessation of all care. To characterize this as "active" euthanasia is to express a truism, since the intention to cause death is implemented by one of two types of deliberate action (deed or cessation).

The expression "passive euthanasia" is sometimes used to designate palliative care which involves the risk of death via analgesics. This expression is unfortunate, in that it leads to confusion; it is better to avoid it.

In the strict sense, euthanasia always involves the *deliberate intention* of directly bringing about death; *this is precisely the heart of the problem*. This intention is not at all present in palliative care. Rather, the latter involves an *activity* that has as its objective the reduction of pain and giving sympathy to the suffering patient, and not the hastening of death. No one will deny that recourse to powerful analgesics, used to reduce pain, can sometimes risk hastening death, even if progress in pharmacology significantly diminishes the instances. Death, even if it should be hastened by the analgesic, is not in any way willed. It is not even indirectly willed, in the sense that the intention of reducing pain would not entail the intention of provoking death by using the legitimate therapeutic means.

It is, therefore, mistaken to emphasize the risk involved in a doctor treating the terminally ill. In fact, this risk does not fundamentally differ from that of a surgeon when called upon to perform justified operations which are known in advance to be delicate. Think of the frequent cases that come up in heart surgery or brain surgery. The surgeon measures better than anyone else the risk involved, but he nonetheless does his best to take care of the patient. Death, if it follows such an intervention, is a consequence suffered but in no way willed.

It is better, therefore, to avoid the distinction between "active" and "passive" euthanasia, for the active element covered by the second expression does not contain the deadly intent essentially characteristic of the first, which is properly called euthanasia.

REFLECTION ON THESE PRACTICES

Clarifying the Debate in the Light of Contemporary Experience

"God created the world but the Dutch created Holland," goes a Dutch proverb. This somewhat caustic joke suggests why the Dutch, who have recovered most of their land from the sea, could have, according to some, a strong awareness of their superiority. Perhaps they share with others even the conviction of being called to play a messianic role on the level of European and world society.

Traditionally a land of welcome, Holland and the Dutch have for a long time shared a common reference point: the Decalog. Nevertheless, from the time of Grotius and above all Spinoza (17th century), this shared reference has become progressively diluted. This evolution has even affected the Calvinist tradition which was originally quite rigorous. Presently the Dutch have pushed tolerance to the point of rejecting practically *every* common principle.

An official statistic coming from the Remmelink report[7] indicates that around 15% of deaths occur by euthanasia every year in Holland. In absolute figures, just under 20,000 people are euthanized, 9% of them without their consent. The situation is all the more astonishing in that euthanasia is not legalized in that country; it is simply tolerated at the present time, which proves that the debate merits reconsideration.

So why should we be surprised? In a society which no longer effectively has any principles or fundamental reference points, any trend becomes possible. There is a recent example in the *Chronique d'une mort annoncée* (Chronicle of an Announced Death), a television program shown on several European networks. What is so distressing is that the euthanizing doctor, who appears in the program, has nothing else to propose to his patient but a lethal injection. Was there nothing else to be done in order to relieve the *pain*? Surely much more could have been done to relieve the moral *suffering* of the person who was sooner or later going to pass away.

As for the "indications" invoked in Holland to justify euthanasia, one sees that they follow an evolution similar to that of the "indications" relative to abortion: the list is endless and increasingly varied.

Now it is no longer a question of only the terminally ill. It is more and more a matter of authorizing or tolerating euthanasia for infants afflicted with malformations, handicaps, mental diseases, etc. When will euthanasia be performed on mongoloids and the sick affected by AIDS?

At the very beginning of this chapter we pointed out that some people are irritated by our recalling particularly somber pages of contemporary history. Yet, rather than crying out in protest against an "amalgam," we must remember the warning given by one of the greatest historians of our century, Arnold Toynbee, who in essence said that "those who ignore history are doomed to repeat it."

Are people aware of the fact that the Dutch television program *Chronique d'une mort annoncée* is but a remake of the film *Ich klage an* (I Accuse) ordered by Goebbels in 1941?[8] The only difference in the Dutch film is that it is a woman who is euthanized. The message the film projects is simple: in the name of the State's interests, of the imperatives of race, of philosophical considerations, etc., it must be permitted to eliminate people considered useless or bothersome.

The fundamental work on this topic was published in Leipzig in 1920 by Bindung, a lawyer, and Hoche, a doctor.[9] The French translation is no longer available, but an English translation of it was published in 1992 in the United States.[10] These two authors were frequently invoked at the trials of the doctors at Nuremberg, especially that of the infamous Dr. Brandt, one of the master designers of the Nazi program for euthanasia and Jewish genocide.[11] The work of Bindung-Hoche already enunciates point by point all the arguments advanced today in favor of euthanasia, and more precisely, assisted suicide: compassion and social utility.

Even if it is unsettling to recall the Nazi precedent, bringing it into the context of today's advocated or observed practices cannot be considered a falsifying amalgram. Today as yesterday, the root of these practices are common theories which must be examined very closely. For, if the same theories produce the same results, we are justified in thinking that we too are involved in a very dangerous and slippery slope. For the remaining "justifications" which are different a distinction matters little since the death-provoking practices are the same.

Put in Philosophical Perspective

The debate over euthanasia can be enriched by discussing several philosophical trends which serve to clarify it. We will limit ourselves here to examining two of them.

The discussion of euthanasia reaches beyond trends currently surfacing in Holland and elsewhere and even beyond Bindung and

Hoche. Above all, we must go back to a philosopher who has left his mark on our whole era, Hegel (1770-1831). As Alexander Kojève,[12] one of the best experts, explains: the philosophy of Hegel is above all a *philosophy of death*. Hegel was tormented by man's condition being finite — like an animal — but who unlike the animal is endowed with reason and free will, all the while conscious of the inevitability of death. Faced with this inescapable situation, and confronted with this "fatal issue," man seeks in the gift of death the affirmation of his sovereign liberty. That is precisely what is achieved in the act of causing his own death by suicide. But if he is the master of his own life and death, why, *a fortiori*, should man be forbidden to act as master of life and death over others, as this is what is already suggested in the famous dialectic of the master and the slave?

Here we stand at the origin of all contemporary lordly moralities, against which all the trends sensitive to the human rights, beginning with those of the weakest, have not ceased reacting. The lords in question, being the powerful, arrogate to themselves the exercise of total mastery over their own life and that of others. This morality leads to diverse forms of oppression, segregation or war, based on the criteria of race or class, of profit, of ability to pay, of usefulness.

Faced with the arrival of death, which is always agonizing for us, would it not be more wise to remain attentive to what Prof. Lucien Israel had to say: "We must always remain open to this part of the mystery of which death is a reminder"?

Philosophers and the Dignity of Man

Because there are essential values, values that we all need to respect and promote in order to insure peaceful community life, we must discern and denounce theories that presage destructive tendencies, and also prevent the establishment of those practices which are their fatal consequences. Now is the time to remember the warnings of the great "prophets" of our time, such as Jaspers, Hannah Arendt, I. Chafarévitch, Claude Polin, Jean-Jacques Walter, to cite but a few.

Although wars have been numerous and the practice of oppression constant, sociability, the social instinct, fraternity, and solidarity have nonethless been moral references that our societies have striven to honor and protect since antiquity. These references always imply a fundamental accord on the equal dignity of men. They provide men with common ground to broaden their discussions. Moreover, every time these references have been misunderstood or flouted, men dedicated to freedom have risen in resistance.

Contribution of Christians

Faced with the question of euthanasia, what can one say from the Christian viewpoint? First of all, we must observe once again that Christians in no way have a monopoly over respect for human life. As far as respect for life goes, the laws in force in Europe have not been imposed by any clerical pressure. In France, the laws condemning abortion go back to Napoleon (penal code of 1810); this condemnation has been repeated and made more precise in the laws of 1920, 1923, 1931, 1951, 1967. We must also remember that from Descartes to Napoleon, including Diderot, Rousseau and Kant, the condemnation of suicide has been constant.

As for the banalization of and legislation regarding euthanasia, this always raises the spectre of the practice first made commonplace by the Nazis. In their verdicts against the doctors at the Nuremberg trials, the judges constantly made reference to euthanasia and cited major reasons for its condemnation. Would the silence surrounding the fiftieth anniversary of this trial suggest that the Nuremberg judges were mistaken in imparting judgment and penalties?

All legislation that authorizes abortion and euthanasia is contrary to the lessons which the Declaration of 1948 drew from the experience of totalitarianism, especially that of the Nazis. By proclaiming and protecting the rights of all men on the international level, it necessarily barred the return of a State that, in the name of "higher interests," violated these rights.[13]

We cannot recommend strongly enough that Christians of today remain mindful of precedents which even some of their own must have taken part in. We must not lose sight of the fact that any weakening of the 1948 Declaration risks opening the way for any totalitarian machine that, in the name of higher interests (e.g., economic imperatives), could violate these rights.

Explicitly echoing this embarrassing past which some would prefer to erase, the Academy of Moral and Political Sciences of Paris, on November 14, 1949, adopted a Declaration in which we read:

The Academy of Moral and Political Sciences:

1) formally rejects all methods aimed at bringing about the death of subjects considered monstrous, malformed, defective, or incurable, because, among other reasons, any medical or social doctrine that does not respect in a systematic fashion the very principles of life fatally ends, as recent experience proves, in criminal abuses;

2) considers euthanasia and, in a general way, all methods which have the effect of causing out of compassion a "gentle and tranquil" death for the moribund must also be ruled out. . . . This categorical opinion rests. . . on the fact that. . . such methods would have as effect the conferring on the doctor a sort of sovereignty over life and death.[14]

The Church fundamentally subscribes to this repugnance which euthanasia inspires in every civilized society. But she adds, along with the whole of Judeo-Christian tradition, that life must be welcomed as a gift. We receive it from our parents and, through our parents, we receive it from God Himself. Unfortunately, it is not rare, by reason of damage incurred through upbringing and other circumstances of life, for some to refuse to welcome this gift for what it is: a marvelous gift. Such damage and personal wounds lead to revolts which block the pathways of hope.

What do Christians do here? They invite people to trust in the hope of resurrection.

The basis of the great clivage between Christians, on the one hand, and deists, agnostics and atheists, on the other, is that Christians firmly believe that Jesus died and rose from the dead. The witnesses, the disciples of Christ, risked their lives to transmit this message to us. And among these witnesses figured some disciples who, like St. Peter had denied Christ during His passion, and who had abandoned Him at the time of His death on the cross. Now these same disciples who had left Him, went and exposed themselves to all sorts of danger after the resurrection in order to proclaim to the whole world that He who had been put to death was alive, and that they had "eaten and drunk with Him after his resurrection from the dead" (Acts 10:41).

This wager of Christians on the resurrection has been described in a magnificent passage the Church proposes in the Office of Readings for the feast of St. Bartholomew. Here is the passage, dating from the end of the 4th century and attributed to St. John Chrysostom:

> How were the apostles, who had never visited cities and their assemblies, able to dream of mobilizing themselves against the entire world? They were fearful and without courage: the one who wrote about them described it well, one who didn't want either to excuse or hide their defects. And that is a very strong proof of truth. What, then, did he say about them? When Christ was arrested, after having performed innumerable miracles,

most of them fled, and he who was their leader (Peter) remained only to deny Him.

These men were incapable of sustaining the assault of the Jews when Christ was living. And while He was dead and buried, when He was still not not risen and thus could not utter a word of encouragement to them, how can you believe they would mobilize themselves against the entire world? Wouldn't they have had to ask themselves: "What's all this? He wasn't even able to save Himself and now He is supposed to protect us? When He was alive, He couldn't defend Himself and now that He is dead, will He lend us a hand? When He was alive, He was unable to subject any nation to Himself, and we are going to conquer the whole earth by proclaiming His name? How is it not unreasonable, not only to try and accomplish that, but to even think of doing it?"

It's evident, then: if they had not seen him risen, and if they had not had the proof of His omnipotence, they would never have undertaken such a risk.[15]

---

[1] Jacques Attali, "La médecine en accusation," in Michael Salomon (ed.), *L'Avenir de la vie* (Paris: Seghers, 1981) 274 f.

[2] See the first few pages of Chapter V.

[3] Yves Ternon, *L'Etat criminel. Les génocides au Xxe siècle* (Paris: Le Seuil, 1995).

[4] See Chapter V, *The Tactic of Derogation*.

[5] See *supra*, Chapter V on the rights of man.

[6] Paris: Laffont, 1989.

[7] See *supra*, Chapter I, *Euthanasia* and note 6.

[8] See J. Lifton, *op.cit.* 68 f.

[9] *Ibid.* 65 f., 67, 130.

[10] *Issues in Law and Medicine* 231-265.

[11] See Alexander Mitscherlich and Fred Mielke, *Medizin ohne Menschlichkeit* (Frankfurt: Fischer, 1989).

[12] *Introduction à la lecture de Hegel* (Paris: Gallimard, 1947) 529-575.

[13] See Chapter V on the rights of man.

[14] Quoted by Maurice Torelli in *La Médecin et les droits de l'homme* (Paris: Berger-Levrault, 1983) 235 f.

[15] Feast of St. Bartholomew, Office of Readings. This text comes from his homily in I Cor 4:3,4 in *Patrologia Graeca* 61:34-36.

CHAPTER IX
TAKING THE FIRST STEP

HAPPINESS AND SOLIDARITY

Today the threats facing human life are not only numerous and diverse, and "justified" by ideologies and even moralists, but they are also advocated by political powers, covered by the law and ultimately executed by medical personnel. These threats reveal a failure in the quest for happiness. If happiness is to love and be loved, it is clear that practices such as abortion, sterilization and euthanasia cannot lead to happiness for either those who undergo them or those who perform them.

An "Intermediate" Relationship

Before this impasse the Christian community must once again sound its call to solidarity.[1] The world today will not come out of its moral destitution, attested to by the contempt for man, except by a flight forward. This implies an authentic conversion of people and societies. The violence which is victimizing human beings today attests to a moral degradation whose perverse effects will continue to multiply if people do not convert in the depths of their heart.

The message of the Church here has the simplicity and radicalness of the Gospel: happiness cannot be found but in an authentic love that reaches out to all men. This universal love, without frontiers, very often occurs by way of institutions, in which one touches numerous brothers whom one will doubtlessly never see; it is this type of "mediate" relationship which we will consider in this chapter. The same kind of love can also be expressed face to face in a direct relationship between persons. We will consider this type of relationship in the exemplary framework of the family.

The Good Samaritan — to return to him once again — offers us an example of both types of relationships: he takes the first step; he himself approaches the wounded man, but he entrusts him then to the care of the innkeeper. Through the mediation of this specialized and paid tradesman the Samaritan still touches the wounded man.[2]

The Church's good news about life in society consists in asserting that happiness is to be found in solidarity. The decision to opt in favor of a solidarity-based society directly entails the future happiness of human society. This solidarity is concretized along the lines of two complementary axes. The *synchronic* axis: solidarity among contemporaries; and the *diachronic* axis: solidarity between generations.

To speak of solidarity is to invite people to share their superfluity; that is to say, the resources of the earth are at the disposition of all.[3] Collective hoarding or monopolization is, then, a form of avarice. Solidarity also requires a sustained attention to the common good. This means that solidarity will never be able to flourish in a society in which private groups are obstinate in trying to make their private good triumph to the detriment of the good of the community. In brief, property including that of nations, must be managed in such a way as to take into account the just needs of the entire human community.

Solidarity also implies that every man can contribute to the human community the benefit derived from the riches of his personality. A society with solidarity is a society in which the differences among men are recognized as riches. Every man effectively has something original to offer to the human community, and each man also has the right to be able to benefit from what all the members of the community offer as original. For the Church, solidarity, far from smothering the singularity of each, stimulates it instead. The Church considers that "man... is given by God to himself."[4] She thus asks that public authorities aid people, families, and intermediate groups — including nations — to express themselves because all of them have riches to offer by sharing in the human community. Hence, there is only a place for solidarity where the requirements of subsidiarity are respected.

The Blinding Sign of the Times

Putting to work these principles depends strictly on the good will of men. The Church thus places all her hope in the ability that all men have to rectify the direction of their lives if they wish to achieve happiness and share that happiness. The Church desires above all else to help men discover the marvelous resources that, all too often, lie dormant in their heart: resources of tenderness and generosity, of inventive imagination faced with the needs of one's neighbor. To each man in particular, the Church says that he possesses in himself underemployed capabilities and qualities. She also says that these capabilities and qualities will be expanded to the extent that each pays more attention to others. The Church invites all men today more effectively to seize the opportunities they have from living at a time when many of the problems that tormented previous generations are solved or are solvable. Many of these problems are entirely avoidable.

But the Church adds right away that this happy circumstance only demonstrates all the more the urgent need for conversion. The real problems which contempt for human life reveals are not problems of the technical order; they are problems of the moral order. The attitude vis-à-vis the weakest is the touchstone of a society's moral caliber. "Progress toward rectifying the problems of the poor constitutes a great opportunity for the moral, cultural and even economic development of all humanity."[5] In this sense, the poor are a great hope for the world; among the poor there figure, understandably, all the unborn infants. The immense hordes of the poor, the innumerable masses of eliminated infants and the mutilated weak constitute today the most *blinding sign of the times*. It calls all men of good will to conversion and to action. The transition from an attitude hostile to these humans to one of respect and love will cause a rainbow to shine over the earth heralding peace and fraternity.

The opportunity offered to us is to profit by the favorable times in which we live, to pull ourselves together morally and to reverse joyously the disastrous dynamic that is corrupting our society. In brief, since the great threat hanging over human life comes from society, Christians are invited to contribute to the formation of a social climate more favorable toward welcoming life. We will now show how some areas of human activity previously mentioned could contribute to this task of moral reconstruction.

TOWARD A POLITICS FOR LIVING TOGETHER

An analysis of both past and contemporary political societies reveals that men have not stopped fighting and even rebelling for the recognition of their dignity. Privileges based on social standing, on fortune, on race, etc., have all been contested. Even in our own century, as the Universal Declaration of the Rights of Man indicates, the Fascist and Nazi regimes have been opposed in the name of the dignity of all men. Nearer to the present time, it was also this perception of the equal dignity of men that imposed itself with the irresistible force of the truth when confronting the communist regimes.

The Slippery Slope of Totalitarianism

The most important action that we can expect from national or international political powers is to respect and make respected this equal dignity of every man. When they legalize abortion, self-proclaimed democratic societies are no longer truly democratic. With this singular legislation they have introduced a principle of unjustifiable discrimination into their interior structure. In so doing, these societies already find themselves on the slippery slope of totalitarianism.

The essential characteristic of a democratic society, a characteristic for which entire peoples have fought and still fight, is the recognition of the same dignity for all. A society that lays down the principle that certain members of the human race do not have this dignity is in the process of regressing into barbarism. It is inadmissible that after so many tears have been shed a human being should be declared an *Unmensch* — a non-man — and treated as such.

Majority rule cannot be validly invoked in this case, for it is nothing but a rule determining behavior rather than the just end of society, namely, equal recognition of all. And the proof that the rule of the majority does not suffice to characterize a democracy is that we have seen only too clearly in contemporary history numerous majorities which have openly invited the most disastrous totalitarian regimes.

As for tolerance, when it is stretched to the point of absolute license, it leads to complete relativism and to a totally agnostic political society. Thus a State or a community of States that, in the name of pluralism, declare themselves agnostic or conduct themselves as such, undermine the very foundations of the fundamental rights which this State or States have the precise mission to defend. Since there are no longer any fundamental rights to be respected, they say, the State is totally disarmed against the assaults confronting these rights. Powerless to react against such assaults, the State itself becomes the victim of the invasion of those who, like the "moles," want to use it and finally lead it to its own destruction.

Once moral norms have been emptied and even denounced as "inadmissible taboos," and the State itself applauds such discrediting, the anarchic claims of individuals invade every level of politics. Since the very idea of moderating principles has been banished, the political arena becomes one of total excess and is transformed into a battlefield. Once the State ceases to be the promoter and vigilant guardian of the basic conditions that make living together in justice possible, might becomes the sole source of right. The rights of the weakest receive no protection; these rights are compromised, even denied. Social life is organized with contempt for all needs of the common good and justice. Strife results from force and then rights are based only on agreements and ad hoc consensus.[6]

It is desirable, then, that as quickly as possible, politicians need to abrogate the iniquitous laws which were passed as a result of cleverly orchestrated campaigns. We should also expect that they continue to work toward humanizing the structure of society. Action aimed at preventing the temptation to abort and favoring the welcome of the child remains to be effected. There is no doubt, of course, that such action must involve good fiscal policy, housing policy, agrarian policy, with a policy for full employment and, above all, a reassertion of the value of a mother in society.

Controlling the Fertility of Couples?

The experience of certain big countries, like China, shows that when the public power arrogates to itself the right to control human life, it does not delay in wanting to manage the fertility of couples, and that it does not hesitate in such situations to have recourse to humiliating and coercive methods. Programs recommending this sort of interference are, alas, even advocated in countries of long-standing democratic tradition. There again we have characteristic abuses of power.

In virtue of the principle of subsidiarity, spouses may never be deprived of their inalienable right to exercise responsible parenthood. Furthermore, the State can and even must intervene so that spouses can exercise this right. Indirect interventions on the part of the State should translate into measures to assist mothers and families.[7]

In no case may public powers, much less private groups, threaten couples with the consequences of their mistakes or incapacity. We must restore the proper indisposability of the human body and reaffirm it is beyond all control and planning on the part of the State or others. For an even greater reason, the human being is not patentable.

In order to create favorable conditions, one must first remember that dictatorships block the process of education and replace it with machines that can be manipulated. We must, therefore, stop supporting despots who obstruct solutions; all men of good will must organize to fight against all forms of corruption. Education of the masses in the domain of political responsibility must teach men to support only representatives concerned with the common good. In this way will people be able to conduct well founded fiscal and family policies leading to a more just distribution of revenue.

Moral Degradation

By reason of the growing interdependence of nations respect for human life has also become an international problem. Various public and private international institutions have come into conflict, sometimes openly, with the Church and those who defend human life. Among these institutions there are some that advocate mass sterilization, making abortion commonplace, and the generalization of contraception — and thereby contribute to the corruption of the young and adults. Certain activists push their audacity to the point of justifying their activity by claiming that problems they are provoking and which people are beginning to recognize are due to old taboos, to the "old paradigm," to a "Victorian morality," and to a "mentality closed to any progress."

The Christian community can no longer allow itself to have recourse to "diplomatic" language to denounce this situation. The programs of action of different international institutions are converging. All these activities are connected and aim at one same global project. If one advocates one such project, he is immediately involved in advocating all the others. People are first neutralized, then won over and finally become accomplices. Silence itself is a form of complicity; if it is the price paid in the vain hope of mollifying the Adversary, it is unworthy of the Gospel. The Christian community must and can find a new language to explain with courage what these organizations are doing and what the motives are that inspire them.[8]

What these organizations are doing is grave on two levels. First, by definition, it is a grave wrong to sterilize, to abort, to promote and make contraception commonplace — all of this must be denounced.

But what these international agencies (public and private) are actually doing is still more serious. What they aim at destroying in fact, is not only physical integrity but psychological and moral integrity. It is the young and the poor that are targeted, physically, psychologically and morally. From a process of deprograming-reprograming, they press on toward degradation and perversion. For the young themselves and the future of the human community, this is even more terrible than any physical mutilation.

It is inadmissible that public international organizations, pressured from within and without by lobbies that do not respect human life, allow themselves to be led to change their orientation and their raison d'être. Some of these institutions go so far as to abuse their power by posing as supranational authorities. We have already indicated which among them exert open or veiled pressure on national governments in order to force them to follow demographic policies incompatible with the respect due to men's rights and the sovereignty of nations. These organizations should not contribute to setting up a system of planetary control of men and things. We must remember in this regard the subsidiary role, not only of the State, but also of these public international organizations. By this we mean that, just as the State must respect the proper autonomy of intermediate bodies and the family, so too must public international organizations respect the sovereignty of the State.

LAW, PROTECTOR OF THE WEAK

The Need for Values

Parents and educators are unanimous in stating that children need values. All the young have the right to them to help them find what is true, good, beautiful and correct, and to avoid evil and all that leads to it. But in this matter the condition of adults and societies does not differ fundamentally from that of children: they also need guidelines. A society that, in the name of pluralism, affirms individual liberty to the point of paroxysm, is a society that is losing its bearings.[9] In such a society, guidelines acknowledged by all no longer have a place. This society founders first in *skepticism* and then in *cynicism*; it ends up decaying, becomes gripped by anarchy, and eventually becomes a jungle.

Once people have eliminated commonly held values, they are reduced to demanding that positive law replace morality.[10] They spontaneously expect law to be just. For example, movements which have sought social reform have struggled so that things would be more just. The tension between morality and positive law is the chief driving force behind the history of political societies as well as the history of rights. But once one accepts the principle that only what positive law dictates is just, then this dynamic tension dissolves and positive law draws its authority solely from the might of those who impose it.

When moral guidelines have been banished, men are persuaded that there is no longer good or evil, true or false, and that the only liberty is that of indifference, since it is no longer possible for society to recognize reference points and to submit to them; one must then take refuge in a "contractural" or "procedural" ethic. The argumentation is well known and goes back to Rousseau: since God as the reference has been banished — practically or theoretically — from society, the sovereign is the people and, through their legislators, they provide themselves with laws, passed by a majority and expressing a general will declared to be infallible. In these laws they acknowledge, then, a civil "sanctity," and anyone who refuses to accept them deserves to be punished for "impiety" vis-à-vis the "sovereign" society.[11]

Resistance to Unjust Law

The legislative texts against life proceed from this conception of the "sanctity" attributed to man's law, a sanctity which has nonetheless not been publicly conferred. That is why currently those who reject such laws are being persecuted by those in power who cannot tolerate the questioning of the civil "sanctity" of laws. As contemporary history shows, this conception of law ends by transforming the legal system into an instrument of totalitarian power, a power which this very same legal process directly contributes toward establishing.

The Church cannot admit this conception of law and power. She considers that no man, no nation, by any title whatsoever, has the right to impose his/its law on others. There is no just law but that which encompasses all the demands flowing from the equal dignity of all men. The Church asks: what kind of a law is it that authorizes the murder of an innocent? What kind of a law is it that in the end destroys love? Only a law in conformity with the demands of justice merits obedience. An unjust law undermines the legitimacy of those who promulgate it and the authority of those who apply it. Such a law calls for resistance.

It is, then by an abuse of language that people sometimes regard the existence of a law, respected by those who govern and those who are governed, sufficient to characterize the State as one of rights. This supposes that the law is in conformity with justice, and that it is good.[12]

Legislation liberalizing abortion reveals, then, a perversion of rights, and this perversion affects in turn social relationships. Rights must be at the service of *all* men and not provide "legitimacy" to a power that abuses people.

Nondisposability of the Body

It is appropriate to recall here that the 1948 Universal Declaration of the Rights of Man includes a very serious warning to which the adversaries of life should pay closer attention., This solemn text explains that it is by having ignored the fundamental rights of man, beginning with that to life (see art.3), that humanity has sunken into barbarism. In order to avoid such evils and prevent them, the entire human community must be involved in promoting these inalienable rights in positive legislation. The right of every human individual to life has been reaffirmed in the Preamble of the Convention on the Rights of the Child adopted unanimously by the U.N. in 1989.

An essential aspect of this Declaration is its universal tenor: it holds true for every human individual. Every attempt to relativize it, to reduce its intent or modify its content; — for example, in the name of cultural considerations — would be condemned in advance to failure.[13]

Legislation hostile to life seriously deviates from the tradition expressed in this Declaration and even regresses to the horrors which this Declaration wanted to render impossible. We must, therefore, hope that this legislation, today in the service of death, will quickly give way to juridical instruments at the service of life. What is asked for here is something of great simplicity: it is that the human body be declared nondisposable from conception until natural death. Furthermore, this requirement is inscribed in the juridical tradition of Western nations and of those nations inspired by this tradition. Every civilized society must, in effect, offer the weakest the right to an effective protection, with punitive consequences for those who threaten them.

MEDICINE IN THE SERVICE OF LIFE

For more than a century now medicine has achieved remarkable progress for the benefit of humanity and, in particular, for the poor world. Encouraged by clear-sighted governments, campaigns for hygiene and preventive medicine have made infant mortality fall in a spectacular manner and life expectancy has increased almost everywhere. Compared with intensive curative medicine and performance enhancing medicine, preventive medicine is relatively less onerous: it has an excellent cost-effectiveness ratio. Who would dare to complain or claim that these doctors and hygienists have acted contrary to the good of the populations they serve?

These achievements which do honor to the medical profession are in sharp contrast to other activities that have been practiced since the beginning of the 20th century in which doctors are involved in actions against human life as practitioners and sometimes also as ideologues.

Unfortunately, the direct involvement of numerous doctors in anti-life campaigns is of such a nature as to weaken profoundly the trust which has been spontaneously given by the public at large to the medical profession for centuries. In effect, it is somewhat the same with medicine as it is with the law. Just as one expects that the latter serve justice, so one also expects that medicine be at the service of health. Yet, at the cost of abusing language, some claim that prescribing contraceptives, sterilization, abortion or euthanasia constitutes medicine at the service of health.

The Church asks, then, that all medical personnel remember their Hippocratic oath and recall the manipulative circumstances into which some of their predecessors have fallen. The honor of the doctor is to serve people weakened by disease, accidents or age. The doctor increases his stature when he refuses to place his art at the service of trends opposed to life.

It is particularly desirable that doctors and biologists pursue their work in such a way as to be able the better to help couples desiring responsible parenthood through honorable means. In this spirit, we must encourage them to pursue research which has been more than promising, regarding the application, simplification, and promotion of natural methods of regulating fertility. One of the greatest services that the medical corps could render to the human community would be to relieve the latter of the weight of anti-life practices and to initiate all couples in this elevated form of liberty, which the natural control of fertility genuinely is.

And then we must appeal to the moral conscience of certain pharmacologists, doctors, biologists and businessmen who, moved by scientific interests or by less worthy forms of temptation, have rushed into research programs involving contraception, sterilization, abortion and euthanasia. It is urgent that they cease research whose objective is to sterilize temporarily or permanently, the poor from whom they often extract consent, or to cause the death of millions of innocents.

It is also urgent that public and private international organizations, especially UNFPA, WHO and IPPF and the big pharmaceutical firms, stop supporting research programs or activities inimical to life.

Finally, it is time for the medical world to reconsider the social dimension of its activity. One can, in effect, sometimes wonder whether, with the support of the media, there isn't too much of a tendency to exaggerate the value and spectacular performance of certain medicines. The prowess and the inventors certainly acquire great prestige and value, but can the same be said of the patients and human life in general? In the determining which research ought to be undertaken and the allocation of budgets, it would clearly be desirable to rectify certain options in order to meet a greater number of requests emanating from the whole of the human community.

ADJUSTING THE AGRO-ALIMENTARY SECTOR

Sensational Progress

Along with biomedical research, research in the agro-alimentary domain has also made sensational progress. Because it is less spectacular, this progress receives less attention from the media. However, it does indeed merit being hailed and encouraged. Nonexploited lands have been cultivated; arid soil has been made fertile; production has been increased; new strains have been produced; and methods of management have been modernized.[14] This progress is not only due to discoveries in agronomy; it is also the result of contributions from chemistry and veterinary medicine, from improvements in the food industry and in the distribution and care of the land.

It is, nevertheless, well known that progress in agriculture sometimes comes up against age-old habits. The latter are difficult to change because, one finds, they offer a minimum guarantee for food sufficiency. This proves the need and urgency of encouraging education for the rural masses in order that, while avoiding impoverishment of the soil, they can attain productivity levels that will put their family beyond an obsessive fear of hunger.

However, the modernization of agriculture, especially in poor countries, is a long-term task. Improvement in the conditions of nutrition in the world requires a heavy investment. Is it utopian to suggest in this regard that we allocate to agriculture a portion of the investments applied to medicine for artifical life preservation? Such investments, of course, call for a sustained political determination.

Before envisaging such promising eventualities, some measures to stabilize the distribution of world farm production must be looked into. Surplus production of foodstuffs among some, penury — even famine — among others is one of the most scandalous problems of our times. Given the lack of political determination, this situation, which is avoidable, brings to light what little energy and enthusiasm politicians and businessmen employ to facilitate access to the means of elementary subsistence for all people. It is morally inadmissible that rich countries use their surplus in foodstuffs to control world prices and to check the integration of poor countries into a more equitable international market. Because of these surpluses, as well as to the combined effect of customs and stimulants to exportation, rich countries can manage to prevent poor countries from benefiting from comparative advantages that would improve their economy.

Patents and the Rights of Farmers

Also entirely inadmissible are the repeated attempts made by rich countries, above all by the United States, to dispute farmers' rights. It is well known that native populations in the Third-World possess species of natural plants that have precious properties: resistance to disease, medicinal powers, etc. Presently, some firms established in the developed countries harvest these species free of charge or at a very cheap price. They withdraw the resistant genes and introduce them into other varieties of the same species which, in turn, become resistant. They then patent this new species and offer the delivery to farmers for an elevated price. Farmers are thus despoiled of their rights over the natural species which they cultivate in their own countries. They are deprived of the technical know-how that would permit them to place an added value on the species found among them. They must, then, buy the genetically-manipulated species at a high price from the Northern hemisphere countries. The process in question can obviously be indefinitely extended to vegetable and animal species.

There we observe that the resources of genetic engineering lend themselves to uses totally opposed to their spirit and ends. They can serve to improve quantitatively and qualitatively the agricultural productiveness of the farmers of the Third-World. But they can also be used as a weapon to control populations weakened by low farming output.

Such an international racket that *extends to all natural resources* deserves the anathema thundered by the prophet Isaiah against the Assyrian powers: "Woe to the Assyrian! He has a heart only to destroy and to cut off nations not a few. For he has said: 'By the strength of my own hand I have done it and by my own wisdom I have understood. And I have removed the boundaries of the peoples and pillaged their treasures. My hand has seized like a nest the riches of nations. As one takes the eggs left alone, so I took in all the earth; no one fluttered a wing.'"[15]

An Agriculture Against the Farmer

The habitual situation of farming thus reveals the pressures that rich countries exert on the poor ones in all sectors of economic life. The pressures aim at rapidly modernizing the poor countries' agriculture with an eye — they claim — at integrating them into the great international market. It is thus necessary to do away with traditional methods of farming and adopt superproductive methods. The consequence they are not slow to observe is that an abundant but little qualified source of labor constitutes an obstacle to this modernization. Such labor then must be brought to benefit from strict programs of family planning.

For the rich countries, the proposed modernization presents important advantages. It makes the agriculture of poor countries depend on the technology of rich countries; it makes the marketing of agricultural products of the Third-World depend on the circuits controlled by the wealthy countries; the price-fixing of products eludes the poor countries. Finally, the poor countries are deprived of comparative advantages from which they could benefit were they not subjected to the abusive pressures of the wealthy countries, and if the latter did not further impose on the international so-called free market rules aimed exclusively at protecting their own interests. Briefly, the poor populations expect the policy decision-makers and businessmen to provide them with a better organization of economic life. The market must be for the benefit of all men; it is an aberration to calibrate the beneficiaries in function of the standards of particular conception of the market — excessively liberal as it happens to be.

A MARKET ACCESSIBLE TO ALL

Like all scientific disciplines, economics with its own method explores one sector of reality and activity. Economic science is often put to the service of profit-making, the liceity of which cannot be contested given certain conditions, which are examined in *Centesimus Annus*.[16] It would nonetheless be opportune again to reflect in depth upon the art of managing the house common to all men, namely, the earth. This reflection, to which economists and scholars in different fields can contribute, should deal not only with the question of surplus, but also with debt, the world monetary problems, and the integration of the poor into the marketplace.[17]

Toward a Global Economy?

Faced with the increasing globalization of economic life, we must state that it is normal for some to wonder and worry about the "new world economic order." We will limit ourselves here to a consideration of its central aspect.

For some time already, we have been witnesses to the spread of *multinational companies*. Many of these companies have such great power that they exercise a determining influence on the economy of certain nations. It happens that, because of them, governments lose a large part of their freedom of action. There exists the risk, then, that, while invoking freedom of international commerce, certain enterprises in fact impose rules of commerce that take too little account of the common good or of those enterprises of lesser scope.

We must, then, hope for a redoubled effort to improve international trade. We cannot ignore the fact that presently there exists a real peril of domination by certain countries under the guise of obeying the imperatives of free trade. Some economically strong nations invoke free market principles to impose self-serving rules on international commerce. The "deregulation" advocated by the neoliberals does not necessarily benefit the whole world!

We must, then, avoid condoning a situation that permits some nations to control, not only the agricultural sector — including fishing — and international commerce in general, but also investments, the media, service industries, and, ultimately intellectual property.

In this vast area what is said in the encyclical *Laborem exercens* regarding the indirect employer is applicable.[18] It is up to international organizations to intervene as indirect employers to determine the norms that will aid nations to establish relationships among themselves that are more just. It is necessary for these organizations to be authorized to exercise impartially this role on which depends greater justice in international economic relations. Is it too optimistic to hope that this role will be played especially by the World Trade Organization?

If an international consultation in economic matters is called for, it cannot achieve success without respecting the principle of subsidarity. The deserving initiatives of economically weak nations, in particular the fragile enterprises of these countries, must not be sacrificed on the altar of an international market having effectiveness as the principal, if not the sole rule. To the extent to which one makes effectiveness the supreme criterion governing economic life and even political life, one determines a principle of exclusion that affords a "legitimation" and a "justification" for attacks on human life. Due proportion observed, what is said in *Centesimus Annus* is applicable to the relations among nations: "Even prior to the logic of a fair exchange of goods and the forms of justice appropriate to it, *there is something due to man because he is man*, by reason of his lofty dignity."[19]

Indebtedness

For analogous moral reasons competent authorities should also take up the problem of indebtedness.[20] In effect, we find ourselves at present in a paradoxical situation: indebtedness affects the wealthy countries as well as the poor ones. Nonetheless, faced with this indebtedness, rich and poor find themselves in very different situations. The wealthy benefit from strong currencies and monetary specie that they supply at their pleasure, and which are the principal means of international transactions. Very different is the situation of the poor countries, whose economies are weak and little diversified, and whose currencies are frail and constantly devalued.

Unlike the poor countries, the wealthy countries don't have to submit to the pressure of insistent creditors: they control the supply of their own money. Moreover, they use it to consolidate their power. Through the intermediary of international money organisms, e.g., the International Monetary Fund, the wealthy countries offer loans in strong currency to the poor countries. While living beyond their means, the lenders flaunt their charitable aid. But at the same time the loans are often badly used, capitals of poor countries secretly enter strong money in numbered accounts, and the loans' maturity dates are the occasions of many pressures on the politicians and public opinion in the debtor countries. It is also known that the international agencies consent to the loans on condition that the "beneficiary" countries accept programs of demographic control determined by the rich sponsors.

And we know what happens: the politicians accept the pressures and public opinion becomes accustomed to the idea, propagated by the media, that such poor countries are overpopulated and that, as a result, they will never be able to pay back the debt unless they curb their demographic growth by every possible means. Poor countries are thus blamed for the very indebtedness which is used to keep them under control. An indebtedness which, from a human standpoint, they will never see the end of, these new Sisyphus.

It is nevertheless necessary to take into account that the attacks on human life in this context arise from blatant injustices that affect the international monetary system in which the voice of rich countries is predominant.

Once more we are confronted with structures of sin resulting from men's actions which, consequently, men can intervene to amend.

A HUMAN ECOLOGY

If one admits that all material goods have been destined by the Creator for the whole of humanity, we should be delighted with the efforts undertaken to protect the environment in recent decades. According to God's plan, the material world was made for man and not man for the material world. God made man the manager of creation[21] and gave him the indispensable light for the reasonable and responsible exercise of this stewardship. We must, therefore, broadly subscribe to the preoccupations of those who are concerned about an ordered equilibrium in the ecosystem, and we must plead for a "human ecology."[22] However, we observe that, under the influence of certain ideologies, respect for the environment is sometimes invoked to *reduce* man's place in nature. The habitual saying in this regard is well known: "World population is too great and it is the cause of the great environmental problems which have arisen. The remedy is, therefore, clear: we must control the growth of the world population."

In fact, the growth of the population in the poor world is presented as "the" cause of the "degradation" of the environment, while the wealthy countries specously point to this demographic growth with an eye to protecting their own security.[23] Yet it is the rich countries that pollute the most and who should, therefore, make the greater effort in this area. But these countries believe they can be relieved of their responsibility by explaining that they recycle certain materials, that they control or impose a tax on pollution. The field thus cleared, they shift the responsibility for polluting the world onto the population of poor countries. The need to protect our milieu — declared for the moment as the "common patrimony" of humanity — is then invoked for justifying the globalist project of the new world economic order. And one hastens to add that the realization of this project requires that one not compromise on the need to plan the demographic evolution of humanity. Now the attainment of this *globalist* project entails particularly grave consequences. The first is paradoxical: far from attenuating it, the project would consolidate and freeze the cleavage between the rich and poor, the North and the South. The second is that, in the name of "globalist" requirements the just sovereignty of nations would be contested in its essence to the point that, in the end, these nations would be threatened with disappearance.

SHARING KNOWLEDGE

The Advantage of Knowledge

In his *Lives of Illustrious Men*, Plutarch reports a curious reproach that Alexander the Great addressed to his mentor Aristotle.[24] In substance he said: "If what you teach me in private you publish in books that anyone could buy, what advantage will I still have over the others by following your private lessons?" Alexander realized that knowledge was advantageous, that it is power, and that is why he was worried when he saw his teacher offer it to all who would read his works.

Alexander's reaction is not unique in history; we have seen, for example, colonial governments, though passing for "enlightened" people, refuse to install printing presses in their overseas possessions. Among others, Pombal knew that the slaves' ignorance made for the tranquillity of masters.

In ancient societies, in effect, the power in an enterprise was concentrated in the hands of those who had knowledge. It was not for the simple performers of jobs that were essentially piecework. In general, the directors, and especially economic entrepreneurs, took advantage of their knowledge to support social divisions in which there was little place for social mobility.[25]

The general spread of quality elementary education entailed a cumulative process that happily put an end to this frozen situation. We should recall here the pioneering role of certain saints as, for example, St. Angela Merici, St. Joseph Calasanctius, St. John Baptist de La Salle, St. John Bosco, St. Anthony Mary Claret and so many others. The role of numerous religious institutes in this domain cannot be overlooked. Nor can we neglect to acknowledge the foresightedness of public powers in making instruction general, in fact obligatory, and entrusting it to competent and dedicated teachers.

The Faces of Poverty

Among the reasons invoked for "justifying" anti-life practices, poverty is very often mentioned. Now progress in the field of education, in scientific research and technical advances permits us to take in account that the current forms of poverty vary according to the circumstances of time and place.

The heirs of Malthus consider poverty the privation of material goods, food and other things necessary for life. Obviously one cannot challenge this analysis. But it must be completed. For there exists today a still more radical poverty than indigence. It is that in which man finds himself once he is intellectually and morally entirely disarmed before his indigence. The progress of industrialized countries is in large part the fruit of a generous sharing of knowledge, and of that which is its consequence, the exponential increase of this knowledge. Knowledge is a good which, by its very nature, lends itself much more to sharing than do material goods. The great cause of poverty in the world today is not to be sought in an unbridled demographic growth — ultimately a fallacious diagnosis which is contradicted every day by the objective analysis of demographic phenomena. The great cause of poverty is found in the inability of the poor populations to face their problems of survival and daily life. This is, however, an avoidable situation. Some countries such as Korea, Taiwan or even Japan, still regarded as underdeveloped after fifty years, have engaged in systematic efforts in education which bear the fruits we all know of. *No more than hunger is ignorance an inevitability.*

If one holds that the goods of the earth have been put by the Creator at the disposition of all men, we must realize that the goods in question are not only material goods. Intellectual, moral and spiritual goods are also a part of these goods destined for all.

The discussions which have recently taken place in some international forums on world commerce, and the lessons that some believe can be drawn from the Persian Gulf War, however, reveal a lack of will to share these very goods.

Some examples offered by very diverse scientific disciplines lead to the conclusion that certain international organizations or certain wealthy countries are tempted by new forms of avarice to hide their knowledge to the point of hindering access to it on the part of countries desirous of developing.[26] There are even some who take umbrage at developing countries which, by their policy of research and technological progress, try to free themselves from the scientific segregation that afflicts them. How is it possible not to see in this concealment of know-how a new cause of poverty emerging? A new discrimination is in an advanced stage of consolidation: one that separates those who know from those who do not know. This phenomenon is all the more dramatic in that it survives in an era when development is more and more tied to the ability to take part in knowledge and its derived techniques.

Moreover, this concealment of knowledge is often aggravated by a characteristic *abuse of intellectual power*. Some wealthy countries and international organizations in possession of considerable resources claim to have "scientific knowledge" which neither ordinary citizens nor, above all, the poor are able to master. Furthermore, it is too often this knowledge which is referred to in order to impose on these very same poor people policies presented as "scientifically founded."

As a result of this kind of oligopoly of knowledge, wealthy countries are able to make their *northern* vision of the world prevail everywhere, thereby strengthening the opinion of those who regard poor nations and the poor in general as living "a life unworthy to be lived," and who believe that, consequently, there is no reason to impede the propagation of their vision.

THE RISK OF LOVING

The drama of poor countries is precisely that they are more and more subject to external controls. They must accept all that the international organizations and most powerful States dictate. The poor are managed, in their resources and in their very life, according to utilitarian criteria imposed on them from outside. They are exposed, individually and collectively, to an alienation without precedent in history.

However, one cannot place the responsibility for poverty on the poor, much less on unborn infants. Like the proletariat of the nineteenth century, the poor are victims of an "undeserved destitution." That four-fifths of humanity are affected by this situation is a tragedy without precedent in the history of humanity, but it is nonetheless an avoidable tragedy. And what demonstrates the moral dimensions of this tragedy is that it survives at the very moment when a minority of men produce more than they can consume and jealously protect their scientific and technical superiority.

This drama, which affects above all the poor, is just as horrifying for the rich. The poor are victims of a refusal to share what is necessary for them and what for the rich is superfluous. The wealthy have the misfortune of considering happiness as consisting in the jealous possession of material or intellectual goods, whose possession, nonetheless, cannot suffice to procure true happiness. The drama of the rich is that they pretend that they are loved while not taking the risk of making the first step, the risk of loving.

[1] See the encyclicals of John Paul II, *SC* and *CA*.
[2] See Lk 10:35; and *supra*, Chapter VII, *The Good Samaritan*.
[3] See *CA* 30-43, 58.
[4] *Ibid*. 38

[5] *Ibid.* 28.

[6] See *supra*, Chapter III, *Procedural Justice*.

[7] See *infra*, Chapter XI, **GUIDELINES FOR A FAMILY POLICY**.

[8] See *TTL*, 37-61, and *supra*, Chapters III and IV.

[9] *Ibid.* 65-76.

[10] See *BPCV* qu. 59-78.

[11] *TTL*, 175 f., 203 f.

[12] See *BPCV* qu. 44.

[13] See *supra*, Chapter V. Esp. **THE RELATIVIZATION OF RIGHTS**.

[14] The progress and perspectives that are opening, according to diverse hypotheses, in the developing countries have been brought to light in a report published in 1984 by FAO of the U.N. See G. M. Higgins et al (ed.), *Capacité potentielle de charge démographiques des terres du monde en développement. Rapport technique du Projet Int/75/P13. "Les ressources en terre des populations de demain"* (Rome: FAO, 1984)

[15] See Is 10: 5-17.

[16] *CA* 35.

[17] The Pontifical Council for Justice and Peace already looked into these problems, and its work could stimulate further research.

[18] See n.17 of this encyclical.

[19] *CA* 34.

[20] See *TTL*, 112-118.

[21] See Gn 1:28.

[22] *CA* 38. On this question see the precious collection: Giovanni Paolo II, *La visione cristiana dell'ambiente. Testi del Magistero Pontificio scelti a cura di Padre Bernardo J. Przewozny* (Pisa: Giardini, 1991).

[23] Such is the central theme of the document NSSM-200/1974, sometimes called "The Kissinger Report" entitled *Implication of Worldwide Population Growth for U.S. Security and Overseas Interests*. See on this subject *TTL*, 57-58; *BPCV* qu.84, 100-102.

[24] See Plutarch, *Vie d'Alexandre le Grand* in *Les Vies des hommes illustres* t. 2, La Pleiade (Paris: Gallimard, 1968) 330.

[25] This theme was developed by Alvin Toffler in *Les Nouveaux Pouvoirs* (Paris: Fayard, 1991). See also *TTL*, 185-186.

[26] See, for example, what was said about protectionism effected through patents, *supra*, Chapter IX, *The Rights of Farmers and Patents*.

CHAPTER X

THE NEW DEMOGRAPHIC ORDER

CONTRASTED SITUATIONS

The world population presents, on the one hand, some general characteristics, but, on the other, great regional diversity.

In a general way, one can observe since 1945 a constant growth in population, a remarkable decline in infant and maternal mortality and an increased life expectancy. The principal cause of the growth in world population is found in the low mortality rate: men live longer and are, therefore, always more numerous while occupying the earth. With a certain lag in time, couples adapt their fertility to these conditions of mortality, and there results a lowering of the birth rate. During this time, called demographic transition, the population grows before attaining a new equilibrium (see Illustration 7).

This situation is the consequence of scientific progress and a better management of public affairs. One can also observe a general tendency toward the growth of urban populations. Without doubt, urbanization is older and more notable in wealthy countries. But, actually, the tendency toward urban concentration is higher in developing countries.

In developing countries one notices in particular that the growth of population results from two factors: first of all, the fall in the mortality rate and also a higher birth rate than in wealthy countries; the latter rate is, however, generally declining. Thus, according to the Brazilian Institute of Geography and Statistics (IBGE), the synthetic index of fertility, that is — simply put— the number of babies per woman of child-bearing age, in 1994 was 2.35; in the metropolitan area of São Paulo it was in the order of 1.9. Now in wealthy countries 2.1 babies per woman are needed to replace the population. One has good reason, then, to estimate that from now on Brazil cannot replenish its population as it grows old. That is but one example (cf. Illustration 8). The same holds true for Mexico where the synthetic index is around the level of 2.5.

Illustration 7

Schema of Demographic Transition

Population, with its births and deaths, is represented as ordinate; duration is represented as abscissa.

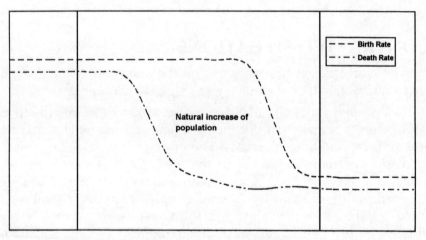

<-Duration of demographic transition->

Source: Schooyans, *Pour comprendre les évolutions démographiques* (Paris: University of Paris-Sorbonne, 1995) p.39.

Again in the Third-World countries, one sees that the median age is clearly lower than in rich countries, and the age for marriage is delayed while the practice of polygamy shrinks.[1]

One also observes heavy internal migration: the poor population flees the countryside to seek employment in the cities and their industrial or administrative centers. This urban concentration sometimes gives rise to the emergence of the megapolises: São Paulo, Mexico City, Bombay, and Cairo. Whatever the cause, the tendency toward urban concentration is universal (See Illustrations 9 and 10). In developing countries these concentrations produce extremely complex problems that affect infrastructure, housing, provisioning, schooling, employment, health, transportation, delinquency, etc.

Very clearly different is the situation in wealthy countries. In all the industrialized Western countries, the synthetic index of fertility rates is below the level of population replacement, which is 2.1 babies per woman of child-bearing age (see Illustration 8).

This level is barely reached in Ireland for instance. The combination of this indicator with, on the other hand, a long life expectancy explains the aging of the population in developed countries.

The difficulties produced by this situation are distinctly perceptible and they come up, for example, in discussions about health insurance, unemployment compensation and, above all, social security at retirement. The difficulty will soon be felt in trying to regenerate an active population.

But the industrialized countries are aware of still further difficulties whose repercussions fall very heavily on demography. One of the most impressive is the increase in divorce. One also sees an increase in juvenile cohabitation, a decrease in the proportion of marriage per inhabitant and an increase of one-parent households.[2] And to that we must add the practice, widespread in some milieux, of homosexuality.

Illustration 8

Synthetic Index of Fertility

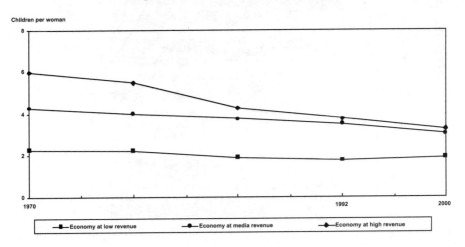

Source: World Bank, *World Development Report 1994*, Oxford University Press, p. 160

Illustration 9

The 15 Largest Urban Concentrations in 1994

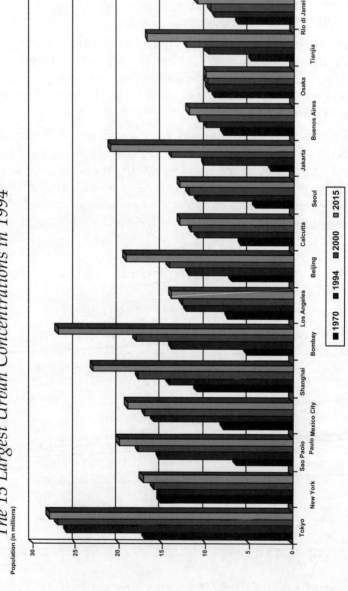

Source: *World Urbanization Prospects. The 1994 Revision* (New York: U.N., 1994) p.5.

Illustration 10

Percentage of the Population Living in Urban Concentrations

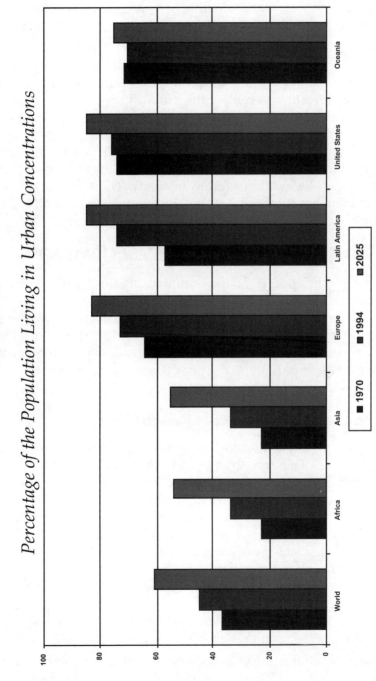

Source: *World Urbanization Prospect. The 1994 Report* (New York: U.N., 1995) p.21.

From this brief listing it follows that demographic phenomena present a great diversity depending upon whether one considers them in the North or South. Now it is precisely by reason of these profound differences, that difficulties arise and risk becoming accentuated in the near future.

In effect, the contrast is striking between the proportion of the young between 1 and 14 years which is less than 20% in developed countries and more than 40% in developing countries. One can also observe a significant lessening of the proportion of the population of developed countries, especially Western Europe, in relation to the entire world population. One also expects a shifting of population from South to North as well as from East to West. In fact, these international migrations have already started, and the difficulties they cause, already perceptible, will not fail to intensify. These migrations will be one of the great challenges of the 21at century, and the difficulties they bring are linked to differences of culture, religion and race.

THE INHUMAN PRICE OF DEVELOPMENT

In the public reports of international organizations concerned with demography, one theme regularly recurs: that of the "excess" of world population. This "excess," we are told, is above all due to the poor countries, "which do not control their fertility." We are told that the interest and security of human society demands that demographic growth, especially in the poor countries, be curbed by every available effective means.

Two Trends: Malthusian and Hedonist

We have already analyzed the ideological bases that inspire demographic fear.[3] The growth of world population would be "exponential" and would constitute a menace for the entirety of human society. Using language that is strongly emotionally charged, they even speak of the "demographic bomb" or of "demographic explosion." The wealthy countries, which are the principal producers of what we have called the "ideology of demographic security," believe that demographic growth in countries of the Third-World presently represents a major threat to their security and to world peace. They point the finger especially at Africa and circulate the names of countries that need — they assure us — to "benefit" from emergency aid for curbing their population growth.

In wealthy countries certain ideologues of demographic control even assert that it is indispensable to liberalize, in these same wealthy countries, all the effective means of population control specifically because the well-known mimicking effects will enable these practices to be introduced and accepted in poor countries.[4] To be credible, rich countries "must give the example" to countries which have — we are assured — the urgent need to curb their population. Being consistent, some of these ideologues go still further by recommending the institution of generalized permits to procreate.[5] If they seem to ignore the fact that this kind of permit had already been set up by the Nazi regime, some do not hesitate, on the other hand, to praise China, which uses it and whose example, according to them, should be followed.[6]

In these ideological "justifications", two distinct trends are intermingled, and it is easy to untangle the threads. The trend used by these ideologues for wealthy milieux — in developed countries as in undeveloped ones — is of a *hedonist* inspiration; it refers to the right to individual pleasure. On the other, the trend used for the poor milieux is one that is typically Malthusian: "overpopulation" is presented as the great obstacle that is opposed to development and security. In its most simplistic formulation, but not less widespread, this last trend maintains that if there were fewer births in the poor counties, the standard of life would soon be better.

This second trend is very broadly disseminated by organizations that consider that the establishment of a new world order supposes the most efficacious mastery possible of the transmission of life. This trend is even interiorized by the governments of poor countries which take it upon themselves to mutilate their populations for the profit of the rich of these same countries and to the benefit of the dominant nations.

The Example of Mexico

Let us take the example of Mexico.[7] In this country in 1982, one counted an effective 1,358,400 women who were sterilized. At thirty years of age or more, the proportion of women living in a sterilized union was 18.7%.[8] The involvement of the public powers in these campaigns of family planning, and especially in female sterilization, is frequently demonstrated in the doctoral thesis of an eminent Mexican demographer.[9]

The involvement of public powers comes out very clearly in Illustration 11, and it needs no commentary.

Similar observations could be made regarding Brazil and a number of other developing countries.[10] Hence, China doesn't have a monopoly on vigorous anti-life policies.

Curb the "New Enemy"

The insistence on the presentation of the poor as a contributing in world disorder, the implacable determination of the fight against demographic growth, and the violent means consistently used — all point to wealthy and influential circles who believe they see in the poor populations of the South a potential enemy which they should curb. After the fall of the communist system, attention was then turned to the mass of poor as the new enemy to confront.[11] Some of

Illustration 11
Mexico: Number of Those Accepting Family Planning Services by Method Year

Year	Sterilization		
	Men	Women	Total
IMSS*			
1984	5,400	160,200	165,600
1985	4,800	161,200	165,800
1986	5,000	166,000	171,000
1987	–	–	168,500
1988	–	–	158,100
1989	–	–	153,800
1990	10,000	168,400	178,400
1991	13,000	172,000	185,000
1992	13,500	219,400	232,900
MEXFAM**			
1984	0	600	600
1985	0	3,500	3,500
1986	300	12,500	12,700
MDS*			
1984	–	–	23,300
1985	–	–	25,000
1990	700	34,000	34,700
1991	700	36,300	37,000
1992	700	40,100	40,800

*IMSS: Instituto Mexicano de Seguro Social
**MEXFAM: Fundación Mexicana para la Planeación Familiar
***MDS: Ministerio de la Salud
(-) means data unknown.

Source: John A. Ross et al., *Family Planning and Child Survival Programs as Assessed in 1991* (New York, 1992), p. 92.

the measures used to curb the communist menace were quickly redirected to control the threat coming from the "South."

Many convergent indications lead to believing that the bloc of wealthy countries, themselves tormented by internal tensions, had to find their cohesion again by facing what the bloc perceived as the new menace: the poor populations. Under pressure from the wealthy bloc, some old international organizations broadened their competence in order to exercise a tighter control on natural resources, food production, international commerce, — particularly between North and South, — and the sharing of knowledge and technology. New institutions arise, private or public, that interfere in the internal affairs of poor countries. The condition of indebtedness of the latter is often exploited to demand the application of measures that national governments hardly have time to endorse, so great are the pressures to which they are exposed.

Finally, organized with great reinforcement from media orchestration, numerous international conferences are convoked without always clearly demonstrating the mandate which brings them together or with what authority they draw their conclusions or recommendations. This doesn't prevent these conclusions and recommendations from regularly being presented as "directives" that States would do well to follow, since, they say, "it concerns the good of all human society."

In this decade alone, many big international conferences have been organized, and still more are planned. The reports already published by the organizations that prepare them leave no doubt about their objectives and the decisions which are to be put into effect. The only unknown factor is the origin for the funding of these programs.

What appears behind these initiatives is that wealthy nations more and more openly consider the poor truly incapable of taking care of their own destiny in a responsible fashion. They insist that this inability is demonstrated above all in their demographic conduct.

Faced with this "alarming" situation, the wealthy countries feel they must redefine their role as international leaders. They must suggest, and eventually impose, measures of every appropriate kind to guarantee international security. In order to build the new international economic order, we must first of all insure the new world demographic order. Such, in the eyes of rich nations, are the best guarantees of peace and development for the world at large.

By What Right?

It is here that serious questions must be asked. By what right, and in virtue of what mandate, are the large international institutions investing so many resources in programs of contraception, sterilization and abortion? By what right do these institutions want to lead poor countries to adopt directives whose acceptance and implementation will signal the end of their sovereignty? By what right do certain institutions and nations want to have the U.N. itself endorse world programs to curb population? Unfortunately, we are forced to admit that here we have characteristic abuses of power. Neither in the letter or spirit of the San Francisco Charter is it provided that the U.N. or its agencies should busy themselves with the curbing of population. And the Universal Declaration on the Rights of Man in 1948 can in no way be invoked in this sense.

Since there already exist parallel powers that exercise a de facto rule over international commerce, forestalling the development of poor countries, we are astonished to see established, also de facto, supranational authorities arrogating to themselves powers that neither member nations or individuals ought to give up. The U.N. and the large international institutions resulting from World War II were created precisely for the purpose of safeguarding peace, promoting the rights of man, and stimulating the development of all peoples. Instead of that, we observe that now these institutions, whose actions are enlarged by a multitude of governmental organizations, fuel a war of the North against the South, defy the rights of man to life and physical integrity, and maintain a strong hold over the development of poor peoples.

We must, then urgently return to the spirit that inspired those who, after the Second World War, wanted to construct peace on the basis of justice and build a world community with respect for the rights of man and national communities. Without doubt, it is due in great part to the wisdom of these builders of peace that the cold war did not give way — on the military level at least — to a worldwide explosion which would have amounted to a slaughter.

Nonetheless, the lessons of 1945 and 1948 always remain valid. No less than before, we cannot now hope to ensure peace where the most elementary right of man, namely, the right to life, is threatened by the very ones whose primary mission is to protect it. For having ignored such an elementary truth, the "peace" which we know today is but window-dressing, since the price paid for it every year is the life of many millions of innocents deprived of all protection as well as the physical and psychological integrity of innumerable defenseless being.

Hence, institutions as well as men must learn to get a hold of themselves and convert. We must call upon all national and international institutions, public and private, to renounce before God and men the anti-life practices they advocate. Thus liberated, they will be able to muster their energies with the sole objective that is truly worthy of them: the promotion in men of complete respect for their dignity.

FOR AN "ELITISM" OF SERVICE

Interdependence: An Opportunity and a Risk

The encyclicals *On Social Concerns* (nn.9, 22, 26, 36-39) and *Centesimus Annus* (nn.27, f., 51, f., 58) have greeted the ever-tightening interdependence of men and human societies. The tendency toward socialization observed in *Mater et Magistra* by John XXIII[12] is confirmed to such a point that it has been extended to the entirety of humanity. For the first time in history men and societies are discovering how much this interdependence is an opportunity to be seized.

Without doubt. It is first of all in the family that men get the experience of this interdependence: it is in this contact, as well as in the contact with other loved persons, that men forge their personality and contribute to the formation of others' personalities. With due proportion, the same holds true for groups and among groups, for nations and among nations. It can also hold true on the world level if all men and all communities decide to respect each others' differences, exchange their richness and work together toward building a society in which all find the best conditions for happiness. For Christians, this interdependence is a sign of the times, an opportunity not to be lost. But in order to seize this chance, it is indispensable that there be, on the part of all men and all communities, an unshakable will to respect each person in his originality and to love each other.

For, if it is an opportunity, interdependence is also a risk. If, instead of resolutely opting for respect and love, people opt for suspicion and rivalry, the differences will continue to be accentuated and the opposition will be exacerbated.

Unfortunately, this is what can happen if the present dynamic is continued. In effect, the poor perceive more and more clearly that the possibilities of their developing are blocked by the consequences of the conduct of the wealthy. And the rich cultivate the sentiment that, by their numbers, the poor are going to threaten their comfort. Interdependence in this case is perceived as entirely negative. We find ourselves back at the direct origin of the alarmist campaigns regarding poor populations, whose "explosion" should be halted by all means.

This pessimistic conception of interdependence causes profound worry among Christians who cannot espouse such an option. From the Christian viewpoint, it is distressing to see that this trend spreads evil between North and South, and there could never be a question of resigning oneself to a dual world, a humanity evolving at two speeds.

Faced with such a gigantic challenge, the Church must first of all confess her poverty. Without yielding to any masochism in which certain people would like to involve her, she must confess the errors and omissions of certain of her members — without complacency — and above all draw from them teaching relevant to the present hour. But this teaching the Church intends to draw from the Gospel as well as the exemplary involvement of so many Christians who from the very beginning have fought and continue to fight so that the integrity and dignity of every man will be better recognized and protected.

For the Church, the present demographic phenomena must be approached in the light of the most elementary demands of human and evangelical morality.[13] It is the duty of the Church and Christians to point out the impasses, to set markers, and to trace the paths. All this is part of her mission. The contribution Christians offer has its foundation in an anthropology that places value, here below, on the body and soul, the person and the community.

The Cost of a Child

Certain questions also crucial for the future of humanity must be urgently treated with calm. Furthermore, alarmist and dramatic language must be regarded as harmful and suspect. It is imperative that we give more consideration to certain pertinent facts that are all too little emphasized in the discussions of demographic questions.

The first thing to do, and this is capital, is to make a reflection full of tenderness on the popular adage that "every baby brings a loaf of bread." Note first of all that it was already the grandmothers who said this long before they had at their disposal the resources to which one has access today. The infant is not a burden. It is itself first of all a gift, the most beautiful gift possible from a woman to her husband, and from him to his spouse, from the family to society. The child is always a promise of happiness, an investment of tenderness, who is called to bear fruit.

This investment of tenderness is not only gratifying to the parents; it is also a gift for society. The infant is good for the parents as well as for society. Without doubt, as we have already explained, at its birth it produces nothing; it brings in no revenue. But it is a powerful stimulant for its parents. They desire to provide it with a good environment, a careful education, clothing, vacations, etc. The infant also arouses the public powers to improve infrastructures, educational resources, and to respond to new demands. In this way, the child, already stimulating for the family, is also a stimulant for economic, social and political life.

Hence, it is aberrant to pose as a simplistic principle that a sterilization or an abortion is "economically preferable" to a birth. It is also aberrant to give preferential aid to families with less than two children and to penalize families with more.

Development and Demographic Density

No serious study has ever produced the evidence for a correlation between the number of inhabitants of a country and its (under) development. This is shown in Illustration 12.

The lack or excess of population is always expressed in terms of lack or excess of goods necessary for the satisfaction of basic needs. There are countries in which the demographic density is less than 20 inhabitants per square kilometer and in which the people do not succeed in feeding themselves properly, or caring well for their children, housing them, or educating them, etc. Then there are countries whose demographic density is above 300 inhabitants per square kilometer and where the people succeed in eating well, caring well for their children, etc. Mozambique, with 21 inhabitants per square kilometer, is a poor country.

Holland, with 458 people per square kilometer, is a rich country. On the other hand, India, with 319 people per square kilometer, is a poor country; and Australia which has 2, is a rich country.[14] Demographic density is not a critical variable that would permit an estimate about development. their alimentary, health, and educational problems in a satisfactory way. There are means for analyzing the reasons and applying a remedy. This is suggested and confirmed by the example of two rich countries, Holland and Australia. In these two the relationship between population density and ability of the people to solve their problems has not always been what it is today. This relationship had effectively evolved: it is not immutable. In brief, there is no sense in speaking of overpopulation in the absolute.

Illustration 12

Demographic Density and Basic Necessary Products per Inhabitant

Country	Density to Square Kilometer	BNP per Inhabitant
Argentina	13	8,060
Australia	2	17,980
Bangladesh	920	230
Belgium	334	22,920
Bolivia	7	770
Brazil	19	3,370
Ethiopia	59	130
France	106	23,470
Germany	234	25,580
Hong Kong	6,419	21,650
India	319	310
Indonesia	110	880
Israel	286	14,410
Italy	195	19,270
Ivory Coast	46	510
Japan	334	34,630
Mexico	50	4,010
Mozambique	21	80
Netherlands	458	21,970
Nicaragua	39	330
Nigeria	114	280
Russia	8	330
Singapore	4,992	23,360
South Korea	458	8,220
Switzerland	178	36,410
Thailand	119	2,210
United States	29	25,860
Venezuela	25	2,760

Source: *World Population Data Sheet 1996*, Washington: Population Reference Bureau.

Supporting Capacity: Relative

For the same reasons, there is scarcely any sense in speaking, in absolute terms, of the "supporting capacity" of the earth. This is neither static or immutable. The capacity of the earth to provide for a given number of men is *relative* to the know-how, itself variable, of the men who people the earth.[15] Besides, this relativity is attested to by the enormous differences that appear in the estimates made in this matter.

In summary, history shows that in rich countries poor people have stopped being impecunious consumers and underproducers. They have been integrated into production systems that are very diversified. This evolution has nothing miraculous about it, nor is it a stroke of luck. It is the result of three converging factors: widespread education, better organization of economic life, and political management that is more concerned with justice and is more effective.

From Privileges to Service

Whence come new data to take into further account. From the moment one observes that the demographic growth does not pose insoluble "problems," provided there is the will to solve them, we have to admit that this growth is advantageous.

This is what history confirms, particularly contemporary history. During this century prodigious scientific discoveries, technological progress, and economic growth have all directly benefitted from a healthy demographic situation combined with effective teaching systems. In fact, the decision to universalize primary education broke the vicious circle of pauperism; it permitted the discovery of the most gifted children in every social stratum. This resulted in a social mobility which had previously been unthinkable. From this situation emerged an array of learned people of the highest level from every discipline, whose achievements have revolutionized the standard of living. But, to construct this pyramid, it was obviously necessary to form a base as broad as possible so that each person, to the best of his intellectual and moral abilities, could make his personal contribution to the common good.

Moreover, to consider — as one does in reactionary circles — that development is measured on the basis of possession of material goods, we must recognize that a developed society is characterized above all by the cross-fertilization of complex information, of which men, in the final analysis, are the only carriers.[16] This cross-fertilization occurs along two axes: diachronic and synchronic. On the one hand, we need a large population to collect and reactivate the human religious patrimony transmitted by past generations. On the other, we also need a large population so that the efforts and original contributions of each will benefit from the efforts and contributions of the greatest number and be profitable to the greatest number.

We should also note in this regard that the transmission of information in human apprenticeship is not ever a purely passive process. Each individual who learns becomes, by definition, capable of enriching the knowledge he receives. This part of personal creativity in the process of learning becomes even greater by the growing number of people having access to the computer. As shown by the example of so many countries and so many urban concentrations, yesterday and today, a large population which are offered quality educational resources, is obviously favorable to the communication and exchange of knowledge. An elevated demographic density certainly does not suffice of itself to guarantee progress in knowledge, but it creates the conditions that are favorable to it. It stimulates exchange and this, in turn, renders research fertile.

Breaking the vicious circle of poverty has been the result of a moral motivation along with an effective political will. Moved by the same motivation and will, we can break the vicious circle of ignorance in which poor populations have been confined and stuck. Making human life respected implies that men and societies be equipped to resolve the vital problems they face.

From that results the urgency of reconsidering the allocation of the resources available to big international organizations and the wealthy nations of the world. In his encyclical *Rerum Novarum*, Pope Leo XIII justly denounced the concentration of wealth in the hands of a few industrialized nations of the epoch.[17] This denunciation must be reprised and broadened today: it is not admissible that a few nations, taking advantage of or even abusing international organizations, control and accumulate the greater part of the wealth of possessions and knowledge.

Rather than allocate enormous human and financial means to morally inadmissible programs of birth control, we should encourage every private and public initiative aimed at basic education in a vision that is in accord with human dignity. It is inadmissible that, as so often happens today, one more easily finances, through subsidies and grants research aimed at demographic planning instead of research bearing on education, hygiene, agronomy, and management, etc.

It is inadmissible that institutions like the population division of the U.N.,[18] the World Bank, the U.N. Fund for Population, and the U.N. Program for Development present as a factor in underdevelopment the fact that a given percentage of the poor population doesn't have access to programs of demographic control which they propagate. It is also entirely deceitful and inadmissible to brandish the myth about the providing capacity of the earth to deplore the "lack of resources," when all the while it is precisely well-trained men who transform, for example, sand into electronic equipment or optic fibers, or the sea into fertile land.

In sum, Christians are urged to apply the great principles that inspire the social teaching of the Church to problems of population. This *rejects all elitism of privilege and proposes an elitism of service*. She desires a more fruitful development of each man's talents in view of the greater service to be rendered to the community.

BACKWARD FLOW AND EXCLUSION

To understand the demographic growth of developing countries, we must take into account two forces that exercise opposite influences. On the one hand, this growth results from the beneficial effect on populations that the progress of preventive and curative medicine has had. On the other hand, however, the educational effort that should accompany health efforts is dramatically insufficient. Just as one has worked effectively on the health variable, one can also work effectively on the educational variable. It is, therefore, not population growth as such which is the cause of poverty. *It is the distortion provoked by an unsound and incoherent program* which, after having fortunately prevented the sickness or death of millions of human beings, unfortunately does not insure that those who have been saved will have the educational equipment permitting them to solve their own problems. *It is, therefore, totally absurd to divert the resources which would find their proper use in education to anti-life practices.*

Thus the deplorable plunder of developing countries appears in clearer light. One not only hides key knowledge from them, but one even curbs the spread of basic elementary and professional teaching. Fruit of new forms of avarice, ignorance is one of the major forms of poverty in our day. With new avarice comes new poverty.

It would be helpful, then, to examine once again the populations of poor countries by resituating them in their proper context. Togo in 1995, for example, comprised some 54,000 square kilometers and had but 4.4 million inhabitants. How can anyone seriously pretend that the more urgent problem there was curbing the population?

What is necessary is to aid this country and all poor countries to develop themselves as they live with their populations. Here is where international solidarity must intervene.

Induced by a bookish fidelity to Malthus, one even risks yielding to astonishing fallacious arguments. Even today they repeat the controverted "prophecies" of the famous pastor, and continue to foretell famines and other cataclysms *if* the demographic growth of the poor population is not curbed.

Nonetheless, one can observe that the cult of the argument from authority entails a distorting disregard of the concrete situation. Once an inexact or incomplete diagnosis is given, the prescribed remedy is inappropriate and even harmful. Let us take once again the example of Africa. There is where we find some of the poorest countries of the world. The recent famines there have hardly been as extensive as those of other times, but those that have and — alas — continue to cause the most devastation are all the result of local conflicts, wars or political failure. Think of the Sudan, of Ethiopia, or Liberia — the same in Asia, of Bangladesh, etc. These famines, then, in principle are avoidable. In no case can they be invoked in support of the catastrophic theses of Malthus and other merchants of fear.

Here we see with urgent clarity the need to equip international society with institutions that, while respecting the sovereignty of States, would be able, in the higher interest of populations, to prevent these conflicts and, if they arise, promptly put an end to them.

Finally, it is not admissible that wealthy countries or international institutions be ready to aid poor countries to develop *on condition* that the development be achieved in wrongful dependence. How could this possibly succeed, as development precisely implies the affirmation of independence?[19]

Demographic Winter

Despite appearances, the demographic situation of developed countries is much more worrisome than that of poor countries.[20] These countries are victims of legislation that, in the absence of love, is also anti-life. Some even think that in these wealthy countries the "demographic winter"[21] had already begun: below a certain synthetic index of fertility, the resurgence of demographic growth becomes very problematic, if not impossible. Of course, demographic phenomena stretch out over the long term; they possess a great inertia. Looked at over a short or medium run, anti-life practices, like abortion or sterilization, give the impression of contributing to the comfort of couples and to general well-being. But in the long run we can foresee that these measures will produce disastrous effects. And the latter will be all the more aggravated by a decline in the marriage rate and an increase in the rate of divorce.[22] It is important, then, to become better aware of the misfortunes that the refusal of life is in the process of sowing in the rich countries.

Among the wealthy but declining and aging populations the refusal of life is going to exacerbate sentiments of hostility toward the poor, developing populations. It will also provoke the young in wealthy nations to a feeling of revolt against the numerous old people whom the young will be reluctant to support. This situation will be all the more serious in that, in wealthy countries, the refusal of life shows a refusal to share. Grave tensions without precedent will result, and these will be fueled still more by migrations which will henceforth be difficult to control.

Concentrating on concern for their security, the rich will start adopting defensive behavior that will be incompatible with liberty and happiness.[23] They will be slaves to their passion to possess. According to one Hegelian analysis that is well known, as they get old and decline the rich will become more and more dependent of the mass of the poor whom they will obstinately desire to continue to control and master. The Hegelian dialectic of master and slave is then going to receive a new metamorphosis!

We are already beginning to take into account how the anti-life attitude that threatens rich societies leads to impasses. Gradually and progressively, even if it is in the name of a kind of "liberalism," one is led to call into question what has been acquired through social legislation. However, a new phenomenon, still more worrisome, is beginning to manifest itself. Opulent societies that could and should help poor countries to curb poverty, are witnessing a return of this very poverty back into the rich world! If the rich countries endeavor to export their anti-life techniques to the poor countries, these latter wind up by not being able to acclimatize the effective methods of development. Those excluded masses among the poor countries will begin to rise up against the opulent societies, with further exacerbation being caused by the surge of a poverty in the North analogous to that observed in the South. In the end, the credibility of the Western development model risks being compromised everywhere.

To these multiple repercussions will be added all the scars resulting — on the physical level — from the banalization of contraception, sterilization, abortion and euthanasia, and — on the level of the heart — the destruction of the family.

IMPOSSIBILITY OF SILENCE ON THE PART OF THE CHURCH

Superfluity and Necessity

How can anyone expect the Church to assent to or remain silent before such campaigns which are openly hostile to human life? The Church cannot but reject the whole panoply of anti-life practices, first and simply because they are opposed to life, and then because they lead to situations which are already perceptively disastrous. Concern for the common good, cornerstone of all social morality, must be the preoccupation, not only of responsible politicians, but also of all individuals. For the Church, there is no such thing as purely private moral behavior. All personal and familial conduct has an inherently social dimension.[24] The unity of the human community is such that each person can either consolidate it or contribute toward ruining it.

Those who accuse the Church of being responsible for the "demographic explosion" in the world give in to a suspect simplism that fails to take into account the complex situations, the mechanisms of demographic evolution, and all the requirements of human and evangelical morality.

Christian morality is a morality of respect for human life in all its dimensions. To have forgotten this capital precision, some non-Christians and even some Christians have too often reduced the morality of respect for life to sexual morality. In reality, morality involves first of all the reaffirmation of the common good's precedence over private good. As legitimate as it may be, the right to private possession, including on the level of nations or federations of nations, is subordinate to the just demands of the good of the entire human community. Just as it was necessary to denounce, the particularism of classes at the time of *Rerum Novarum*, today we must denounce the particularism of certain nations. Even considered on the level of nations, private property has a social function: it must be managed in a way that takes the entire human community into account.

As legitimate as it may be, private possession on the part of nations cannot be invoked to defeat the universal destination of goods, whether material, intellectual, cultural or spiritual.

Also as legitimate as it may be, this right of private possession cannot cause us to forget that, in her constant social teaching, the

Church has reminded us that we must not only give of our excess goods, but even give from our necessary goods, like the widow in the Gospel.[25]

Those who find the sexual and familial morality of the Church too demanding have not perhaps noticed that social morality is no less so, and, on the whole, that it is not easy. To be seen for what it is, that is, a morality of shared human life and happiness, this morality must be considered in all its richness: personal, familial, social, and international. It is vain to wish to honor the social requirements of the Gospel if one is not at the same time concerned to honor the requirements of life and the family. And reciprocally, the requirements of evangelical morality concerning life and the family cannot be separated from the demands of the Christian involvement in society.

Demographic Police?

In order to save the "new world order" project, it must be considered as a project for happiness, the realization of which all men must be invited to share in, for it is in God's design that authentic happiness begins here on earth. Whatever threatens the poor in the name of fatalism, and whatever infantilizes or demoralizes them — must be denounced and corrected. There is no immanent order in the world to which men must resign themselves in order to be happy. And a liberty that would consent to determinism would be, in reality, a consent to alienation and the "voluntary servitude" denounced by La Boétie.[26] For human liberty is above all freedom to responsibly develop the future in concert with others. It involves first the ability to give assent to the truth about man, and to the values of justice and love that together men want to concretize.

It is, therefore, urgent that we employ all the richness of the principle of subsidiarity, namely, that the affluent nations, inspired by the example of the Good Samaritan, slow down or rather suspend their indifferent march in order to care for the poorest! If no one approaches them to give a hand and help them lift themselves up, how will they acquire a full awareness of their dignity as men and sons of God? And like a mother who, taking her children for a walk, adapts her steps to the pace of her smallest one, the rich must find the means of adapting their pace to that of the poor; without that the poor will be definitively excluded. In the human community there can be no place for first and second class, still less a place for men, subhuman and nonhuman!

In short, the Church says it is a scandal without precedent to abuse the innocence of the poor by offering them anti-life practices, as "aid" under the auspices of *a new international terrorism, the contraceptive terrorism*. No one in the world, no lobby, no nation, no international organization, no person has the right to establish what strongly resembles a demographic police.

In summary, the times we are living are favorable to a fundamental redetermination of solidarity, not only between North and South, but also among the countries of the North. For, if the latter erect themselves into a purely utilitarian common front against the South, they will quickly come to a division among themselves, whereas by reviving their fund of generosity they could gather together all the Samaritans who forget self as they engage in a victorious combat against misery and the injustices that are the principal cause of it.

---

[1] The *median age* is the middle between two parts of the population equally divided: half younger, half older. In developing countries the median age is around twenty years old; in wealthy countries it is around thirty-five. On these different notions see our work, *Pour comprendre les évolutions démographiques*.

[2] On these questions see Jean-Didier Lecaillon, *La Famille, source de prosperité* (Paris: Regnier, 1995).

[3] See *TTL* Part II, 91-220.

[4] See for example René Dumont, *L'Utopie ou la Mort* (Paris: Le Seuil, 1973) 47 f.

[5] The permit to procreate exists in China; it has also been instituted in Vietnam and Singapore. It is examined by Hubert Gérard in "Le point de vue démographique," *L'Explosion démographique au crible des valeurs humaines et chrétiennes* (Louvain: Faculty of Theology, 1972) 16.

[6] On the methods used by the Chinese government see John S. Aird, *Foreign Assistance to Coercive Family Planning in China. Response to Recent Population Policy in China* [by Terence Hull] (Canberra, 1992). We owe to the famous demographer a more recent study entitled *Family Planning, Women and Human Rights in the People's Republic of China, pro manuscripto* (Taipei, 1995).

[7] See the surprising *Programa Nacional de Población. 1995-2000*, published by the Poder Ejecutivo Federal (Mexico City, 1995).

[8] See Maria-Eugenia Cosio-Zavala, *Changements de fecondité au Mexique et politiques de population* (Paris: Harmattan, 1994) 151.

[9] *Ibid.* esp. 165-179, 197 and *passim*.

[10] We have studied the case of Brazil in *TTL* 159-174; see also George Martine, "Brazil's Fertility Decline — 1965-1995, "*Population and Development Review* (New York: Population Council) vol.2, 1 (March 1996) 47-75. See above all the acts of the congress held in Brasilia, Oct. 15-19, 1992, published under the title *VIII Encontro nacional de Estudios Populacionais*, by Associação Brasileira de Estudios Populacionais (São Paulo, 1992): T.2, 9-104. Finally, one will follow with great interest the work led at CRH of the Federal University of Salvador (Brasil) by Prof. Guaraci Adeodato de Souza.

[11] See *TTL* 47-58; *BPCV* qu.88.

[12] See John XXIII, *Mater et Magistra* nn.59-68; *GS* 75,3.

[13] That is what the Pontifical Council for the Family did in a document entitled *Evolutions démographiques: dimensions éthiques et pastorales* (Vatican City: Libreria Editrice Vaticana, 1994).

[14] According to the data of the *World Population Data Sheet* (Washington, D.C.: Population Reference Bureau, 1996).

[15] Taking into account the agronomic methods presently available, authoritative specialists hold that the earth can at present carry more than thirty-five billion people (Colin Clark, Rover Revelle, FAO, etc.). See especially the report of the Food Agricultural Organization, *Les ressources en terre des populations de demain* (Rome: FAO, 1984).

[16] These themes are often taken up by Pierre Chaunu, esp. in *Trois millions d'années* (Paris: Laffont, 1990).

[17] RN 1 f.

[18] See for example *World Contraceptive Use 1994*, a leaflet published by Population Division, U.N. New York, 1994.

[19] See Chapter V, note 27.

[20] These concerns have been expressed for many years in scientific works of first class demographers, but they are too often the victim of academic and media censures. They are more and more shared by a public attentive to the future of our societies. See for example *La Jaune et la Rouge* (review of the alumni of the Polythechnic School of Paris) n.506 (June-July, 1995) the file "La démographie" 22-56; see also *La Nef* (Paris) n. 62 (June 1996) "Dossier sur la démographie" 20-29.

[21] This very suggestive expression was offered by Gerard-François Dumont. See for example *Le Festin de Kronos* (Paris: Fleurus, 1991).

[22] See Jean-Didier Lecaillon, *op.cit.*

[23] On the problems arising in the United States and rich nations in general see the thought-provoking work of John Kenneth Galbraith, *La République des satisfaits. La culture du contentement aux Etats-Unis* (Paris: Le Seuil, 1993).

[24] Marie Hendrickx has demonstrated well the close link between "Famille et société dans l'enseignement du Magistère," *Anthropotes* (Vatican City) n.1 (1996) 99-118.

[25] See Lk 21:1-3.

[26] See Etienne La Boétie, *Le Discours de la servitude volontaire* (Paris: Payot, 1976).

CHAPTER XI
FOYER OF LOVE: THE FAMILY

WHEN LOVE SPEAKS TO US OF GOD

Since God wanted to reveal something of His mystery to men, He used very simple words whose meaning men could immediately comprehend because they correspond to their most profound experience.

Man and Woman

At the heart of this experience is love — more precisely, conjugal love. Already in the Old Testament, Isaiah used that experience to help us grasp the significance of the covenant between God and men. God is Jerusalem's "spouse"[1] and, according to Hosea, it will come to pass that the unfaithful spouse will call Yahweh her "husband."[2] Moreover, from the time of the Canticle of Canticles, the mystics have often spoken of their moving experience with God in terms of a spiritual marriage. The joy of the covenant between man and wife also fills St. John the Baptist with joy.[3] St. Paul also refers to human love in order to help us understand the new covenant between Christ and His Church.[4] The Apocalypse employs the same nuptial language to describe the completion of this covenant at the end-times. It involves a "nuptial banquet" (19:9), spoken of also by St. Matthew (22: 2-14; 25: 1-13): or again the "Spouse of the Lamb", or the "Spouse" (Ap 21:9; see also 21:2; 18:23; 22:17). St. John sums up this revelation in one word which brings us right to the heart of the mystery: "God is love" (1 Jn 4:8, 16).

"Male and female He created them" (Gn 1:27): man is the image of God, of a God who we know from Jesus is Father, Son and Spirit and who are but one, and as such, the three different persons are respected in the unity. To express something of God who is love, men must be many. It is as *man and woman* that they express, incarnate and manifest the image of God who is love.

Human love, then, cannot be understood except in the light of this mystery of love which is the Holy Trinity. "Conjugal love reveals its true nature and nobility when it is considered in its supreme origin, God, who is love."[5] And reciprocally, to grasp something of the God who is one in Three Persons, we can rely on the experience of human love, as Scripture invites us to do.

Human love is rich in meaning for helping us understand the mystery of God. It's not a question of a simple comparison between human love and divine love. The language of human love has been retained and repeated with insistence because between human love and divine love, there is not only a difference, but above all a real connaturality. Human love is the path of sanctification because God, who is love, is holy.

It is in the full human reality of love that something of the love of God is expressed and that His loving design is realized in history. By offering men the prodigious capacity to love, God proposed to associate them with himself "to realize in mankind His design of love."[6] The happiness of men consists in loving as God has taught them to love. For the irrepressible craving for happiness cannot be truly satisfied by possessing or by having the perishable goods of the earth; it can be satisfied only by love. Man aspires to love and to be loved, and this double aspiration itself bears the mark of the infinite.

The Twofold Fruitfulness of Love

And so it is not surprising that God, who has given man a heart capable of loving, has also made his heart sensitive to the demands of love. More than in other areas, man's heart is inscribed with the ability of discerning true love from false love. An interior light reveals to man that human love engages the whole person, not only in the excitement of the flesh and the ardor of his sentiments, but in the impetus of his will that wants to free itself by abandoning self without reserve to the joy of total giving and receiving. Precisely because it is total, love is faithful: it would make no sense to pretend to give oneself totally to many persons.

Furthermore, the human love that is built during the life of the spouses is a love that is *doubly fruitful*. It is fruitful because each spouse offers to the other all the potential that he/she carries within. The wife is given and gives herself to her husband as a "helper made for him" (Gn 2:18). The joy the wife brings to her husband is such that it is compared to that of God, the spouse of Israel![7] As between Yahweh and His people, a covenant is effected between the spouses: the history of their life is a history of love. This first aspect of the fruitfulness of love sets in relief the fact that loving in truth is always being willing to renounce the temptation to prevail over the other, it is always in a way to die to self so that the other can be born and grow to the fullness of his/her personal stature. This self-effacement so that the other can attain existence is evoked in the sleep of Adam, the condition for Eve's entering into life and being given to a delighted Adam.[8]

This loving effacement of spouse before spouse is also brought out by the story of the Good Samaritan (Lk 10:25-37).[9] To make the wounded man his neighbor, the Samaritan had to first efface himself. He was probably on a "business trip", and suddenly, faced with the wounded man, he puts his personal interests to death, and it is even on condition of dying to self that he is able to make the wounded man his neighbor.

The Good Samaritan offers us two familiar lessons. On the one hand, seen from the side of the one who loves, authentic love cannot be subordinated to conditions that the beloved must realize. On the other hand, seen from the side of the one who is loved, authentic love cannot be subordinated to conditions that the lover must fulfill.

Nevertheless, to this personalizing fruitfulness is added the procreative fruitfulness, often greeted as the cause of joy.[10] The common task in which the spouses are engaged is not exhausted in building two personalities, profound as their reciprocal love may be. The spouses who love each other and whose tenderness is expressed in the hearts and bodies of both, as time goes by, build this marvelous reality called the loving couple. Now this couple is not simply a juxtaposition or an association of two loving beings. It is original in two senses: first, it results from a unique encounter of two persons; then it is the source of a total novelty: it is the origin of a new person. In fact, in order to achieve a union of love, the couple must be open to the creation of a new being that will emerge from their embrace.

Once more, the Good Samaritan's conduct can serve as a model, this time for the couple as such. They become truly a foyer of love, since they are disposed to "interrupt their trip," i.e., die to their self-interests, in order to let themselves be called by the poor one par excellence, the unborn infant who is completely dependent. For, from the most secret origins, the very existence of the baby depends, not only on the love of each of the spouses, but on their love as a couple.

The first the question that arises is as spouse, to whom am I to make myself neighbor? The quality of the response to this question concerning the worth of their conjugal love determines the quality of the response to the next question concerning the worth of their parental love: to whom, as a couple, do we make ourselves neighbor?

To Love Unconditionally

Whether it is a question of conjugal love or parental love, for this love to be authentically and fully human, it must be an unconditional love. Conjugal love is mutilated in its very essence when it depends on a condition, for example, that one of the spouses may be infertile or unfaithful. A husband who would claim to love his wife *so long as* she is infertile would not love his wife for herself but for what he would want her to be, accommodated to *his* plan for her. The deliberate refusal to transmit life is always a disquieting symptom, showing that the love potential in the heart of man is willfully restricted to limits which cause it to atrophy.

A wife who would claim to love her husband *on condition* that he authorize her engaging in a few deviations would not love her husband for himself but only for what she wants him to be, accommodated to *her* plan for him.

A couple that would claim to love a child *on condition* that he appear only when he wouldn't disturb them would not love the child for himself but only as he adjusts to *their* convenience. A couple that would claim to love a baby *only if* he is wanted would not love the child for himself but only as adjusted to *their* desires. A couple who claim to love a child *insofar* as he is normal would refuse, in principle, to be a neighbor to the wounded, the feeble, the one whose only hope for happiness is in love that is purely gratuitous.

Man and woman who decide freely to unite by definition start this foyer of love which is the family. In it, human love is fashioned in the two inseparable dimensions that constitute its originality and richness: conjugal love and parental love. If life is attacked in the very sanctuary where it must be born, it is then this familial sanctuary which must be strengthened in order to protect life.

To all men of good will the Church proposes that they take the risk of loving in all truth. The threats that hang over human life attest to the fact that *men are sick of loving badly and of not loving anymore.* The men and women of our time know that love is the way to happiness, but they are so obsessed with pleasure and individual security that they forget, even in their homes, that happiness is received and shared.

AN INVINCIBLE BASTION AGAINST TOTALITARIANISM

The family, then, is called to play a decisive role in society. Entry into the conjugal community and then, beginning with it, the formation of the familial community have a decisive significance for the quality of political society.

The Family: Seat of Resistance

The family is the primordial place where human beings recognize and welcome one another in their diversity It is the place where the weakest human being is first welcomed and then offered for the acknowledgment and welcome of the community. Between family and society, then, the bonds are very strong.

Positively, the family is the first place in which personalities are formed; in their quality depends the contribution that each will make toward building the common good. The experience of resistance to contemporary totalitarian regimes is rich with lessons in this regard. Resistance to enslavement and the rejection of ideological propaganda have been possible above all thanks to the family. Because it is the nourishing soil of personality, it is the best rampart against totalitarian devourers of men.

The political importance of the family finds its negative confirmation in societies in which the family is disintegrating. The banalization of premarital sex, the decline of marriage, the increase of divorce, the refusal of life by families, the option of single parent families, homosexuality: those are but some of the practices that wound first the family, but also seriously compromise the quality of the social fabric and even the future of society.

On the other hand, many States have happily developed political programs in which the family is made the object of priority attention. Inspired by the principle of subsidiarity, such States have taken measures favorable to the family in various domains: the possibility of the mother devoting herself entirely to her home, outside assistance for the mother and child, sufficient family subsidies, fiscal policies, housing policies, education, maternal education, insurance, etc. Such measures do honor to the governments that take them, for they permit the family to be what it must be, the first "basic social community."[11]

However, it must be sadly observed that the political importance of the family is negatively confirmed by the attacks of which it has constantly been the object on the part of regimes with totalitarian tendencies. From Plato to contemporary totalitarian regimes, there have always been unworthy ideologues who want strictly to control the family, to pair off couples, to rule over procreation and, even sometimes, blatantly to break up families. The true reason for this hostility toward the family is simple: the family is the seat where one is loved, and to be loved is to open self to others, and a place to converse. The family is the refuge where one poses questions, where he dialogues, deliberates, plans projects, decides, and then executes together with the other members. In short, it is the place where people work together with dialogue and liberty.

Anti-life practices tend to destroy the family and some of their promoters have even gone so far as to admit this as their ultimate goal. Public or private organizations that incite people to the destruction of life at its source or its development deserve to be regarded as war machines which, killing love and its fruit, destroy the family. Effectively, from the moment the place par excellence for welcoming life becomes one of the places in which life is compromised or refused, the family can only decline. This decline has been begun by the banalization of hormonal contraception, which some saw as the step they had to pass through in order to make abortion commonplace.[12]

Anti-life practices, therefore, pose a twofold danger to the family: they strike a fatal blow to both conjugal love and to parental love. These practices are the expression of "Neomalthusianism" such as it was advocated by Margaret Sanger. Totally separating the unitive aspect of love from its procreative dimension, these practices make it impossible for spouses to become a couple welcoming life, that is, in an enduring union of love. In more simple terms, anti-life practices prevent the spouses from acting like Good Samaritans toward each other, and as a couple toward the child.

Thus, with their exaltation of individualistic hedonism and utilitarianism, the anti-life ideologies have undoubtedly precipitated the crisis of the family institution.

Finally, fron the moment when, in the family, respect for incipient life is made to depend on certain conditions, all life risks being respected only conditionally. Proceeding from conditional love, it is in fact the same logic that discriminates both against those who can be loved or not, as well as against those who can live or not. It is from the same logic that proceeds infanticide, prenatal or during birth, the elimination of little girls (or little boys), parricide out of false compassion, euthanasia of people under care, etc. None of the criteria put forth to "justify" these practices can claim for itself the example of the Good Samaritan.

The Role of the Media

This destruction of the family is still fomented by an unrestrained flaunting, especially on television, of shocking sexual license. Sometimes presented as "education," this so-called freedom is in fact too often an attempt at corruption that distracts youth from discovering authentic love. Under the cover of an initiation in love, it incites the young to premature premarital sexual relations. This perversion is all the more reinforced by the degrading pornography that invades all available media space. To compensate for the effects of this "education," so destructive of love and the family, too many children believe, alas, that they must seek refuge in the paradise of drugs.

The totalitarian regimes that have flourished in this century have striven to alienate man from himself. They have demanded that he sacrifice his life for the Cause and set about physically and psychologically destroying the recalcitrant. All had to be sacrificed to the State, the Race, the Party. The international campaigns directed against human life risk restoring a totalitarianism similar to those which have just been terminated with so much effort. We must urgently protect spouses, couples, families, and the young from the anti-life ideologies. All are subjected to a propaganda that infantilizes them and robs them of the capacity of judging and freely deciding about responsible parenthood. It would be an intolerable abuse of power to condition couples in such a way that they sacrifice their ability to transmit life, and subject life to the dictates of totalitarian ideologies that spread the "morality of race" under the label of "the quality of the species"; restoring the "morality of living space" under the label of quantitative restraints imposed by the environment; reinterpreting the "morality of the fight for life" in the name of an unrestrained market consecrated to the victory of the strongest. Even the pitiless capitalists denounced by Marx had never openly dared to propose depriving the proletariat of their sole riches: their children!

The example of the nations that have put an end to contemporary totalitarianism offer us again a precedent rich with lessons. What precluded many men and women from suffering shipwreck in a Kafkaesque universe was the family. Despite iniquitous laws, despite usurped power exercising a direct control over the sexual conduct of the spouses, the family has been and remains the impregnable bastion of resistance to unjust power. Today, resistance to the powers that kill love and hope by legalizing contempt for life can be developed by revitalizing the family.

GUIDELINES FOR A FAMILY POLICY

From what we have said above it follows that any project aimed at restoring the respect owed to human life necessarily entails a redefinition of family policy. In developing societies, this policy is generally still in its infancy, sometimes non-existent. In societies of abundance, this policy is often confused with social policy; one attaches to it, for example, unemployment welfare, social housing, aid to the handicapped, etc. If there is a connection between social policy and family policy, the latter has a specificity that must be respected. Family policy must be concerned with the long term, for building a family lasts for the duration of a generation, at least, and is even prolonged for two, three, yes, four generations.

Habitually, the family is considered as pertaining to private life. Of course! However, recent studies rightly set in relief the role and importance of the family in society.[13] From that flow good reasons for public powers' aiding the family. In a general way, the family is the primary support of society's memory. Testimony and witnesses are transmitted in its womb. The child is going to learn from the example and insistence of its parents, their simple behavior and actions, which will ultimately awaken their particular vocation and which, in any case, will be very precious for society. Among these activities, we can especially note: personal responsibility, contributions to the economy, discovering the talent that can be developed, taking initiative, respecting schedules, managing personal finances, saving, sharing in household chores, paying attention to others, calming people, pardoning, teaching, caring for the sick, praying, etc. The family is the first foyer of mutual help, the first school of solidarity, the first center for the distribution of revenue, the first little enterprise, the place where the people open themselves to sociability. Through their educational role parents, then, make a contribution of primary importance to society. They awaken in the child qualities which society greatly needs. We must hope, then, that public powers and public opinion will acknowledge this contribution on the part of parents in society. A priority objective, therefore, of a just family policy is to facilitate and encourage this parental activity.

The family is still the seat of memory on the economic level where the sense of saving is developed, and also where parents can shield their children from misfortune. The family discourages ostentatious and wasteful consumption.

It is high time that society measures the contribution made to it by the family, and the great contribution made to it by the mother of the family. One of the most scandalous injustices of our societies consists in ignoring mothers' contributions to society. The mother in the home is designated as "without profession." She is the object of a condescending or even reproving regard on the part of those who believe that there is no economic activity other than commercial. It is, therefore, urgent that public powers and public opinion acknowledge the specific contribution of mothers to society. Such recognition should pave the way for a special status: the mother who chooses to dedicate herself to the education of her children ipso facto renders a special service to society both at present and in the future. With such a status one will be able to react against the anti-life forces that are at once cause and consequence of the too widespread disaffection toward the maternal vocation. Surveys confirm that numerous women desire many children and want to rear them. The least that democratic societies could do is to offer all women the *possibility of making a free choice*. Social justice and distributive justice demand a fundamental revision of the system of family subsidies and of the fiscal policies from which the families suffer.

As for the child, all too often it happens to him as well that he is perceived as being outside of all reference to memory and time. The anti-life movements emphasize that the child costs too much money and doesn't bring in anything. But it is evident — and we must not try to evade this other evidence — that the child is the man of tomorrow. Today it is he who benefits from the natural solidarities; tomorrow he will nourish them. He will produce, earn his living and that of his family, pay taxes, etc. It is urgent, then, that the child be recognized as good, not only for his/her immediate family, but for all of society. Man isn't born a producer; he must learn how to produce, with education and instruction. Society must invest in the child because for society the child is a condition of survival. Like all investments, this one will not produce income until tomorrow, but it will bring in much more than it will have cost.

As recent studies show, this last observation regarding the child, merits being extended to the whole family, to the activity of the parents and especially to that of the mother. In particular we should hope that more and more refined studies measure the contribution of the different actors such as the mother, in the larger market of political communities and enterprises.

---

[1] See Is 54:5-8.
[2] See Hos 2:18.
[3] See Jn 3:29.
[4] See Eph 5:23-32; 2 Cor 11:2.

[5] Paul VI, *Humanae Vitae* 8.
[6] *Ibid.*
[7] See Is 62:5.
[8] See Gn 2:23.
[9] See *supra*, Ch. VI, *The Good Samaritan*.
[10] Cf. Gn 17:15-22; 1 Sam 2:5; Ps 113:9; Is 54:1. etc.
[11] See *On Social Concerns* n.33.
[12] See *EPA* 16 f., 81; *BPCV* qu.122.
[13] See the works of economists and demographers as famous as Jean-Didier LeCaillon, *La Famille: source de prospérité*; Gerard-François Dumont, *Pour la liberté familiale* (Paris: PUF, 1986). Gary Becker, of the Chicago school, received the Nobel prize for economics in 1992 for, among other things, his research on the family. See esp. *A Treatise on the Family* (Cambridge, MA: Harvard Univ. Press, 1981); second ed. enlarged, 1991.

CHAPTER XII
PROCREATION AND DELEGATED WORLD POWER

If one wishes to save the dignity of human life, it is also necessary for men and women as well as societies to rediscover the joy of loving in truth. The child is the fruit of a love which, for being fully interpersonal, resonates joy. Even before needing love and being able to offer a smile, the child of man needs a couple who love each other and to whom it brings, like a treasure, a new reason to love each other more.

This love, inscribed concretely in the flesh, is not, however, reducible to a purely psychological process. Man's vocation to "fill the earth and subject it"[1] can never be invoked to justify man's having recourse to his ability to control and dominate in order to "legitimize" the separation of the unitive end from the procreative end of the conjugal union.

IMAGE OF THE CREATOR

The book of Genesis suggests instead that man is the image of God for two reasons. He is certainly the image of God by reason of the capacity to control and dominate that flows from the divine intelligence he partakes of as a reasoning creature. But it is also manifested in his capacity to transmit life. Man is the image of God because he participates in God's creative power: he is *pro*creator; he received this power from God to give birth to new human beings. And so, at the very heart of his condition as creature, he resembles God the creator.

All the practices that are contemptuous of human life upset this dimension of being an image of God, which every man bears within himself. The grandeur of human love is thus due to the fact that, since Adam, parents transmit to their children the quality of being in the image of God, which was given to them from the beginning.[2] It is significant, in this regard, that the great genealogies attach the human generations to God through Adam. Thus St. Luke stresses the fact that, in their universality, men are images of God in virtue of the divine likeness transmitted to them by Adam.[3]

It is, then, in virtue of the double title of his procreative capacity and his controlling capacity that man is the image of God. However, in the very clarification of this likeness, God gives his first order: "Increase and multiply,"[4] to dominate comes in second place.[5]

It is in virtue of being created in the image and likeness of God that man is distinguished from the animals. This unique relationship to God provides the foundation for the originality of human sexuality and procreation, and justifies the management that man must, by divine delegation, exercise over the animals and material creation in general.

Once man inverts the order of the two senses in which he is the image of God, his "procreative" vocation is relegated to second place after his "dominative" vocation. The door is then opened to a totally dominative use of human reason. The latter is inclined to exercise domination, not only over the earth, the air, the sea and all creatures contained in them, but also over man. The legitimate control exercised over the material world is wrongly turned back against man himself. This disordered summit of technical reason plunges man into a situation in which it is impossible for him to perceive how much his procreative capacity attests to his dignity of being made in the image of God and consequently distinguishes him from the animals.

Thus the inversion of the order of precedence mentioned above is, in the final analysis, a religious fault whose undesirable repercussions in the relations among men are inevitable.

HUMAN PARENTHOOD, RESPONSIBLE PARENTHOOD

In the light of what we have seen regarding the meaning of human procreation, and therefore of love and the family, we can understand what the Church means by responsible parenthood and why she recommends it. The anti-life ideologues often accuse the Church of being simply for having children and sometimes reproaches her with vehemence. Now the Church is in no way a partisan of uncontrolled and irresponsible fecundity. Her doctrine on this point has been clearly formulated by the Second Vatican Council, which underlined the necessity of harmonizing "conjugal love with the responsible transmission of life."[6] This doctrine was made more precise by Paul VI who, in his encyclical *Humanae Vitae*, used the expression "responsible parenthood" and explained its meaning.[7] For the rest, human wisdom already recommends that parents have as many children as they can generously welcome, taking into account the concrete circumstances in which they live.

It is necessary, then, to avoid the very frequent confusion of expressions whose meanings must be carefully distinguished.

First of all, we cannot identify "responsible paternity" (or "responsible parenthood") with "birth control" or "population control." Responsible parenthood, as we have just explained it, gives rise to no particular objection and is morally licit. On the other hand, the expressions "birth control" and "population control" are used by ideologues of overpopulation and demographic security. To reach their goals, these ideologues advocate any kind of means so long as they are efficacious. What counts for them is that couples and families be subordinate to the interests of society such as the technocrats define them.

Furthermore, we cannot confuse "birth regulation," "limitation of births" and "contraception." Here again, precision is needed.

Many people today identify birth *regulation* with *limitation* of births. Now regulation of births can be understood as being in accord with responsible parenthood which the Church recommends. "Birth regulation" is even the explicit object of the encyclical *Humanae Vitae*. If this regulation implies an effort toward self-control and of foresight as well as respect for openness to life, then such regulation is morally desirable. In effect, it appeals to the responsible liberty of the spouses to space births or even limit them through legitimate means and for legitimate motives.

As for limitation of births, it can be understood in two senses. First of all, it can result, as we just said, from a legitimate desire not to further multiply births. If this desire proceeds from proper motives and has recourse to legitimate means and if, furthermore, it is disposed to accept the infant who might eventually come, this desire to limit births is entirely admissible. Entirely different, however, it the situation in which limitation of births would mean, once a quota has been reached, an unyielding limitation having recourse to morally inadmissible means, and not hesitating to suppress a life that has begun.

Unfortunately, in the general conception one too often identifies *contraception* with regulation or limitation of births. Here too, some distinctions will help clarify the problem. If one uses the word contraception in an incorrect way to designate the regulation or limitation of births, this word involves the same moral qualifications just spoken of. But if contraception is understood in its proper sense, that is, as deliberately impeding the very possibility of conception then the word contraception designates above all a firm and constant disposition to prevent the beginning of new life at any cost. This will translate into having recourse to chemical, mechanical, or surgical means which, by their very nature, intention and effectiveness profoundly differ from all the means that leave some chance for life to begin.

The moral problems that the practice of responsible parenthood raise are, then, of two orders: that of the end and that of the means. From the viewpoint of the end, it is clear that wisdom recommends that parents adapt the number of their children to their potential for educating them well. It is also clear that this potential varies according to circumstances and time. In this context, public powers have a possibility of action that, by means of a family policy, either promotes or curbs the reception of life.

However, parents often have a lot of difficulty understanding and agreeing with what the Church says regarding the means that allow them to practice responsible parenthood. This question has already been the object of numerous Church documents, and the doctrine has been clearly explained by Paul VI in his encyclical *Humanae Vitae*. What is important is never to lose sight of the concern the Church has for helping all couples to live their love fully.

When spouses have already welcomed life into their home and have adequate reasons for not wanting any more new births, they can decide to limit their fecundity. Toward this end, they can continue to enjoy communion of heart and body while preventing a new birth by means of natural methods. However, it must be made clear that natural methods are capable of being used, not as a means of regulating births, but as contraceptive methods. Such would be the case of a couple who would refuse to transmit life and have recourse to natural methods to achieve this intent. Use of these methods in these conditions would be incompatible with the aspirations of the authentically loving heart. In fact, they would have as their end to exclude the realization of one of the goods of conjugal union, namely, procreation.

On the other hand, in their morally licit use, these natural methods have the double advantage of respecting the integrity of the spouses and of not thwarting procreation, since, as it happens, this good has already been accepted and will be again in the future when possible.[8]

Many people wonder, however, why the Church, which goes so far as to affirm responsible parenthood permitting couples to limit the number of their children, does not admit contraception in the sense explained above. Why, when the end can be legitimate in certain cases, reject the chemical, mechanical, even surgical means whose efficacy is lauded?

The answer to this difficulty has many points that constitute a coherent whole.

Chemical or mechanical contraception always negatively affects the couple as such because one or the other of the spouses is treated in an unequal fashion. The equality necessary to true love is not respected. For example, chemical means disrupt the woman. When one reads the present authoritative studies in this point, it is dishonest to pass over in silence the harmful effects of these products, and for a greater reason, to deny them.[9] The Church cannot admit that society be more concerned when it is a matter of — please excuse me — forbidding the use of hormones with cattle than when it is a question of preventing the use of hormones with women.

Disastrous effects are also produced by the use of mechanical devices, whether by the woman or the man. When they are used by the man, for example, such means always affect the couple as such because one or the other of the spouses is always treated in an unequal manner with the consequences, especially psychological, which we've mentioned.

The harmful effect of chemical and mechanical means are even such that some women prefer to have themselves surgically sterilized rather than have recourse to them. But female sterilization is a grave and definitive mutilation whose physical and psychological repercussions are profound, and it definitively enslaves the woman to her desire or to the desire of her husband. It goes without saying that these serious reservations apply, for the same reasons, to male sterilization.

For some time now chemical products have appeared and been present as contraceptives, but in fact they have various effects: the effect is sometimes that of a barrier, sometimes contraceptive, sometimes anti-nidatory. The use of such products can in no way be consistent with the dynamic of authentic human love for two very decisive reasons: they disrupt the woman in every case and, it may happen that they disconnect and expel the embryo from the nest which is as indispensable to its life as air is to the life of an adult. Let us call things by their right names: beyond the barrier effect, these preparations have a twofold aim, one contraceptive, the other abortifacient, even if this latter effect is not continuously produced.

Abortifacient chemicals and anti-pregnancy vaccines[10] are always disastrous for the woman and, naturally, for the conceived baby. They are the shame of medicine and of certain contemporary pharmaceutical enterprises. They merit condemnation without appeal, just as the case of all murder of an innocent person does. However, they present a particular gravity resulting from the frozen determination exhibited by the whole chain which, beginning with those who decided to perfect them, ends with those who use them, passing by the lugubrious cortege of those who produce them, finance them, distribute them, prescribe them and apply them.

When governments and public or private international institutions distribute such means they degrade man and woman. They establish inequality within the couple. They organize humiliation, subjection, and mutilation of the spouses. They dishonor marriage, work toward the destruction of the family and, thereby, of the entire human social fabric.

The duty of these governments and institutions consists rather in creating conditions favorable to the happiness of couples and in allowing them to exercise freely and with joy their responsibility as parents.

EXPANDING MAN'S HEART

The Church, then, is well oriented to the heart of men and to their irrepressible aspiration to happiness. Her teaching on responsible parenthood addresses itself above all to the profound nature of human love that blossoms within the family. And the Church expands all of its potential. Without doubt, the heart of man is not that of God: yet it is like God's (see Gn 1:26). Man is then capable of growing in love, namely, of loving with a heart more and more like God's. But in his carnal condition nothing is ever definitively finished, and man can allow the divine likeness in him to become darkened, he can harden his heart, and he can let his capacity for tenderness wither.

The Church's teaching here is entirely oriented toward the exaltation of love and of life. What the Church says about responsible parenthood and the family, then, concerns men's experience in their capacity to love. But this experience the Church explains from what she has learned from her Savior: with grace the heart of man is capable of better, but it is also capable of worse.[11] If the Church compromised on the demands of human love, if she hid the fact that human love, blessed by God, is the common way of happiness and holiness, it would be the sign that she no longer has the courage to help men discover and activate all the reserves of love that they carry in their heart.

The Church must, then, highlight the warning signals, indicate the pitfalls, prevent the diseases of love and the attacks on life, whether they arise from societies or individuals. In brief, she must do all she can to mark out the path to happiness.

The Church is perfectly aware of what her demands require. But these requirements show precisely that these demands are not an invention of men, still less an arbitrary imposition. These requirements are total because the evangelical morality of love is a total demand: to love as Jesus did, one must love "unto the end,"[12] even unto pardon.[13]

The Church would fail in her mission, and even deceive men, if she hid the essential demands of love out of fear or out of concern to please. That is why she cannot be content with referring men to the judgment of their individual consciences alone. Neither in this domain, nor for that matter in any other, can subjective moral choice be erected into a norm of moral conduct.[14] And those who make believe that this could be the case deceive themselves and those with whom they speak. The service which the Church owes to the human community is first of all the service of the truth about man, and it is around this truth that we can build bit by bit a new man and a new humanity.

---

[1] See Gn 1:28.
[2] See Gn 5:3.
[3] See Lk 3:23-38.
[4] See Gn 1:28a.
[5] *Ibid.* 28b.
[6] See *GS* 50 f.
[7] See Paul VI, *Humanae Vitae* n.10.
[8] On these methods see René and Marie Sentis, *Amour et fécondité* (Paris: Fayard, 1986); Mercedes Arzú Wilson, *Amour et fécondité* (BBE, 1986) and *Love and Family* (San Francisco: Ignatius Press, 1996).
[9] See Dr. Ellen Grant, *Amère pillule. Le "contraceptif parfait" est-il sans danger?* preface by Prof. Lucien Israel (Paris: L'OEil, 1988); Dr. Rudolf Ehmann, "Problems in Family Planning," in *Anthropotes*, Rome, n.1 (1991) 95-126.

[10] See *supra*, Chapter I, *Abortion*.
[11] See Mt 15:19; 1 Jn 5:20.
[12] Jn 13:1.
[13] See Mt 5:44; Lk 6:27; Rm 12:14, 20.
[14] We refer here to the central themes of the encyclical of John Paul II *Veritatis Splendor* of 1993.

CHAPTER XIII
WHAT IS TO BE DONE?

HOPE IN THE HEART OF THE POOR

The attacks on human life today show that profound problems have not been considered in time to permit all people of the world to develop. The anti-life programs are thus presented as curative measures aimed at warding off the consequences of past errors and omissions. Now this fearful attitude cannot but aggravate the evil, since, when all is said and done, anti-life measures lead to imprisoning the poor in the very conditions that are the cause of their poverty.

Fearfulness is also a conservative attitude; it consecrates a sort of intellectual and moral blurring that inhibits the inventive capacity which is now more than ever indispensable. In order to invent a better future, we must have the courage to question securities of the present. This is why, to invent the future, one must hope, and to hope one must have the heart of the poor which is not cluttered by these securities.

Since the present problems proceed from an unsatisfactory anthropology,[1] a better future cannot be built except on the basis of an anthropology recognizing the right of every man to aspire to complete happiness. If one wants to motivate men and lift poor populations, it is evident that this anthropology must not exalt the cult of sterility and death. Men must, then, begin by liberating themselves from their morbid phantasms so that the cell to happiness may flower.

"NO DISPARATE COUPLINGS!"

Liberty in the Face of Idols

Jesus did not leave any doubt with regard to the radicalness of His message and His demands. He came to bring fire (Lk 12:49) and the sword (Mt 10:34); He came to divide daughter from mother (Lk 12:53). "You have heard it said..." He told them adding right away, "But I tell you..." (Mt 5:21-43). The controversy between the Pharisees and Jesus shows that it is impossible to claim to be a disciple of Jesus while clinging to legalistic rationalism. Faced with Jesus, we are obliged take sides (Jn 6:66). This great decision of attachment to Jesus *by faith* is absolutely central in the epistles of St. Paul.

From the beginnings of Christianity there have thus appeared two choices which we cannot avoid: "You cannot serve both God and mammon" (Mt 6:24). We must obey God rather than men, said Peter and the apostles (Acts 5:29; 4:19). The Apocalypse shows how far the tension between fidelity to God and the claims of a tyrannical and cruel power can lead (Ap 17-18).

The history of the Church is highlighted by the testimony of a multitude of Christians who chose to say no, even at the cost of their lives, rather than lose the treasure they had discovered in Jesus (see Mt 13:44; Phil 1:21).

In our century still this sovereign liberty afforded by faith in Jesus led Christians victoriously to resist the new idols. "Fear not!" Jesus repeats in the Gospel (Mt 1:28; Lk 12:7; Mk 6:50; Jn 6:20; 12:15, etc.). And this recommendation has often been recalled by John Paul II. Men today have a right to expect Christians to give proof of their courage in the witness they are called to give, in favor of the divine gift of life.

No more than in ancient or more recent times must Christians today permit themselves to be abused by ideologies hostile to life. They must not yield to a misunderstood tolerance which would make them sink into an anthropological agnosticism, skepticism and moral subjectivism. Christians are *in* the world without being *of* the world (see Jn 15:19; also 1 Jn 5:5). The Lord's call does not take Christians out of the world: it is *in the world* that they respond to their vocation. Jesus prays that the Father guard them from the Evil One (see Jn 17:15; Jas 1:27), but He then sends them into the world (Jn 17:17).

The Christian, then, is called to the "folly of the cross" (1 Cor 1:18), the cross "by which the world is forever crucified to me and I to the world" (Gal 6:14). He cannot seek vain glory which only serves to divide (see Gal 5:3-26), nor "carnal wisdom", but the wisdom that comes from on high, that is, the grace of God (see 2 Cor 1:12). For the Christian, security cannot come from the world: it comes from the glorious cross.

Such are the specific foundations which dictate the practical attitude of Christians before the threats facing human life. There are lines of rupture which the Christian cannot cross without putting himself in direct opposition to communion with Christ.[2]

Refusing Conformity

The Christian must therefore reject all conformity: he cannot adopt either the behavior or attitudes characteristic of the world (see Rm 12:2). He must reject all opportunism that would lead him to "speak like the world" (see 1 Jn 4:5) or to "form disparate fellowships with nonbelievers" (see 2 Cor 6:14). He must also reject any ambiguity with regard to his beliefs: "let your speech be yea, yea; no, no; anything beyond that comes from the Evil One" (Mt 5:37; see also Jas 15:12; Gal 2:11-21).

Hence, how can we not regret that some Christians have become lukewarm with regard to human life in the vain hope of pleasing the world (see 1 Cor 1:17-22) or of escaping persecution (Gal 6:12-15). The conformist, opportunist or ambiguous Christian ceases to challenge the world by means of a proper conduct that calls into question the behavior of others. Furthermore, "love of the present world" can lead Christians to "abandon" (see 2 Tm 4:9) or to prefer "the glory of men to the glory of God" (Jn 12:43).

May the warning of St. Paul not be applied to today's Christians: "There will be a time when [men] will not be able to endure sound doctrine, but according to their own desires and itching ears, they will seek numerous teachers who will turn their hearing away from the truth in order that they may be turned to fables" (2 Tm 4:3 f.).

From that follows a twofold obligation of resistance: first the duty of passive resistance, and even at times active, to unjust laws and orders; then the global duty of resistance to those agents who push society toward organizing itself in a manner hostile to life. Christians are sent into the world to change it (see 1 Cor 5:10) and to be witnesses to *both* the truth (see Jn 17:18) *and* to love (1 Jn 4:17).

However, on the human level, we shouldn't have any illusions. In their commitment to life, Christians will have to face the hostility of the world (see Jn15:18); they will be persecuted (see Gal 6:11). They will even be seduced and led astray by the false coiners of liberty (see 2 Pt 2:19 f.).

The Christian, then, will have to give proof of his patience when faced with trials, knowing that it belongs to the Lord to separate the good grain from the weeds (Mt 13:24-30, 36-43). But during this time of trial, this same Christian has faith in Jesus as his weapon, for he has conquered the world (see 1 Jn 5:4 f.), and also the strength derived from being a son of God, while bearing the Holy Spirit within him (1 Jn 4:4).

Hence, it is in this world, where the passion of the Lord is continued, that Christians are called to be the salt of the earth (Mt 5:13) and the light of the world (*Ibid.* 14); they are called to collaborate with God in the creation of the new man (Eph 4:24); to "shine as centers of light" (Phil 2:15); to "reconcile all things in Christ" (Col 1:20); and to bring about the unity of all men in Christ (see Rm 12:5; 1 Cor 12:13; Gal 3:28; Eph 4:4-6).

After the example of the great prophets, Isaiah (Is 6), Ezechiel 9Ez 3:16-27), Amos (Am 7:12-17), Jeremiah (Jer 1:17-19) as well as John the Baptist (see Mk 6:17-28), but above all fortified in his faith in Him who died and rose for us, the witness of God must dismiss all fear — that fear which Cardinal Tomasek said is "unworthy of the Christian." We are reminded of this lesson by a saint only recently canonized, who lived in a milieu in which, as good courtiers, Christians cared more about pleasing the world than God. It was St. Claude de la Colombière who wrote: "At worst, the Christian must die in serving God and neighbor; I do not see that that should give rise to fear in anyone."

LIFE, LIKE DEATH, NEEDS INSTITUTIONS

Public and Private Institutions

International organizations, including private ones, together with States and public powers, if they are genuinely concerned, must reconsider the entirety of their policies regarding human life. This step requires exceptional intellectual and moral courage. But this twofold courage may find motivation in the hope it will give birth to, as well as the happiness it will enkindle.

This reconsideration is especially pressing for the European Union. Europe is the region that has been the cradle of the most inhuman totalitarian ideologies history has known; it has also been the first to suffer from the totalitarian regimes that were incarnated by them. While all the tears are not yet dried and so many wounds remain to be dressed, Europe should not be advocating new and insane ideologies that claim to "legitimize" the final solution to the problem of the poor. It shouldn't be pushing the most delirious aberrations to their paroxysm; nor should it forget that one genocide can conceal another!

The reassessment of policies regarding human life is also obligatory for politicians who, in every nation — not excepting the poorest

— are responsible for the common good. These politicians are the most exposed to both internal and external pressures, sometimes with tempting advantages added, which aim at making practices that harm life legal. Politicians of every country, and especially those who exercise authority in poor countries, must not compromise the legitimate victory gained from the struggles for national independence. On a point as decisive as the population of their nation, they cannot allow the just sovereignty of the State to be victimized; or let immoral decisions, sometimes backed by threats and blackmail, be imposed from outside authorities; or let their entire populations be exposed, without defense, to the sterilizing commands.

The best counterattack against those abuses consists in bringing morality back into political life in order to fight against corruption and, in a general way, to dedicate oneself to the common good. This dedication implies, as expected, that priority be given to man's integral education, for a man or woman who has discovered his true value and the worth he has in the eyes of others and before God is immunized against any regression toward slavery!

In this struggle for life, which we see unfolding on a world scale, the nation has an irreplaceable role.[3] No head of state, no nation can be made an outcast by the international community for defending respect for life from its beginning to its end. Examples of appropriate resistance to multifaceted pressures will make other nations reflect. According to the given circumstances, these other nations will be led to reestablish laws guaranteeing the right of all to life.

Doctors

It is still indispensable that all associations of doctors solemnly reaffirm their will to serve human life from conception to natural death. It is the honor of the medical profession to be at the service of life without showing favoritism to anyone. Examples from contemporary history, however, show that doctors have participated in repression and torture. These appalling examples ought to lead the members of the medical profession to see that they can still be implicated today in collaborating with programs similar to those in which only recently some of their confreres were involved.

Let all the world medical associations unite in an indestructible force for human life! By reinforcing their unity vis-à-vis human life, doctors will continue to rank as primary defenders of the dignity of man.

Raising the conscience of the medical corps should also, it is understood, reach all midwives and nurses in the entire world. The power of dissuasion and prevention on the part of certain highly qualified persons has been such that numerous human lives have been saved, even though medical or public authorities have decided on death.[4]

Finally, it is urgent that those who practice anti-life interventions abandon their false compassion.[5] Let them renounce monetary gain acquired at the expense of blood and, following the example of others, place themselves totally at the service of life!

The madness that through present times has led certain doctors to practice euthanasia should open the eyes of the medical family in its entirety. Today as formerly, euthanasia appears as the last step of a continuous process, punctuated with headstones, that begins when doctors dry up life at its source. The honor of the medical profession is such a precious asset that it seems that totalitarian power is always desirous of tarnishing it!

Lawyers

As for lawyers, they will be able to have recourse to all the resources of law in order to assure the juridical protection of human life — a protection to which it has both a right and a need. Why should not law, including international law, consecrate the principle of the nondisposability of the human body from conception to natural death? In effect, the legal profession becomes distorted when it forgets that one of its first raisons d'être is to insure respect for the weakest by the strongest.

Alas, the same rules seem to apply for law as for medicine. Contemporary history is full of examples of cynical lawyers who have placed their talents at the service of the most abject causes. All the dictatorships, all contemporary totalitarianism, have enjoyed the collaboration of lawyers, sometimes obliging, sometimes mercenary, who have asserted that the most elementary rights of man, beginning with the right to life, could not be given priority when the "higher interests" of the State, Race or the Party came into play.

The ideology of demographic security is often presented as the heir apparent of these trends. This is evident whenever this ideology takes up the themes of Fascism, Naziism, or Communism and translates them into a new language.

Farmers

How can we not rejoice at seeing specialists in food production apply themselves to increasing production so as to improve the quality and the distribution of foodstuffs which are not only indispensable to subsistence, but also to a healthy physical constitution? It is first of all on them that national or regional communities depend for access to self-sufficiency in foodstuffs, sign and condition of a wider autonomy. Should we not express the wish that the activities of these specialists receive still more support from international organizations and national authorities? Among specialized international organizations, it frequently occurs that the greater part of their budget goes to pay for their functionaries. It also happens that only a minority of these functionaries actually work in the field. Such is the case with the FAO. It is plain for all to see that better allocations deserve to be considered, not only of international experts who give their best in the field, but also, for example, of better technical training for the small farmers of the poor world. Between the dereliction to which many peasant populations are abandoned and the precipitous modernization of agriculture with all its entailed distortions, there is, without doubt, a place for intermediate solutions.

In any case, these solutions often require profound reforms in the structure of ownership of land. It is inadmissible to impute guilt to a claimed excess of population for those ills which can be remedied by means of agrarian, fiscal and educational reforms. "Ownership of the means of production, whether in industry or agriculture, is just and legitimate if it serves useful work. It becomes illegitimate when it is not utilized or when it serves to impede the work of others in an effort to make a profit which does not benefit the overall expansion of work and the wealth of society but rather is the result of curbing them and of illicit exploitation, speculation or the breaking of solidarity among working people. Ownership of this kind has no justification and represents an abuse in the sight of God and man" (*CA* 43).

Economists

Since considerations of the economic order are invoked to "justify" attacks on life, the prevention of this aggression ought to be served by the ingenuity of which economists have often given proof.

As in law and medicine, economics is a discipline that explores an area of reality and by that fact places itself at the service of man: the economy is made for man.

However, along with Malthus, some believe that "at the great banquet of nature, the table was not set for everybody."[6] Malthus focused his attention on destitution in food. His present heirs enlarge this trend and invoke ecological considerations. They alert everybody to the disparity between the growth of world population, on the one hand, and the scarcity of material resources and the deterioration of the environment on the other.

This perspective that seeks to make the earth's resources the principal source of wealth must obviously always be taken into consideration. Nevertheless, we have the opportunity of living in an era in which the problem of scarcity does not arise anymore as it did at the beginning of the nineteenth century. In an updated vision of economics we cannot attribute to natural resources, especially foodstuffs, the place that Malthus once gave them. Yet it is precisely this vision of the famous pastor that continues to captivate the Malthusians of today.

Demystifying Malthus

The return of Malthus, however, is in no way explained by the pertinence or actuality of his analyses, which have been largely contradicted by facts. This return is explained by the usefulness today of Malthus to the liberal ideology. His theses are reprised today and amplified for two complimentary reasons. First of all, reference to Malthus conceals the economic and social failures of classical liberalism. The contemporary Malthusian explains these failures by pointing to a scapegoat. The poor, we are assured, are not victims of the failures of a liberal economy; their poverty is the result of their irresponsible multiplication. It follows that the wealth of the entire world, which flows from the liberal ideology and enjoys its effectiveness, is not to be blamed when we see the mass of poor people stagnating in underdevelopment.

It is thus proven urgent to subject the present expressions of Malthusian liberalism to a severe and demystifying critique. In essence, to the extent that ideologues succeed in using Malthus to conceal the true causes of liberalism's failures and to absolve the profiteers, they acclimatize people to the simplistic and false idea that the poor are responsible for their poverty, and that therefore their multiplication must be must be curbed whilst placing them under guardianship. If this process of ideological mystification were to be swallowed, the demands for greater justice and development in greater solidarity would be deprived of any object.

Workers

We must not, therefore, hesitate to unmask such a reactionary ideology that presents the poor as an inexorable given. The determinist portrayal of poverty is all the more unacceptable as we concur in acknowledging, not only the role of work in the economy, but also the role of the worker, that is, of human capital.[7] John Paul II has illuminated the fact that "In our time there exists another form of ownership which is becoming no less important than land: the possession of knowledge, technology and skill. The wealth of the industrialized countries is based much more on this kind of ownership than on natural resources." (*CA* 32).

Like the poor of the nineteenth century, the poor of today are deprived of material resources, but they suffer still more from being deprived of knowledge, of technology and know-how. Hence, it is highly desirable that economists study the best means of hastening the advent of the day when the poor from around the globe will have access to such knowledge. As a result, one will no longer be able to reproach economists for being useless and even harmful in today's world which is organized to serve a paying minority. The well-to-do of this world will then perhaps stop demanding that the poor countries sell their natural resources at cheap prices — the only resources they have a right to at present — to settle their debt. We also expect from economists, particularly monetary specialists, some bold suggestions for stabilizing the international monetary system.[8]

For the short and intermediate terms, it is nonetheless urgent to break the shackles that confine too many poor people to the periphery of humanity. Economists are well placed to propose to governments and enterprises realistic solutions in order to satisfy the "many human needs which find no place in the market."[9] In brief, no human solidarity worthy of the name can be constructed on a humanity which has had some of its members removed beforehand.

Finally, to restore the respect due to human life, one must note that there are no easy recipes: it is a genuine conversion of heart that is required. The Good Samaritan gives us the example of such conversion. Making oneself neighbor to every human being for the simple reason that he is human is what is required of spouses and families at the very moment when a new life announces itself. But honoring this immediate relationship does not exhaust the demands of love for the one whom one wishes to make a neighbor. The Good Samaritan does not limit himself to caring for the wounded man himself and placing him on his horse; he entrusts him to the hospitable solicitude of the innkeeper and commits himself to pay the bill.

It is thus indispensable, not only for men to relearn the joy of face-to-face encounter, but also to discover this joy of encounter through the intermediary of political, medical, and economic organizations as well as juridical institutions, etc.

---

[1] See *supra*, **A NEW ANTHROPOLOGICAL ERROR** in Ch. VI.
[2] See *supra*, *Rejection of the Two Commandments* in Ch. VII.
[3] See *CA* 13, 49.

[4] See Ex 1:7-22. There is a present appreciable collection *Charte des personnels de la santé* published by the Pontifical Council for Health Services (Vatican City, 1995). It is a precise and practical vade-mecum devoted to procreation, life and death.

[5] This is what Dr. Bernard Nathanson did. See also Germaine Greer, *Sexe et destinée* (Paris: Grasset, 1986).

[6] We quote the famous *Apology of the Banquet* by Malthus in our *TTL* 139 f.

[7] It was not by accident that Gary Becker, Nobel Prize winner for economics, (1992) came to study the family after having perceived its importance in developing human capital. See esp. *Human Capital* (New York: Columbia University Press, 3rd ed., 1993). See also Alvin Toffler, *Les Nouveaux pouvoirs* (Paris: Fayard, 1991).

[8] See *CA* 35.

[9] See *CA* 34a.

CHAPTER XIV
FAITH AND WORKS

UNITY OF FAITH, UNIVERSALITY OF LOVE

Signs of the Times

The Second Vatican Council insisted that Christians be attentive to the signs of the times.[1] In practical terms, this attentiveness is directed above all toward men and the concrete conditions in which they live. From the beginning of the Church this attentiveness allowed Peter and Paul to understand better that, in the Lord's design, salvation is offered to all men without exception. Throughout the centuries, the Church has constantly redefined the concrete content of her mission by accepting the challenges that came from these signs. Still today the Church is anxious to read the signs of the present time. It is in the light of these that she can define the present priorities of an evangelization that is always new. Impelled by these signs, the Church scrutinizes the riches of the Gospel, drawing from this the treasure both "new things and old" (Mt 13:52). Moved by the Holy Spirit, she develops a language that finds the way to contemporary man's heart.

The contempt in which human life is held today is undoubtedly the most important sign of the times that forces itself on the attention of Christians. Confronted with this situation that in fact expresses a profound despair, Christians are invited to give unanimous witness to the dignity of every man in the plan of God. What nourishes the unity of Christians in their witness is the truth about man in the divine design. In the final analysis, what makes every man loveable for the Christian, what places upon each individual the obligation to love, is that every man is the image of God. The unity of faith establishes the universality of love (see Gn 5:6).[2]

Based on the unity of faith, the Christian's witness, however, calls for a rich multiplicity of activity. Let us recall here the grave warning of Paul VI: "The great sin of Christianity is faith without works."

Giving witness to life through action means, first of all, to respect and cause to be respected the integrity of every man in the framework of conjugal relations and the family. It also means giving specifically Christian witness to all the organizations concerned with the respect due to life. Less than ever, can Catholics resign themselves to take refuge in a privatizing religion, which would leave the field open to the forces of death in society. The appropriate autonomy of earthly realities (see *GS* 37) cannot be invoked to allow or tolerate simply any kind of practical politics. It was the immorality of the nineteenth-century society that Leo XIII denounced, and it is immorality that must still be denounced today.

We rejoice seeing flourish, in so many countries, organizations that actively fight in defense of human life. Many of these organizations are Christian; others, together with Christians fighting alongside them, also welcome members with diverse outlooks. These organizations are a sign of hope for the future of humanity. They deserve to be effectively and openly supported. By means of their public and discreet action, they contribute greatly toward the eradication of the culture of death (*CA* 39) to the benefit of the culture of life.

It is normal that the activity of these organizations is specialized according to the way they perceive the political, juridical and medical world or the public at large. It is also normal that different sensitivities manifest themselves among these organizations. However, by reason of the importance of the stakes, these different sensitivities should remain in their proper place, namely, secondary. Experience shows, in fact, that these sensitivities sometimes give rise to tensions, even conflicts, that weaken and sometimes ruin the fundamental unanimity indispensable for witness on behalf of life. A magnificent task, then opens up before Christians: that of giving, in the name of love for man, a testimony to unity. There should be no doubt that such a witness would receive the support of numerous men of good will who wish only to express themselves in favor of life.

Defending life supposes that Christians support very generously, both on the material as well as moral level, movements dedicated directly to respect for human life. It all too often happens that these movements are limited in their potential for action due to a lack of resources. When deciding on the allocation of gifts as well as to their amount, those activities which favor life deserve priority. If we want

Christians' witness to permeate hearts and institutions more, it is indispensable that militants for life have resources at their disposal that will be sufficient for effective action. This suggestion concerns not only individuals, but also private businesses and public powers. To make human life respected — what more noble cause could move the heart of sponsors and stimulate their generosity?

Another task that still faces us is the pursuit of research in the field of natural regulation of births.[3] The results already achieved in this matter are so remarkable that the number of couples desirous of being informed about these methods has not stopped growing. These methods can be explained to groups of families and taught in medical faculties. It is not illusory to envision in the end that these methods will eventually eclipse the artificial methods predominant today. What a victory that would be for couples and for love!

All these initiatives in favor of life deserve to be better known, and that is why it is comforting to see some of the media increasingly committed to a struggle whose issue depends on a certain conception of justice and right.

A special effort should be made regarding adoption. Since St. Peter Nolasco and St. Raymond Nonnatus, many Christians have fought for the redemption of captives. St. Vincent de Paul sent the Daughters of Charity into the streets to collect abandoned children. St. Peter Claver devoted his best to the slaves of America; it is also in this same spirit that St. Maximilian Kolbe offered his life.

Such examples can inspire new initiatives in order to reinforce a world network of solidarity in view of facilitating adoption, notably by a simplification of legislation regarding this matter. Some remarkable initiatives have already been taken in this direction, and they deserve to be encouraged by reason of the respect they show for the child and the help they offer mothers in difficulty, and also by reason of the treasure of tenderness thus offered to the affection of the adopting couple.

Education for Life

Since education plays a primordial role in the prevention of attacks on human life, Christians in the entire world must mobilize to enlighten individuals, families and those responsible for civil society. Christians who often play an outstanding role in teaching and education have, here again, a magnificent role to play. This role flows from the importance of sharing knowledge and know-how with a view toward an integrated action in favor of human life.

Having taken account of this objective, numerous religious institutes could redefine their goals and methods so that human life would benefit from the experience they have accumulated since their beginnings. This could include whatever would permit the poor to escape their situation of misery, and prepare them for a better perception of their dignity and their parental responsibility.

Investment needs to be made in new Christian educational forces in basic education, including that of adults. Examples given by the saints, such as St.John-Baptist de La Salle, St. Anthony Maria Claret, St. John Bosco, etc. remain the beacons for educators today.

In these educational tasks, special attention must be given to women, too often victims of discrimination in schooling. There again examples of sanctity give by St. Jeanne de France, St. Angela Merici, St. Madeleine Sophie Barat as well as St. Maria-Dominic Mazzarello show that commitment to Christian education can be a path of perfection.

Some Catholic institutions are directly concerned with respect for life. In New York, Cardinal John O'Connor founded a congregation which devotes itself completely to welcoming life. Such must be the case with nursing orders. The quality of their witness and their credibility require that they be examplary in what concerns respect for life. This quality of witness is also expected of Christian insurance groups, which cannot, by any stretch of the imagination, intervene financially in anti-life operations.

The same goes for Catholic universities from which the Church expects an irreproachable witness. To these universities falls a special effort of reflection on respect for life, beginning with the complementary clarifications offered by philosophy, theology, law, political science, economics, demography, agronomy, etc. By reason of their special responsibility, Catholic medical faculties must be irreproachable in all cases in which human life is threatened. Despite some public counter-witness that discredits the authorities who cover it up, today as in its beginning, the Church can count on legions of Christians to whom abuse of power is repugnant and who walk the path of the Good Samaritan of the Gospel.

Hospitals, insurance groups and universities need specialized pastoral attention to which all who serve in these institutions or have recourse to them have a right.

Option for the Poor

From its beginning, the Church has been invited by the Master to show a preferential but nonexclusive option for the poor. All through the centuries this option has been constant in the life of the Church. To effect this option is first of all to listen to the poor. The Lord identified with them (see Mt 25:34-36; 26:11, etc.): we must, therefore, pay attention to what He says to us through them. He effectively shows us the example through the widow and her mite (see Mk 12:41-44; Lk 21:1-4), and the widow of Sarephta (1 Kgs 17:9-24; see also Lk 4:25 f.). To be poor means also to be able to forgive (see Gn 50:19-21; 1 Sm 25:35; 2 Cor 2:10). Finally, to be poor means to accept dependence on others and on God. Contrary to the anxious foresight of the wealthy (see Lk 12:16-21), the lack of foresight disposes the poor to hope (see Mt 6:25-33; Lk 12:22-31; 1 Tm 6:17-19).

As for the rich, it is recommended that they follow the example given by the Lord Himself: welcoming the poor (see Lk 14:13 f.), a counsel given with a promise: "You will be repaid at the resurrection of the just." It is also recommended that those rich who have amassed their fortune through ill-gotten means reconcile themselves vis-à-vis the poor(see Lk 16:9).

In this way, Jesus traced the two lines of behavior to be adopted toward the poor. First, an attitude of humbly listening. Everywhere in the world the poor show the meaning of welcoming, hospitality and sharing. They are not inclined to sharing of their superfluity, for they haven't got any, but they share out of their substance. This habitual disposition of heart on the part of the poor is expressed, not only in their attitude toward newborn life, but to human life in general. "The poor are our teachers," St. Vincent de Paul used to say, because they teach us to love and serve the frailest child, the sick person whose health is on the decline, parents in their old age — or again by adopting the orphan, the abandoned baby, to help their neighbor by means of systems of mutual aid, and to love their neighbor by helping to build his house or to work his land.

Relearning to respect human life means, then, to relearn how to see life through the eyes of the poor, and to use the goods one has following the priorities flowing from the preferential option for the poor. Today the poorest of the poor is incontestably the unborn baby and, for this reason, he deserves the best place in the heart of men. However, if the unborn babies are the victims of anti-life campaigns, they are not the only ones. Anti-life campaigns always begin with systematic attacks on adults who are psychologically defenseless.

This situation reminds us of what Leo XIII said about workers in the ninteenth century. And, adapting the recommendations of *Rerum Novarum*, it is necessary for all actual or potential victims of campaigns hostile to life to associate and organize among themselves to ensure that their fundamental rights are respected. By reason of the extreme gravity of the situation, this action needs to be undertaken without delay. It will permit us to restore the cult of human life in all milieux, national and international, and in particular among all men who have the direct responsibility of building a society of justice and peace.

FOYER OF HAPPINESS: THE FAMILY

The crisis of the family incontestably contributes to the deterioration of the respect due to life. Reciprocally, this deterioration contributes toward accentuating the crisis of the family. To break this vicious circle, it is clear that action in favor of the family must be taken without delay. Since the family is the basic cell of society and is, par excellence, the foyer of human happiness, it is urgent that all men of good will exert themselves toward improving its status. A society built upon such foyers of love will be a society in which living together will be agreeable and in which the joy of the couple welcoming life will resound within the whole community.

Truth be told, this movement of reestablishing the value of the family has already been started. Efforts of renewal achieved in the Church's pastoral activities in marriage and baptism deserve to be greeted with joy.

Preparation for marriage is, in effect, a privileged occasion that is offered to prospective couples in order for them to understand the full human meaning of love, of sexuality, of fidelity and fecundity.[4] Preparation for marriage introduces them to the discovery of unsuspected facets of human love. It brings to life the most profound aspirations that God has placed in the heart of man. During the marriage preparation sessions, the young fiancés meet older people who are disposed to help them perceive, along with the demands of love, the graces that will permit them to respond to them.

Preparation for marriage is the ideal occasion for couples to discover that a baby is the most excellent gift that couples can offer each other and that is offered to them as a couple. During the preparation for baptism, the wonder over new life if doubled with the joy of obtaining the entrance of the child of men into the greater family of the children of God. It is in the name of God that the parents give to their child a name chosen with love. The wonder aroused by the baby is sung in Scripture which sees it as a gift of God (see Ps 127:3-5; 128:3-6), a divine blessing (Prov 10:1; 15:20; 17:6; 23:24; 27:11; 29:3) and foreshadowing the gift that God makes of his Son (Jn 3:16; 6:32 f.; 2 Cor 9:15).

How is the reestablishment of the value of the family conceivable without rediscovering the meaning of paternity? In human life, the father is, so to speak, called to be the revealer of the divine paternity. This specific role of the father is evoked in the story of creation. Created in the image of God, Adam becomes, in turn, the father of children who, like him, are the image of God (see Gn 5:1-3). Through the generations, the father is the link in the chain that attaches all men to the divine paternity.[5]

The teaching of the New Testament on Christ and the Church, as well as on man and woman, cuts short here any "macho" interpretation of the place of the man in the family. The sole privilege which the husband is able to take advantage of would be that of leaving father and mother and clinging to his spouse and that of serving and loving her as he loves himself (see Eph 5:25-33). The husband doesn't attain the fullness of his masculine humanity except through his spouse. If the unity of the couple supposes a complementarity of roles, this complementarity, in turn, excludes questioning the equal dignity of the spouses.

The first and the most basic duty of the husband vis-à-vis his wife is, therefore, to respect her for what she is and not for what he would want her to be. The second duty is to defend her — and at the same time to defend himself — against all who, under various pretexts, would want to interfere in their most intimate exchanges, and in their decisions and plans for transmitting life.

FOR AN AUTHENTIC FEMINISM
What Kind of Liberation for Women?

Apart from the unborn baby, the woman is the principal and most habitual victim of anti-life practices: victim, obviously in her flesh, but more so in her heart. Knowing very well, in effect, how much the heart and body of the woman are the marvelous jewel box in which a new man will be born, adversaries of life have presumed even to "dematernalize" the woman. Maternal sentiment is but a "cultural" given, and just as this fact appeared in history, it can disappear; this process can even be hastened.[6]

Already bludgeoned by Malthusian, neo-Malthusian, utilitarian and hedonist ideologies, woman is on the point of being mutilated in her heart. Once "dematernalized," "liberated" not only from the child but from every maternal instinct, woman is brought down to the level of personal pleasure and her availability for the pleasure of others. The "machismo" that is concealed behind these anti-life ideologies has this perversity in that it wants to pass off as the "right of women" what is really the ownership of the woman who may then be used by men at their discretion.[7]

It is high time that the half of humanity consisting of women, organize themselves before this world campaign that aims at nothing less than dispossessing them of their identity. We must unmask the lie that offers women the "new right," of letting themselves be filled with hormones, sterilized or aborted.

Very happily eyes are beginning to open and protests are being raised.[8] But it is also time that, being already humiliated or on the point of being humiliated, women of the entire world become conscious of the dangers that threaten them and which, through them, threaten the family and human society. For, as Mother Teresa of Calcutta liked to say: "In a society in which a mother is 'authorized' to kill her baby, anything becomes possible."

The world today needs an authentic feminism that reaffirms the specificity of the feminine nature and which strives to protect for women their inalienable role in the formation of the family and society.[9]

In this vast movement of mobilization, the collaboration of all women of good will is indispensable. In order to mobilize international public opinion, it is indispensable that all persons who have been sterilized or suffered pressure toward this end organize themselves in the name of their dignity and in the name of respect for life. To be effective, this mobilization must take place on a worldwide scale. In some rich countries, for instance, Germany, there is a growing trend already evident in many poor countries, namely that a certificate of sterilization is sometimes required in order to get a job.[10] After sterilization for racist motives there now appears sterilization for economic motives. Such practices, odious in themselves, are also odious, not only for the woman, but for her husband and her home. As for the State that closes its eyes or for employers who encourage these practices, the memory of some tragic precedents ought to lead them to see the error of their ways.

Women who, either willingly or by force, have abortions deserve a very special solicitude. The greater number of them feel permanently wounded and many bitterly regret what has happened. They must know that their repentance goes straight to the heart of God. The merciful Father is readily disposed, if they ask Him, to offer them pardon and peace in the sacrament of reconciliation. Following Christ who spoke to the sinful woman, the Church says to them: "Neither do I condemn you. Go; sin no more" (Jn 8:11). Perhaps, despite this pardon, Rachel will continue to weep for her children, for they are no more (see Jer 31:15; Mt 2:18). However, the memory of their little ones, who in heaven "constantly look upon the face of the father" (see Mt 18:10), should be a sign of hope for them: the hope of one day finding their child in the joy that fills the house of God.[11] The Church even recommends that these women commit themselves generously to the movements for life, where they will be welcomed fraternally. Through this commitment to life, crowned perhaps by the advent of other children, these women will be able to find again their pride in being women and the happiness of being mothers.

It would also be desirable if one could, without immediately being accused of simplistic antifeminism, propose that *women be offered the real possibility of choosing to remain at home or of a balanced adjustment between family life and work*. Spouses who choose to devote themselves entirely to their home and the education of their children habitually suffer pressure or unacceptable discrimination.[12] However, we should remark that some countries, which are among the most developed in the world, count but a small percentage of women among the active working population and these countries have a rate of unemployment markedly lower than others. Such is the case in Japan. Such examples merit closer study and, by means of certain adjustments, they could suggest other analogous initiatives.

From Power to Love

Finally, how could one erase what humanity has always known? By her very constitution and her psychology, woman is naturally inclined to make the relationships of love prevail over those of force.[13] In a world obsessed with success, riches and power, woman must be protected. She must be able to remain herself so that humanity will remember that there is no happiness except in loving and being loved.

Nine months are required for a baby to be formed in its mother's womb. If during this period and beyond the woman is plunged into a feeling of insecurity, if she no longer has reason to believe her husband will be faithful to her, and that together with her he will educate their child, in short, if she fears not being loved for always, how can she welcome the child with joy and why would she give herself over to the joys of being a mother?

The quality of a society can also then be measured according to the acknowledged place of the mother. The mother is always the first to recognize deeply within herself the beginning of a new human being.[14] It is she who offers this being, who is all weakness, to the acceptance of the father, the family, and society.

Human maternity is, then, not only an event of the personal and familial order, *it is also a political event*. This child welcomed by the mother, is presented for the recognition and welcome of society. It is still mandatory that society ratify this choice for life, which the mother has the inalienable privilege to express by making herself the first neighbor to this smallest of all human beings.

Salvation history had the same beginning. Informed by the angel, the young girl, Mary, one day recognized and welcomed the presence of a being within herself whom she then offered to the world (see Lk 1:26-38). Since that day, between the Blessed Virgin Mary and all mothers of the world, there has existed a relationship that nothing can destroy, for each infant born diffracts, in an absolutely unique fashion, the Light which impelled the shepherds to hasten to the crib.

THE CHURCH: SIGN OF HOPE

Direct attacks on human life express an extremely profound malaise in certain sections of human society. They are the visible tip of the iceberg: they show that the problem of development is much more profound than we have thought until now — namely, that men sometimes prefer to renounce their freedom rather than fight to earn it, and that the passion for exploiting and dominating is sometimes, so to speak, insatiable. They also show that the ideologies that immersed the twentieth century in fire and blood, far from being extirpated, are perhaps in the process of being radicalized. They reveal, finally, a practical atheism, analogous to that which, after having been enthroned in the cult of the State, the Race and the Party, is trying to enthrone the "idolatry of the market"[15] and is restoring the pagan cult of Mother-Earth toward this end.

The ideology that inspires practices hostile to human life boasts about offering the final solution to the problem of poverty. It is, nevertheless, the greatest deception of our times, since it turns man against himself and asks the powers of death to build the future of humanity.

The Church not only rejects this ideology but also the practices it inspires. She also rejects the unjust accusations the adversaries of life hurl at her because she refuses to accept the "evidence" concocted in certain neognostic secret societies and which are then swallowed whole and broadcast by the media, which is all too easily manipulated.

Before such "evidence," the Church asks very simply that people examine *all* the data of this certainly difficult problem, but whose solution is within the powers of men of good will.

The Church does not ignore the complexity of the demographic phenomena. But she takes into account the diversity of demographic situations according to various regions. She also states, with still more force than her detractors, that if the present dynamic continues, humanity is headed toward catastrophe. This dynamic leads to the destruction of humanity.

But the Church further states that, at their foundation, all questions relative to demographic situations are first questions of a moral nature and that is why the challenges must be raised and considered with realism. Christians take note of the "growing awareness of the interdependence among individuals and nations' (*On Social Concerns* 38), and they know that the path to happiness consists in building a world of solidarity. John Paul II wrote: "It is above all a question of interdependence, perceived as a *system determining* relationships in the contemporary world in its economic, cultural, political and religious dimensions, and accepted as a *moral category*. When interdependence becomes recognized in this way, the correlative response as a moral and social attitude, as a 'virtue' is *solidarity* (*Ibid*. 38). Further: "The 'evil mechanisms' and 'structures of sin'... can be overcome only through the exercise of the human and Christian solidarity to which the Church calls us and which she tirelessly promotes" (Ibid. 40).

Transgressions against human life, then, appear as transgressions against solidarity among men and against solidarity between men and their Creator.

That is why practices against human life and laws that claim to legitimize them call for resolute resistance on the part of all who defend and believe in justice. Such laws and practices are opposed to the common good and do injury to man, who is the image of God. This resistance can undoubtedly be offered by way of conscientious objection, but it can also encompass morally correct methods of opposition that all tyranny merits.

The church does not, however, confine herself to these warnings, as opportune as they may be. She wants to be sign of joyful hope among men. She proclaims the Gospel of life: the infant, she proclaims, is a source of joy; as children of the same Father, all men are called to be brothers. People have been made stewards of creation by God. God has not burdened them with insolvable problems, when we consider the capacities with which He has endowed men.

Finally, to announce the dignity of all human life is an essential aspect of the *new evangelization*. Faced with new forms of idolatry, the Church is, once again, put to the challenge. In the same breath, she must proclaim God and she must proclaim man. She must proclaim God in order to defend man; she must proclaim man so that, beginning with the understanding of his dignity, he can once again find the way to God.

This God who loves us is contemplated by all the innocents who, since the time of Herod, have been victims of the malice of men. This God who loves us has also given to each of us a mother in the Virgin Mary who, as she carried Jesus, carries each of us inside her heart. In this combat in which St. Michael the Archangel once again lends a strong hand to the Mother of the Savior, it is Mary whom the Church implores to intercede with her Son, so that He may give to everyone the joy of giving thanks for life both received and shared.

---

[1] See GS 4, 11; the decree on ecumenism of Vatican II, *Unitatis Redintegratio* 4; and the Council's decree on the ministry and life of priests: *Presbyterorum Ordinis* 6, 9.

[2] On this subject see Cardinal Ratzinger, Chapter I, note 22.

[3] On natural methods, see the works cited in Chapter XII, note 8.

[4] The Pontifical Council for the Family has published a precious brochure, *Préparation au sacrement de mariage* (Vatican City: Libr. Edit. Vaticana, 1996.

[5] See *supra*, Chapter XII, **Image of the Creator**.

[6] See *supra*, Chapter II, *The Influence of Structuralism*.

[7] See *BPCV* qu. 19.

[8] *Ibid.* qu 96, 121.

[9] The most important pontifical document devoted to the Christian vision of woman is without doubt the Apostolic Letter of John Paul II, *Mulieris dignitatem* (1988). Among more recent documents let us mention his message for the World Day of Peace (Jan. 1, 1995) *La Femme éducatrice de paix*; the discourse of Gertrude Mongella, secretary general of the Beijing conference (May 16, 1995), *La Dignité de la femme*; the Letter to Women, *La Dignité et les droits des femmes à la lumiére de la Parole de Dieu* (June 29, 1995); *L'Engagement de l'Eglise en faveur de la jeune femme et de la petite fille* (Aug. 19, 1995).

[10] See *supra*, *Life Dried up in its Source*.

[11] See the beautiful page devoted by John Paul II to mothers in his *Evangelium Vitae* n.99.

[12] See *supra*, Chapter XI, **Guidelines for a Family Policy**

[13] This is what Marie Hendrickx emphasizes in "Quelle mission pour la femme? *Louvain* (Louvain-la-Neuve) n.4, April 1989, pp.15 f.

[14] *Ibid.*

[15] *CA* 40.

ACKNOWLEDGEMENTS

In the pluralist milieu of publishing Mr. Jean-Claude Didelot preserves a place for freedom: a rare treasure for which he knows well the price! For this reason, as well as many others, we thank him for having welcomed us yet again into the Fayard Editions, among the prestigious collections which he directs and animates.

Miss Anne-Marie Libert, with degrees in philosophy and theology, has helped us find and scrutinize abundant and first-hand documentation from international organizations and specialized institutions.

For Chapter II to V, we have largely made use of interviews, documents and analyses placed at our disposal by Miss Marguerite A. Peeters. These reports are disseminated by the Interactive Information Service (IIS) of the Center for the New Europe (CNE) of Brussels (Email: m.peeters@cne.be). Moreover, Miss Peeters kindly reread these chapters in our manuscript and offered us helpful observations and suggestions.

Miss Anne-France Saglio, of Fayard Editions, has, with competence and devotion watched over every step of this edition.

May all three kindly accept our warmest gratitude!

BIBLIOGRAPHY

Abortion. A Tabulation of Available Data on the Frequency and Mortality of Unsafe Abortion, 2nd ed., document WHO/FHE/MSM93-13. Geneva: WHO, 1994.

Abortion Policies: A Global Review, New York: U.N. Department of Economic and Social Development, 3 vols. 1992, 1992, 1993, 1995.

John S. Aird, *Family Planning, Women and Human Rights in the People's Republic of China*, report of 34 pp., pro manuscripto. Taipei, Sept. 1995.
Foreign Assistance to Coercive Family Planning in China. Response to Recent Population Policy in China by Terence Hull (Canberra, 1992).
Death by Default. A Policy of Fatal Neglect in China's State Orphanages. New York: Human Rights Watch, 1996.

Maria Jose Alcalá, *Compromosos para la salud y los derechos sexuales y reproductivos de todos. Marco de acción. Sobre la base de los acuerdos y convenciones internacionales pertinentes, incluidas las conferencias de Beijing, Copenhague, El Cairo y Viena.* New York: Family Care International, 1995.

Louis Althusser, *Lire le Capital*, I-II. Paris: Maspero, 1966.

Mercedes Arzu Wilson, *Amour et fécondité*. BBE, 1986.

Jacques Attali, "La médecine en accusation," in Michael Salomon (ed.), *L'Avenir de la vie*. Paris: Seghers, 1981.

Associação Brasileira de Estudios Populacionais, *VIII Encontro nacional de Estudios Populacionais*, Acts of the Congress held at Brasilia, Sept. 25-29, 1992 (São Paulo, 1992).

Elizabeth Badinter, *L'Amour en plus*. Paris: Flammarion, 1980.

World Bank, *Rapport sur le développement dans le monde 1993. Investir dans la santé*. Washington, 1993.

The World Bank Research Program 1995. Abstracts of Current Studies. Washington, 1995.

Gary Becker, *A Treatise on the Family*. Cambridge, MA: Harvard Univ. Press, 1991.

'*Human Capital*. New York: Columbia Univ. Press, 3rd ed., 1993.

Beijing Declaration and Platform for Action. Beijing Conference, Sept. 15, 1995.

Karl Binding, Alfred Hoche, "Permitting the Destruction of Unworthy Life," in *Issues in Law and Medicine*, Vol.2, n.8 (Autumn, 1992).

Ellen Brantlinger, *Sterilization of People with Mental Disabilities*. Westport, CT.: Auburn House, 1995.

Rodolfo A. Bulatao, *Key Indicators for Family Planning Projects*. Technical Paper 297. Washington: World Bank, 1995.

Antonio A Cançado Trindade, "Memoria da Conferencia Mundial Direitos Humanos (Viena, 1993)," in *Revista brasileira de Estudios Politicos* (UFMG, Belo Horizonte) n.90 (Jan. 1995) 149-224.

Giovanni Cardascia, *Les Lois assyriennes*. Paris: Cerf, 1969.

Anne Carol, *Histoire de L'eugénisme en France. Les médecins et la procréation, XIXE-XXe siècle*. Paris: Seuil, 1995.

Philippe Caspar, *Penser l'embryon d'Hippocrate à nos jours*. Paris: Edit. Universitaires, 1991.

Charte de personnels de la santé. Vatican City: Lib. Edit. Vaticana, 1995.

Pierre Chaunu, *Trois millions d'années*. Paris: Laffont, 1990.

Warren Christopher, *American Diplomacy and the Global Environmental Challenges of the 21st Century*. Palo Alto, CA: U.S. Dept of State, 1996.

Sandra Coliver, *The Right to Know. Human Rights and Access to Reproductive Health Information*, United Kingdom, Article 19. University of Pennsylvania Press, 1995.

Maria-Eugenia Cosio-Zavala, *Changement de fécondité au Mexique et politiques de population*. Paris: L'Harmattan, 1994.

Stig Dagerman, *Notre besoin de consolation est impossible à rassasier*. Actes Sud, Hubert Nyssen, 1981.

Daniel-Ange, *Sida: safe-sex ou save sex*? Paris: Fayard, 1997.

Ton corps fait pour. . . un même corps? Paris: Fayard, 1997.

Godfried Danneels, *Le Christ ou le Verseau*. Malines, 1990.

"La démographie," in *La Jaune et la Rouge* (Paris) n.506 (June-July, 1995) 22-56.

Donum Vitae in *DC*, n. 1937 (April 5, 1987) 349-361.

Yixin Duan, "Valuing International Assistance," *Integration Journal* (Tokyo) 32 f.

Gerard-François Dumont, *Pour la liberté familiale*. Paris: PUF, 1986.

Le Festin de Kronos Paris: Fleurus, 1991.

"La science peut-elle être neutre? Le cas de la démographie," in *La Famille: des sciences à l'éthique*, Paris: Bayard, 1995 pp. 27-40.

Le Monde et les hommes. Les grandes évolutions démographiques. Paris: Litec, 1995.

René Dumont, *L'Utopie ou la Mort*. Paris: Seuil, 1973.

Rudolf Ehmann, "Problems in Family Planning," in *Anthropotes* (Rome) n.1 (1991) 95-126.

Friedrich Engels, *L'Origine de la famille, de la propriété privée et de l'Etat* [1884]. Paris: Editions sociales, 1954.

Evolutions démographiques: dimensions éthiques et pastorales. Vatican City: Libr. Edit. Vaticana, 1994.

Anne Fausto-Sterling, "The Five Sexes. Why Male and Female are not Enough," *The Sciences* (March-April, 1993) 20-24.

Marylin Ferguson, *Les Enfants du Verseau. Pour un nouveau paradigme.* Paris: J'ai Lu. 1995.

J. Ferin, "Communication," in Charles Robert (ed.), *L'Homme manipulé*. Strasburg: Cerdic, 1974; see pp. 25-34.

Xosé Figueroa Custodio, "La Francomasoneria hermetica," *Excelsior* (Mexico City) Dec. 7, 1991, p.11.

Giorgio Filibeck, *Les Droits de l'homme dans l'enseignement de l'Eglise: de Jean XXIII à Jean-Paul II*. Vatican City: Libr. Edit. Vaticana, 1992.

Shulamith Firestone, *The Dialectic of Sex. The Case for Feminist Revolution.* New York: Bantam, 1971.

U.N. Fund for Population Activities (UNFPA) *Inventor of Population Projects in Developing Countries Around the World*. New York: UNFPA, 1994.

The State of World Population 1995, New York.

Michel Foucault, *Histoire de la sexualité*. Paris: Gallimard, 19976. T.I: *La Volonté de savoir*; T.II: *Le souci de soi*, 1984.

Naissance de la clinique. Paris: PUF, 1963.

Gaudium et Spes in *Concile oecumenique Vatican II*. Paris: Centurion, 1967.

Hubert Gerard, "Le point de vue du démographe," in *L'Explosion démographique au crible des valeurs humaines et chrétiennes*. Louvain, Fac. of Theology, 1972.

Giovanni Paulo II, *La visione cristiana dell'ambiente. Testi del Magistero Pontificio scelti a cura di Padre Bernardo J. Przewozny*. Pisa: Giardini Editori, 1991.

René Girard, *Le Bouc émissaire*. Paris: Grasset, 1982.
Quand ces choses commenceront... Paris: Arléa, 1994.

Mary Ann Glendon, *Abortion and Divorce in Western Law. American Failures, European Challenges*. Cambridge, MA: Harvard Univ. Press, 1987.
"Woman's World: Beijing and Beyond," in *Church* (New York) Summer, 1996, 19-24.
Rights Talk. The Impoverishment of Political Discourse. New York: The Free Press, 1991.

Ellen Grant, *Amère pillule. Le "contraceptif parfait" est-il sans danger?* Paris: Oeil, 1988.

Germaine Greer, *Sexe et destinée*. Paris: Grasset, 1986.

David Griffin, "The Immunoregulation of Fertility — Changes in Perspectives," *American Journal of Reproductive Immunology* n.35 (1996) 140-147.

David Griffin et al., "Anti-Fertility Vaccines: Current Status and Implications for Family Planning Programmes," *Reproductive Health Matters* n.3 (Geneva: WHO, May 1994) 108-114.

David Griffin, Julie Milstien and J. W. Lee, "Damage to Immunization Programmes through Misinformation on Contraceptive Vaccines," *Reproductive Health Matters*, n.6 (Geneva: WHO, Nov. 1995) 24-28.

Robert E. Hall, *Abortion in a Changing World*. New York: Columbia Univ. Press, 1970.

Heidi I. Hartman, "Capitalism, Patriarchy and Job Segregations by Sex," in M. Blaxall and B. B. Reagan (Eds.), *Women in the Workplace. Implications of Occupational Segregation* (Chicago: Univ. of Chicago Press, 1976) 137-169.
"The Unhappy Marriage of Marxism and Feminism. Towards a More Progressive Union," in L. Sargent (Ed.), *Women and Revolution* (London: Pluto Press, 1981) 40-53.

William A. Haseltine, *Exposé fait à l'Academie des sciences à Paris*, Nov. 16, 1992, pro manuscripto (Via Aurelia 218, I - 00165 Rome).

Marie Hendrickx, "Le Magistère et la peine de mort. Réflexions sur le Catéchisme et *Evangelium Vitae*," in *Nouvelle Revue Théologique* (Namur) 118, 1 (Jan-Feb. 1996) 3-22.
"Famille et société dans l'enseignement du Magistère," *Anthropotes* n.1 (Jan-Feb. 1996) 3-22.
"Quelle mission pour la famille?" *Louvain* n.4 (April 1989) 15 f.

G. M. Higgins et al. (Ed.), *Capacité potentielle de charge démographique des terres du monde en développement. Rapport technique du Project Int/75/P13. Les ressources en terres des population de demain.* Rome: FAO, 1984.

Hippocrate de Cos, *De l'art médical.* Trans. By Emile Littre. Paris: Livre de Poche, 704 LP 18, 1994.

Interactive Information Service (IIS), Center for New Europe (Brussels), various reports 1995-1996. Email: m.peeters@cne.be.

International Planned Parenthood Federation (IPPF), *Informe Annual.* London.
Plano estratégico. Visión año 2000. London, 1993 and ff.

Stephen Isaacs (ed.), *Politique de population. Un manuel pour les planificateurs et les responsables politiques*, 2nd ed. New York: Columbia Univ. Press, 1991.

Alison M. Jagger, *Feminist Politics and Human Nature.* Totowa, NJ: Rowman & Allanheld, 1983.

Karl Jaspers, *La Bombe atomique et l'avenir de l'humanité.* Paris: Buchet-Chastel, 1963.
La Culpabilité allemande. Paris: Minuit, 1948.

John Paul II, *Redemptor Hominis* [1979], DC n.1761 (April 1, 1979) 301-323.
Laborem exercens [1981], DC n.1815 (Oct. 4, 1981) 835-856.
Apostolic Exhortation *Familiaris Consortio* [1981], DC n.1821 (Jan. 3, 1982) 1-37.
Discours au Congrès des médecins catholiques [Oct. 3, 1982] DC n.1840 (Nov. 21, 1982) 1029-1032.
On Social Concerns [1987], DC 1957 (Mar. 6, 1988) 233-256.
Apostolic letter *Mulieris dignitatem* [1988], DC n.1957 (Nov. 20, 1988) 1063-1088.
Centesimus Annus [1991], DC n.2029 (June 2, 1991) 518-550.
Veritatis Splendor [1993], DC n.2081 (Nov. 7, 1993) 901-944.
Evangelium Vitae [1995], DC n.2114 (April 16, 1995) 351-405.
Journal of the Group of 77. P.O. Box 20, New York, NY 10017.

Daniel J. Kevles, *Au nom de l'eugénisme. Génétique et politique dans le monde anglo-saxon.* Paris: PUF, 1995.

Alexandre Kojève, *Introduction à la lecture de Hegel.* Paris: Gallimard, 1947.

Hans Küng & Karl Josef Kuschel (eds.), *Manifeste pour une éthique planétaire. La déclaration du Parlement des religions du monde.* Paris: Cerf, 1995.

James Kurth, "Hacia el mundo posmoderno," *Facetas* (Feb. 2, 1993) 8-13.

Etienne de La Boétie, *Le Discours de la servitude volontaire*. Paris: Payot, 1976.

Philippe de La Chapelle, *La Déclaration universelle des droits de l'homme et le catholicisme*. Paris: Librairie Général de Droit et de Jurisprudence, 1967.

Jean-Didier Lecaillon, *La Famille, source de prospérité*. Paris: Regnier, 1995.

Gaston Legrain and Pierre Delvoye, *La Planification familiale pratique et opérationnelle*. Paris: Hatier, 1994.

Jerome Lejeune, *L'Enceinte concentrationnaire, d'après les minutes du procès de Maryville*. Paris: Fayard, 1990.

Leo XIII, *Quod Apostolici Muneris* (1878), in Emile Marmy, *La Communauté humaine*, 66-77.
Diuturnum illud (1881), *ibid.* 447-463.
Immortale Dei (1885), *ibid.* 464-486.
Libertas Praestantissimum (1888), *ibid.* 36-65.
Rerum Novarum (1891), *ibid.* 295-334.

Claude Lévi-Strauss, *Anthropologie structurale*. Paris: Plon, 1958.

Robert Jay Lifton, *Les Médecins Nazis. Le meurtre médical et la psychologie du génocide*. Paris: Laffont, 1989.

Magaly Llaguno, *Homosexualismo y Sida*. Vida Humana Internacional, 4345 SW 72nd Ave., Suite E, Miami FL. 33155.

Judith Lorber and Susan A. Farrell (eds.), *The Social Construction of Gender*. Newbury Park, CA: Sage, 1991.

Henri de Lubac, *La Postérité spirituelle de Joachim de Flore*. Paris: Lethielleux, T.I: *De Joachim à Schelling*, 1978; T.II: *De Saint-Simon à nos jours*, 1980.

Elizabeth S. Maguire, *Evaluating Reproductive Health Programs: Perspective for the U.S. Agency for International Development. Pro manuscripto*, Annual Meeting of the Population Association of America, San Francisco, CA, 1995.

Halfdan Mahler, *Global Strategy for Health for All by the Year 2000. The Spiritual Dimension*. Geneva: WHO, EB 73/15. Oct. 21, 1983.

Thomas Robert Malthus, *Essai sur le principe de population*. Paris: Institut national d'études démographiques, 1980.

Emile Marmy, *La Communauté humaine selon l'esprit chrétien*. Friburg-Paris, 1949.

George Martine, "Brazil's Fertility Decline — 1965-1995," in *Population and Development Review* (New York: Population Council) vol.2, n.1 (March 1996) 47-75.

Karl Marx & Friedrich Engels, *L'Idéologie allemande* (1846). Paris: Editions Sociales, 1968.

Robert S. McNamara, *Une politique démographique mondiale pour promouvoir le développement humain* au XXe siècle. (New York: UN, 1991).

James A. Miller, "Baby-Killing Vaccine: Is It being Stealth Tested?" *HLI Reports* (Gaithersburg, MD) June-July, 1995, pp.1, 2, 8.

Alexander Mitscherlich and Fred Mielke, *Medezin ohne Menschlichkeit*. Frankfurt: Fischer, 1989.

Theodore Mommsen, *Le Droit pénal romain*. T. XVIII of *Manuel des Antiquités romaines*. Paris: Fontemoing, 1907.

Henrietta Moore, *A Passion for Difference. Essays in Anthropology and Gender*. Cambridge, UK: Polity Press, 1994.

Stephen D. Mumford, *The Life and Death of NSSM 200*. Center for Research on Population and Security, P.O. Box 13067, Research Triangle Park, North Carolina 27709, 1994.

Charles Murray and Richard Herrnstein, *The Bell Curve. Intelligence and Clan Structure in American Life*. New York: Free Press, 1994.

Josette L. Murray, *Gender Issues in World Bank Lending*. Washington: World Bank, 1995.

Hiroshi Nakajima, *Allocution au conseil exécutif de l'Assemblée mondiale de la santé*. Geneva: WHO, Jan. 14, 1991, A44/DIV/4.

Allocution au conseil exécutif de l'Assemblée mondiale de la santé. Geneva: WHO, Jan. 21, 1992, A45/DIV/4.

Allocution au conseil exécutif de l'Assemblée mondiale de la santé. Geneva: WHO, May 3, 1994, A47/DIV/4.

Ethique de la santé au niveau mondial. Rôle et contribution de l'OMS. Geneva: WHO, EB95/Inf. Doc/20. Jan. 23, 1995.

Lennart Nilsson, *A Child is Born*. New York: Doubleday, 1989.

O Codigo de Hammurabi. 2nd ed. Petropolis: Vozes, 1976, pp.89-90.

Dale O'Leary, Gender: *The Deconstruction of Women*. Pro manuscripto, P.O. Box 41294, Providence, RI 02940.

Overview of USAID Population Assistance 1993. Washington: USAID, April 1994.

Blaise Pascal, *Pensées et Opuscules*. Paris: Hachette, 1945.

Paul VI, *Discours à des évêques américains*, May 26, 1978, in DC 1744 (June 18, 1978) 553.

Peiyun Peng, "A Long Way to Go," *Integration Journal* (Tokyo), 2-5.

Plato, *Oeuvres complètes*. Paris: Gallimard, 2 vols. 1950.

Plutarch, *Vie d'Alexandre le Grand* in *Les Vies des hommes illustres*, t.II Paris: Gallimard, 1968.

Population Reference Bureau, *World Population Data Sheet*. Washington, DC: 1875 Connecticut Ave., NW Suite 520.

Préparation au sacrement de mariage. Vatican City, Lib. Editrice, Vaticana, 1996.

Programa nacional de población, 1995-2000. Mexico City: Poder Ejecutivo Federal, 1995.

Programme of Action of the United Nations International Conference on Population and Development. Cairo Conference, Sept. 5-13, 1994.

Propuesta para una Declaración Universal de los Derechos Humanos desde una perspectiva de género. Lima: CLADEM, 1994.

Joseph Cardinal Ratzinger, "Le relativisme est aujourd'hui le problème central de la foi et de la théologie," in DC 2151 (Jan 5, 1997) 29-37.

Review and Appraisal of the World Population Plan of Action. 1994 Report. New York: UN 1995.

Fenneke Reysoo et al., *The Incentive Trap. A Study on Coercion, Reproductive Rights and Women's Automony in Bangladesh*. Leiden: Rijks University, 1995.

Adrienne Rich, *On Woman Born*. New York: Norton, 1976.

"Compulsory Heterosexuality and lesbian Existence," in *Blood, Bread and Poetry. Selected prose, 1979-1985*. New York: Norton, 1986.

Judith Richter, *Vaccination against Pregnancy. Miracle or Menace?* Amsterdam: van Lennepkade 334 T; Health Action International, 1993.

Norberto Rivera Carrera, *Instrucción pastoral sobre el New Age*. Mexico City, Archbishop's House, 1996.

John A. Ross et al., *Family Planning and Child Survival Programs as Assessed in 1991*. New York: UN, 1992.

J. Roux, *Précis historique et théorique de marxisme-léninisme*. Paris: Laffont, 1969.

Joaquim Carlos Salgado, "Os Direitos Fundamentalais," *Revista Brasileira de Estudios Politicos* (Belo Horizonte) n.82 (Jan. 1996) 15-69).

U. Schaz & I. Schneider, *Antibodies Against Pregnancy*. Video from Bleicherstrasse 2, Hamburg, 1991.

Philippe Schepens, *L'Euthanasie. Pourquoi en Hollande?* Ostende: World Federation of Doctors who Defend Life, 1995.

René & Marie Sentis, *Amour et fécondité*. Paris: Fayard, 1986.

Michael Serres, *Le Contrat naturel*. Paris: Flammarion, 1990.

Pierre Simon, *De la vie avant toute chose*. Paris: Mazarine, 1979.

Simon Stanley & Sarah Hyde, *Handbook on European Union Support for Population and Reproductive Health Programmes*. New York: UNFPA, 1995.

Pierre-André Taguieff, "Sur l'eugénisme: du fantasme au débat," *Pouvoirs* (Paris) n.56 (1991) 23-64.

Technical Definitions and Commentary. WHO, Division of Family Health and Special Programme of Research and Research Training in Human Reproduction, Geneva-Cairo, 1994.

Yves Ternon, *L'Etat criminel. Les génocides au XXe siècle*. Paris: Seuil, 1995.

A. De Tocqueville, *Democracy in America*. Vol. I: New York: Knopf, 1948.

Alvin Toffler, *Les Nouveaux pouvoirs*. Paris: Fayard, 1991.

Maurice Torelli, *Le Médecin et les droits de l'homme*. Paris: Berger-Levrault, 1983.

Stephen Trombley, *The Right to Reproduce. A History of Coercive Sterilization*. London: Weidenfeld & Nicolson, 1988.

UNICEF, report on *La Situation des enfants dans le monde 1996*. New York, 1996.

U.N., *Declaration et Programmes d'action de Vienne*. June 1993. New York, 1995.

Rodrigo Vera, "Controversia en torno de la vacuna antitetánica," in *Proceso* (Mexico City) n.971 (June 12, 1995) 32-35.

Albert Verdoodt, *Naissance et signification de la Déclaration universelle des droits de l'homme*. Louiain-Paris: Nauwelaerts, 1963.

Jacques Verhaegen (ed.), *Licéité en Droit positif et Références légales aux valeurs*, Brussels: Bruylant, 1982.

Jean Vernette, "Sectes, nouveaux mouvements religieux et nouvelles croyances," *Esprit et Vie* (Langres) n.36 (Sept. 7, 1995) 481-491.
Le Nouvel Age. A l'aube de l'ère du Verseau. Paris: Téqui, 1990.

Jean-Jacques Walter, *Les Machines totalitaires*. Paris: Denoël, 1982.

Max Weber, *Le Savant et le Politique*. Paris: Le Monde, 1959.

H. T. Wilson, *Sex and Gender. Making Cultural Sense of Civilization*. Leiden: Brill, 1989.

C. E. A. Winslow, *Le Coût de la maladie et le prix de la santé*. Geneva: WHO, 1952.

Elizabeth Wollast & Marcel Vekemans, *Pratique et gestion de la planification familiale dans les pays en voie de developpement*. Brussels: De Boeck, 1995.

World Contraceptive Use 1994, pamphlet published by the U.N., Department for Economic and Social Information, Population Division, New York, 1994.

World Health Organization, *Towards a Paradigm for Health*, DGO/91.1, Geneva: June 19, 1991.
Reproductive Health: A Key to a Brighter Future. Geneva: WHO, 1994.
Challenges in Reproductive Health Research. Biennial Report 1992-1993. Geneva: WHO, 1994.
Documents fondamentaux, 40th edit. Geneva: WHO, 1994.
Rapport sur la santé dans le monde 1995. Réduire les écarts. Geneva: WHO, 1995.
Reproductive Health Priorities. Safe Motherhood. The Mother-Baby Package. Geneva: WHO, 1995.
Mother-Baby Package: Implementing Safe Motherhood in Countries. Practical Guide. Geneva: WHO, 1995.
Achieving Reproductive Health for All. The Role of WHO. Geneva: WHO, 1995.
Ethics and Health, and Quality in Health Care. Report by the Director-General to Executive Board, 97th session (Geneva) document EB97/16, Jan. 9, 1996.

World Urbanization Projects. The 1994 Revision. New York: U.N., 1994.

Index

A

Abzug, Bela 26
Adeodato de Souza, Guaraci 174
Aird, John 26, 81, 174, 219
Alcalá, Maria Jose 80, 219
Alexander, Samuel 60
Alexander the Great 149
Althusser, Louis 26, 219
Arendt, Hannah 129
Aristotle 57, 97, 149
Arius 61
Arzú Wilson, Mercedes 193
Attali, Jacques 123, 132, 228

B

Bachelard, Gaston 49, 57
Badinter, Elizabeth 27, 219
Bahamon, Claire 15
Baufle, Jean-Marie 119
Baulieu, Etienne-Emile 2
Becker, Gary 186, 204, 220
Bel, René 15
Bentham, Jeremy 19, 44
Binding, Karl 14, 54, 91, 228
Blaxall, M. 26, 222
Blayo, Chantal 14
Boné, Edouard 60
Boutros-Ghali, Boutros 64, 65, 80
Bouzon, E. 119
Brantlinger, Ellen 26, 220
Brunschvicq, Léon 104
Bryant, John H. 47
Bulatao, Rodolfo A. 47, 220

C

Cançado Trinidade, Antonio 220
Candau, Marcolino 30
Caprile, Giovanni 119
Cardascia, Guillaume 119, 220
Carol, Anne 26, 220
Caspar, Philippe 119, 220
Chafarévitch, Igor 129
Chaunu, Pierre 175, 220
Christopher, Warren 60, 220
Cicero 77
Clark, Colin 175
Clement of Alexandria 110, 114
Coliver, Sandra 220
Cosio-Zavala, Maria-Eugenia 174, 220

D

Dagerman, Stig 15, 220
Daniel-Ange 220
Danneels, Godfried 61, 220
De Greef, Etienne 8
Delvoye, Pierre 15, 224
Driesch, Hans 60
Duan, Yixin 25, 220
Dumont, Gérard-François 81, 86, 104, 175, 186, 221
Dumont, René 16, 174, 221
Durkheim, Emile 26

E

Ehmann, Rudolf 193, 221

Engels, Friedrick 21, 22, 23, 26, 221, 225

F

Farrell, Susan A. 26, 224
Fausto-Sterling, Anne 26, 221
Ferguson, Marilyn 50, 51, 52, 54, 59, 60, 61, 221
Ferin, J. 119, 221
Feuerbach, Ludwig 17
Figueroa Custodio, Xosé 61, 221
Filibeck, Giorgio 119, 221
Firestone, Shulamith 26, 221
Flavius, Josephus 113
Foucault, Michel 26, 49, 50, 60, 221
Friedan, Betty 26

G

Galbraith, John Kenneth 175
Galton, Francis 19, 44, 45
Gérard, Hubert 174
Girard, René 15, 222
Glendon, Mary Ann 81, 120, 222
Grant, Germaine 193, 222
Greer, Germaine 204, 222
Griffin, David 14, 222
Grotius, Hugo 127

H

Hall, Robert E. 16, 222
Hammad, A. 31, 32
Hammurabi 113, 119, 225
Hartman, Heidi I. 26, 222
Haseltine, WIlliam A. 15, 222
Hegel 129, 132, 223
Hendrickx, Marie 120, 175, 216, 222
Herod 111, 216
Herrnstein, Richard 26, 225
Higgins, G.M. 152, 223
Hippocrate de Cos 119, 223
Hitler, Adolf 9, 124
Hoche, Alfred 14, 128, 129, 220
Hyde, Sarah 80, 227

I

Isaacs, Stephen 16, 223
Israel, Lucien 129, 193

J

Jagger, Alison 27, 223
Jaspers, Karl 14, 15, 129, 223
John Paul II 78, 91, 114, 115, 120, 151, 194, 196, 202, 215, 216, 223
John XXIII 174
Justinian 120

K

Kaplan, Ed 14
Kelsen, Hans 124
Kevles, Daniel J. 26, 223
King, Maurice 60
Kissinger, Henry 11, 152
Kojève, Alexandre 129, 223
Kuhn, Thomas S. 49, 60
Küng, Hans 60, 223
Kuschel, Karl Josef 60, 223
Kurth, James 25, 81, 224

L

LaBoétie, Etienne de 173, 175, 228
LaChapelle, Philippe de 80, 228
LaColombière, Claude de 198
LeCaillon, Jean-Didier 174, 175, 186, 224
Lee, J.W. 14, 222
Legrain, Gaston 15, 224
Lejeune, Jérôme 119, 224
Lenin 18
Leo XIII 6, 104, 168, 206, 209, 224
Lévi-Strauss, Claude 26, 224
Lévy-Bruhl, Lucien 26
Lifton, Robert J. 125, 132, 224
Llaguno, Magaly 15, 224
Lorber, Judith 26, 224
Lubac, Henri de 61, 224
Lycurgus 113

M

Magazzeni, G. 80
Maguire, Elizabeth 16, 224
Mahler, Halfdan 29, 224
Malthus, Thomas 18, 19, 149, 170, 201, 202, 204, 224
Marmy, Emile 224
Martine, George 174, 225
Marx, Karl 18, 21, 22, 23, 26, 44, 183, 225
McNamara, Robert S. 11, 16, 225
Mielke, F. 132, 225
Miller, James A. 14, 225
Miller, Janice 15
Millett, Kate 26
Milstien, Julie 14, 222
Mitscherlich, Alexander 132, 225
Molay, Jacques de 61
Mommsen, Theodore 113, 119, 225
Mongella, Gertrude 216
Moore, Henrietta L. 26, 225
Morgan, Conwy Lloyd 60
Mumford, Stephen D. 16, 225
Murray, Charles 26, 225
Murray, Josette L. 27, 225

N

Nakajima, Hiroshi 29, 31, 32, 41, 42, 48, 57, 59, 68, 225
Napoleon 130
Nathanson, Bernard 204
Newton, Isaac 15, 50
Nilsson, Lennart 119, 225

O

O'Connor, John J. 208
O'Leary, Dale 26, 225

P

Pascal, Blaise 104, 225
Paul VI 114, 186, 189, 190, 193, 206, 226
Peeters, Marguertie A. 41, 46, 80, 81, 217

Peng, Peiyun 25, 226
Philip the Fair 61
Piel, Anthony 68, 81
Plato 18, 182, 226
Plutarch 149, 152, 228
Polin, Claude 129
Przewozny, J. 152, 221

R

Ratzinger, Joseph 15, 216, 226
Rawls, John 45
Reagan, B.B. 26, 222
Reysoo, Fenneke 226
Rich, Adrienne 27, 226
Richter, Judith 14, 226
Rivera Carrera, Norberto 226
Robert, Charles 119, 221
Robin, Leon 25
Ross, John A. 160, 226
Rousseau, Jean-Jacques 130, 140
Roux, Jean 226

S

Salgado, Joaquim Carlos 80, 226
Salomon, Michel 132, 219
Sanger, Margaret 24, 182
Sargent, L. 26, 222
Schaz, U. 14, 227
Schepens, Philippe 14, 227
Schneider, I. 14, 227
Schwarzenberg, Léon 125
Sentis, René 193, 227
Sentis, Marie, 193, 227
Serres, Michael 51, 60, 227
Severus, Septimus 113
Simon, Pierre 13, 16, 45, 48, 61, 227
Smuts, Jan Christian 59, 60
Solon 113, 124
Speth, Gustave 33
Spinoza, Baruch 127
Stanley, Simon 80, 227
Stuart Mill, John 45

T

Taguieff, Pierre-André 26, 227
Teilhard de Chardin, Pierre 51, 52
Teresa of Calcutta 212
Ternon, Yves 15, 132, 227
Tocqueville, Alexis 104, 227
Toffler, Alvin 152, 204, 227
Torelli, Maurice 46, 104, 132, 227
Trombley, Stephen 14, 227
Türmen, Tomris 81

V

Vaher, Ado 33
Veil, Simone 66, 119
Vekemans, Marcel 15, 228
Vera, Rodrigo 14, 227
Verdoodt, Albert 80, 227
Verhaegen, Jean 227
Vernette, Jean 61, 227
Vigne, C.H. 30

W

Walter, Jean-Jacques 15, 129, 227
Weber, Max 45, 48, 228
Wilson, H.T. 26, 228
Winslow, C.E.A. 46, 228
Wollast, Elizabeth 15, 228

Index of Subjects

A

Ability to pay 42, 129
Abortion 1, 2, 3, 4, 7, 9, 11, 12, 13, 14, 15, 16, 24, 32, 51, 66, 79, 87, 94, 102, 103, 105, 107, 108, 109, 112, 113, 114, 115, 116, 117, 118, 119, 120, 121, 122, 123, 129, 131, 132, 135, 137, 139, 142, 146, 167, 170, 178, 183, 192, 194, 228
Adoption 207, 211
Aging 35, 155, 171
Agnosticism 46, 97, 118, 196
Agro-alimentary 143, 200
AIDS 4, 15, 71, 128
Arianism 55
Attali 228

B

Bachelard 49
Binding 54, 91, 228
Body 7, 24, 45, 51, 56, 65, 70, 72, 77, 79, 89, 90, 92, 99, 100, 106, 107, 117, 137, 140, 141, 164, 190, 200, 211

C

Child 2, 31, 58, 69, 70, 88, 93, 100, 101, 102, 105, 111, 112, 113, 117, 119, 137, 141, 153, 155, 160, 164, 165, 180, 181, 182, 184, 185, 187, 207, 209, 210, 211, 213, 214, 225, 226
CIOMS 29, 30, 37, 47, 48
Class struggle 18, 20, 21, 24
Consensus 53, 66, 67, 81, 92, 119, 137
Contraception 4, 9, 11, 12, 13, 24, 83, 100, 101, 102, 138, 142, 162, 171, 182, 189, 190, 191
Conviction 45, 46, 103, 122, 127
Culture 15, 23, 24, 38, 40, 44, 46, 49, 53, 56, 69, 72, 80, 95, 96, 97, 111, 158, 175, 206
Curbing of population 160, 162

D

Death 2, 3, 4, 6, 7, 15, 16, 17, 26, 33, 34, 36, 38, 44, 47, 51, 71, 79, 80, 85, 88, 89, 91, 92, 93, 94, 95, 96, 97, 98, 99, 100, 101, 102, 103, 104, 107, 109, 111, 112, 113, 116, 121, 122, 124, 125, 126, 127, 128, 129, 130, 131, 141, 142, 154, 169, 179, 195, 198, 199, 200, 204, 206, 214, 219, 225
Debt 145, 147, 203
Delvoye 224
Demographic density 165, 168
Demography 26, 79, 155, 158, 208
Derogation 66, 124, 132
Development 2, 9, 11, 12, 14, 16, 27, 30, 31, 33, 36, 37, 38, 39, 41, 56, 65, 73, 74, 75, 76, 80, 84, 85, 87, 98, 112, 135, 150, 155, 158, 159, 161, 162, 165, 167, 169, 170, 171, 174, 182, 202, 214, 219, 224, 225, 226
Discrimination 42, 67, 71, 79, 119,

136, 150, 208, 213
Divorce 99, 100, 101, 120, 155, 171, 181, 222
Doctors 13, 14, 19, 57, 79, 121, 125, 128, 130, 141, 142, 199, 200, 227

E

Ecology 148
Education 19, 22, 54, 71, 79, 87, 106, 112, 137, 143, 149, 150, 165, 167, 168, 169, 181, 183, 185, 199, 207, 208, 213
Elitism 163, 169
Engels 225
Equality 22, 31, 46, 48, 63, 64, 67, 68, 69, 71, 72, 73, 78, 100, 112, 191
Ethics 32, 37, 38, 39, 40, 44, 45, 46, 47, 48, 57, 68, 90, 107, 120, 228
Eugenics 19, 21, 26, 43, 48
Europe 2, 71, 76, 77, 78, 130, 158, 198, 217, 223
Euthanasia 3, 7, 12, 14, 43, 83, 93, 99, 116, 118, 119, 121, 122, 123, 124, 125, 126, 127, 128, 130, 131, 132, 133, 142, 171, 182, 200
Excommunication 115

F

Fairness 32, 35, 37, 39, 40, 45, 46, 47, 48, 67, 69, 70, 71, 73, 78
Family 12, 14, 15, 20, 22, 23, 24, 25, 26, 31, 32, 38, 47, 53, 56, 66, 67, 68, 69, 80, 81, 96, 102, 105, 108, 112, 117, 118, 133, 138, 139, 143, 145, 152, 159, 160, 163, 164, 165, 171, 173, 174, 177, 180, 181, 182, 183, 184, 185, 186, 188, 190, 192, 193, 200, 204, 206, 210, 211, 212, 213, 216, 219, 220, 221, 222, 226, 227
FAO 152, 175, 201, 223
Fecundity 99, 189, 190, 210

Fecundity index 155
Fidelity 20, 93, 99, 101, 102, 170, 196, 210
Freemasonry 13, 58, 59, 61

G

Gender 17, 21, 22, 23, 24, 25, 26, 27, 44, 55, 81, 104, 224, 225, 228
Globalization 43, 46, 145
Gnosis 56
Golden rule 97, 107
Grafts 3

H

Hammurabi 225
Health 2, 4, 15, 16, 21, 29, 30, 31, 32, 33, 34, 35, 37, 38, 39, 40, 41, 42, 43, 44, 45, 46, 47, 48, 51, 52, 54, 60, 64, 65, 66, 68, 70, 71, 72, 80, 81, 87, 98, 104, 142, 154, 155, 165, 169, 204, 209, 220, 222, 224, 226, 227, 228
Hedonism 182
Herrnstein 225
Holism 15, 29, 51, 54, 58, 59
Homosexuality 4, 24, 155, 181
Hyde 227

I

Image of God 56, 59, 88, 89, 96, 102, 108, 109, 110, 112, 115, 177, 178, 187, 188, 205, 211, 215
In vitro fertilization 2, 101
Interference 38, 137
International organization 4, 9, 11, 18, 21, 29, 37, 75, 78, 87, 138, 139, 142, 146, 150, 151, 158, 161, 168, 174, 198, 201, 217
IPPF 9, 12, 14, 16, 40, 66, 74, 80, 142, 223

J

Juridical positivism 77, 79, 124
Justice 9, 45, 71, 73, 77, 78, 81, 87, 97, 98, 111, 116, 120, 121, 136,

137, 140, 142, 146, 147, 152, 162, 167, 173, 185, 202, 207, 210, 215

L

Life expectancy 34, 37, 47, 71, 83, 84, 141, 153, 155
Lobbies 54, 138
Love 9, 20, 22, 42, 83, 88, 89, 90, 92, 93, 94, 97, 98, 99, 100, 101, 102, 105, 106, 108, 109, 110, 111, 113, 114, 115, 133, 135, 140, 163, 170, 173, 177, 178, 179, 180, 182, 183, 187, 188, 189, 190, 191, 192, 193, 197, 203, 205, 206, 207, 209, 210, 213

M

Malthusianism 19, 20
Market 3, 13, 20, 21, 22, 43, 72, 79, 94, 95, 144, 145, 146, 183, 185, 203, 214
Media 8, 13, 16, 55, 116, 118, 121, 142, 143, 146, 147, 161, 175, 183, 207, 214
Median age 34, 158, 174
Medicine 14, 30, 35, 38, 43, 50, 79, 87, 132, 141, 142, 143, 169, 192, 200, 201, 220
Memory 4, 7, 57, 184, 185, 212
Messianism 18, 20, 54, 60
Migration 154
Mortality rate 52, 153

N

Natural methods 142, 190, 191, 216
Naziism 7, 68, 75, 77, 87, 91, 200
Neomalthusianism 48, 182
Networks 45, 49, 53, 54, 55, 58, 59, 76, 87, 127
New Age 44, 49, 50, 51, 52, 54, 55, 56, 57, 58, 59, 60, 61, 76, 226
Nongovernmental organization 29, 48

O

Organism 44

P

Paradigm 15, 17, 21, 29, 31, 33, 41, 42, 43, 44, 45, 46, 47, 48, 49, 50, 51, 52, 54, 55, 56, 57, 58, 59, 68, 70, 76, 138, 221, 228
Parental responsibility 208
Pelagianism 51
Permit to procreate 174
Pill 2
Pluralism 97, 118, 120, 136, 139
Plutarch 228
Poverty 13, 19, 37, 149, 150, 151, 164, 168, 169, 171, 195, 202, 214
Prenatal diagnosis 117, 118
Priorities 29, 32, 33, 35, 38, 42, 46, 52, 70, 71, 205, 209, 228
Procreation 3, 20, 24, 182, 187, 188, 190, 191, 204

Q

Quality of life 21, 26, 31, 69, 71, 72, 118, 120

R

Relativism 15, 44, 136, 226
Resistance 9, 38, 129, 140, 144, 181, 183, 197, 199, 215
Responsibility 6, 8, 13, 16, 21, 31, 39, 40, 45, 54, 93, 120, 137, 148, 151, 184, 192, 208, 210
Resurrection 131, 209
Rights of man 25, 37, 39, 40, 57, 63, 64, 65, 66, 69, 70, 71, 72, 74, 75, 76, 120, 132, 135, 140, 141, 162, 200
Rights of the Child 141

S

Salami tactic 54
Samaritan 109, 110, 111, 112, 113,

133, 134, 151, 173, 174, 179,
182, 186, 203, 208
Slavery 70, 107, 117, 199
Solidarity 41, 74, 129, 133, 134, 170,
174, 184, 201, 202, 203, 207,
215
Solvency 34
Sovereignty 20, 46, 73, 74, 77, 78,
131, 139, 148, 162, 170, 199
Sterilization 3, 4, 7, 9, 12, 13, 14, 15,
26, 32, 79, 83, 101, 102, 119,
133, 138, 142, 159, 162, 165,
170, 171, 191, 212, 220, 227
Structuralism 22, 23, 44, 46, 48, 60,
216
Subsidiarity 46, 72, 134, 137, 173,
181
Suicide 4, 6, 15, 99, 122, 123, 128,
129, 130
Supporting capacity 167

T

Totalitarianism 15, 75, 94, 96, 124,
130, 136, 181, 183, 200

U

U.N. 1, 9, 11, 14, 15, 16, 24, 25, 32,
33, 38, 40, 50, 68, 72, 73, 76, 80,
87, 141, 152, 156, 157, 162, 169,
175, 219, 221, 227, 228
UNESCO 29
UNICEF 11, 16, 33, 227
Universality 35, 63, 71, 75, 77, 188,
205
UNPD 33
UNPFA 9
USAID 11, 16, 225
Utilitarianism 44, 100, 182

V

Vaccine 14, 225
Violence 6, 8, 20, 51, 92, 95, 96, 98,
101, 102, 133

W

War 7, 8, 51, 58, 61, 75, 78, 87, 94,
96, 123, 129, 150, 162, 182
WHO 2, 4, 9, 14, 15, 29, 30, 31, 32,
33, 34, 35, 37, 38, 39, 40, 41, 42,
43, 45, 46, 47, 48, 49, 50, 51, 52,
59, 80, 142, 219, 222, 224, 225,
227, 228
Women 12, 26, 174, 211, 212, 216,
219, 222, 225
World Bank 11, 27, 29, 30, 33, 35,
36, 37, 47, 52, 74, 84, 85, 155,
169, 219, 220, 225